D0777205

AMERICAN ARBITRATION

AMERICAN ARBITRATION

Its History, Functions and Achievements

By FRANCES KELLOR
First Vice-President of the American Arbitration Association; Author of *Arbitration in Action*

Foreword by
JAMES R. ANGELL
President Emeritus, Yale University

HARPER & BROTHERS PUBLISHERS
New York and London

AMERICAN ARBITRATION

FIRST EDITION

E-X

To

LUCIUS R. EASTMAN and FELIX M. WARBURG

FOUNDERS OF THE AMERICAN ARBITRATION ASSOCIATION

and to

SPRUILLE BRADEN and THOMAS J. WATSON

FOUNDERS OF THE INTER-AMERICAN COMMERCIAL ARBITRATION COMMISSION

This story of the organization of American Arbitration is dedicated with the affection and appreciation of the author for the opportunity to have been of service in so great an adventure in so goodly a company.

Contents

FOREWORD

by James R. Angell

President Emeritus, Yale University

This highly important volume supplies a need in the literature of arbitration which has long been recognized as urgent. Under the form of a presentation primarily historical, it offers the most illuminating analyses of the issues involved and the reasons for the several forward steps which have from time to time been taken, in replacing costly and time consuming litigation with the more effective and less expensive procedures of arbitration. Similarly, it points out the requirements still unfulfilled which must be provided before the full impact of arbitration as an indispensable element in sound national and international commercial relations can be realized. The intelligence, foresight, courage, and devotion of those, our author among them, who have given themselves over the last quarter century to promoting the arbitration faith are beyond all praise, and now that so much of the critical territory has been occupied, it is to be hoped that adequate public recognition may be accorded them. The repercussions of successful commercial arbitration upon political issues and the peaceful methods of dealing with them, especially at the international level, can hardly fail to be increasingly felt. In a less tempestuous period of international affairs they would of a certainty be widely and joyfully acknowledged and accepted, and yet ironically enough these are exactly the conditions in which the need for arbitration is most acute.

The necessity for effective and world wide educational procedures is throughout the book vigorously and rightly stressed. Effective arbitration is not something which to be adopted has only to be proposed. It cannot be effective, indeed it cannot be generally employed, save as its principles and its methods are thoroughly studied and understood. Mere good will and sentimental approval is no satisfactory substitute for searching scholarly instruction. Like many other intrinsically sound social processes, it can be greatly harmed by ignorant and ill-timed publicity. Publicity is certainly still needed, but to avoid damage and destructive misapprehension well organized and wisely promoted teaching is essential.

As a corollary of this general doctrine, emphasis is repeatedly put by the writer on the wisdom of proceeding slowly in the promotion and spread of arbitration, lest its advocacy get too far ahead of full public understanding and of the appropriate legal and other provisions to assure its successful practice.

No careful reader of this text can come away with any misconception of commercial arbitration as a self-starting and self-executing process. Its demonstrable and extremely important values are clearly set forth as dependent upon exhaustive research and shrewd and informed drafting of procedures, with constant corrections to improve practice and avoid needless friction, disappointment, and subsequent distrust.

The author is to be complimented on the excellent organization of her material and the lucid and effective exposition of both facts and principles. Her work cannot fail to increase the intelligent understanding of arbitration and to expand the area where it is in operation.

Preface

On Rockefeller Plaza, overlooking a scene made gay by skaters and solemn by the flags of all nations, where a fountain plays in summer and Christmas trees are lighted and carols are sung in winter, there functions an institution unique in the history of keeping peace and goodwill among men.

It is the first of its kind in civilization. It is the headquarters of national and international systems of arbitration, set high among the thousands of organizations and leaders that constitute the commercial interests in Rockefeller Center. It is peculiarly American in that, in a busy center where competition thrives and ideas flow like magic, there should be an institution that brings tranquillity and happiness out of the chaos which disputes make in the lives of men and of nations.

This institution is the headquarters of the American Arbitration Association and its affiliated systems. Its leaders constitute as unique a body of men as ever made American history. They are the commercial and international and labor leaders of the nation.

There follows the story of how this institution came into being, how it functions, what are its ideals and philosophy, and whither it leads. The story is written as a tribute to the thousands of men and organizations that have built the Western Hemisphere Systems of Arbitration, and who stand ready year after year to serve in the cause of peace and justice.

Perhaps not before in any nation have so many men from so many different walks of life, of high and low degree, of wealth and position and of common and diverse heritage, labored without thought of profit to bring accord out of discord, to replace enmity with friendship and to strengthen goodwill toward men.

The National and Special Panels of the Association and of its affiliated international systems of commercial arbitration best exemplify the participation and achievement of these many men from all walks of life. They are commercial and industrial peace officers of the nation, and in the other countries of the Western Hemisphere they comprise a body of men devoted to taking discord and misunderstandings out of inter-American and Canadian-American trade. Altogether, a body of approximately 15,000 men are enlisted as members of National and Special Panels.

In the last Chapter, an attempt has been made to indicate some of the outstanding builders of American arbitration. The only regret is that the thousands of members on the panels of arbitrators cannot also receive their due share of recognition for to them the nation is indebted for solving many disputes and differences and for advancing public welfare through their service.

In the twenty years which this record covers, thousands upon thousands of civil, commercial and industrial difficulties and disputes have been brought to the American Arbitration Association. Through both national and foreign trade channels has gone forth word of the miracles of reconciliation and justice which have been wrought.

To Charles L. Bernheimer and Moses H. Grossman, inspirers of the American plan; to the late Felix M. Warburg and Lucius R. Eastman, founders of the American Arbitration Association; and to the late Dr. L. S. Rowe, and to Spruille Braden and Thomas J. Watson, pilots of the Inter-American adventure; to Brooke Claxton and D. L. Morrell, architects of the Canadian-American system, and to the hundreds of friends of international commercial arbitration, the success of the adventure of arbitration owes much of its inspiration and encouragement.

To Mrs. Lucius R. Eastman, who through the Lucius and Eva Eastman Fund, Inc., and to Mrs. Felix M. Warburg, who through the Felix M. and Frieda Schiff Warburg Foundation, have contributed the funds to make this publication on American Arbitration possible, the Association owes special appreciation of their continuing interest and generosity.

It is, however, to the teamwork of its staff that the final achievement has been largely due. It is their staunch upholding of the ideals and policies of these Western Hemisphere institutions and their efficient and faithful work that make it possible to present this story of achievement.

With J. Noble Braden, George N. Butler, Martin Domke, Paul Fitzpatrick, Antonia Hatvany, J. S. Murphy, Rufus S. Paret, Ferris Faulkner, Jr., present staff officers and department heads, and with Frances V. Church, Executive Assistant to the First Vice President and Catherine G. Salisbury, the author shares whatever praise or blame there may be found in this story of a new era in national and international arbitration. In the spirit in which Kipling wrote "L'Envoi," we have worked together:

And only the Master shall praise us, and only the Master shall blame;
And no one shall work for money, and no one shall work for fame;
But each for the joy of the working, and each, in his separate star
Shall draw the Thing as he sees It for the God of Things as They Are!

FRANCES KELLOR

New York, January 1948.

Part I

THEORY AND ORGANIZATION OF AMERICAN ARBITRATION

CHAPTER I

The Historical Pattern

«««« »»»»

OF ALL mankind's adventure in search of peace and justice, arbitration is among the earliest. Long before law was established, or courts were organized, or judges had formulated principles of law, men had resorted to arbitration for the resolving of discord, the adjustment of differences, and the settlement of disputes.

Out of the dim recesses of fable and mythology, it appears that upon Mt. Ida the royal shepherd Paris was called upon to deliver a famous award. The dispute concerned the competing claims of Juno, Pallas Athene and Venus for the prize of beauty. All other means of settlement having failed, Paris, by agreement of the parties, decided the issue.

If the course of arbitration, begun presumably on Mt. Ida, could be traced through the centuries, it would be found in the most primitive society as well as in modern civilization. Commercial arbitration was known to the desert caravans in Marco Polo's time and was a common practice among Phoenician and Greek traders.

Civil arbitration also flourished. In the Homeric period, chiefs and elders held more or less regular sittings in places of assembly to settle the disputes of all persons who chose to appear before them. In the middle of the sixth century B.C., Peisistratus, the Athenian tyrant, furthered his policy of keeping people out of the city by appointing justices to go on circuit throughout village communities. They were authorized to give binding decisions if they failed to effect a friendly settlement.[1]

[1] See, Gertrude Smith, "The Greeks Had a Word For It—25 Centuries Ago," *Arbitration Magazine*, Vol. I, Nos. 4-5 (1943), p. 5.

International arbitration was also known to the ancient world, for many political disputes seem to have been thus settled. In a controversy between Athens and Megara, about 600 B.C., for the possession of the island of Salamis, the matter was referred to five Spartan judges who allotted the island to Athens. A dispute between Corinth and Corcyra for the possession of Leucas (480 B.C.) was settled by Themistocles as arbitrator. A boundary line in dispute between the Genoese and Viturians was settled by arbitration (117 B.C.), the decision having been recorded upon a bronze tablet unearthed near Genoa. There are also instances in which a third strong power compelled other powers to resort to arbitration. Sometimes the arbitrator was an individual as Themistocles; or an institution such as the Areopagus at Athens; or a state. The tribunal might, therefore, be an individual, a group of individuals, a state, or a large number of citizens chosen from within a state.

Industrial controversy was also arbitrated in such matters as master and servant relations, terms of employment, working conditions and wages. One of the first disputes submitted to the earliest known American arbitration tribunal, organized in 1786 by the Chamber of Commerce of New York, involved the wages of seamen.

It is important to recall these early uses of arbitration at this time when, in the midst of a rising tide of controversy, doubts arise and arbitration is sometimes thought to be something new and untried and hazardous to good public relations; or when its organization seems to be detrimental to judicial institutions that seem older but are in reality next of kin.

So soundly was arbitration then conceived, and so generally was it applied to all kinds of controversy, that little change in its fundamental principles has taken place over the centuries. Despite efforts to narrow the early concept or to put its practice in a legal strait jacket, arbitration remains the voluntary agreement of states or persons to submit their differences to judges of their own choice and to bind themselves in advance, to accept the decision of judges, so chosen, as final and binding. This natural right of self-regulation is a precious possession of a democratic society, for it embodies the principles of independence, self-reliance, equality, integrity, and responsibility, all of which are of inestimable value to any community.

It was inevitable that in the absence of the organization of the idea or of the processes of arbitration, and without available records of its early use, a period of confusion should have prevailed. The primitive idea that parties in dispute chose a judge to render a final and binding decision on the merits of the controversy and on the basis of proofs presented by the parties (which process was then called arbitration) later became confused with other processes for the amicable settlement of disputes. These were not judicial, but bargaining processes, and were in the nature of mediation or conciliation. They were intended to effect compromises rather than to administer justice; or to bring the viewpoints of the contestants into sufficient accord for them to settle the matter henceforth by themselves. As the general term arbitration was rather indiscriminately applied to all of these processes, the effect was to lessen confidence in arbitration as a judicial process and to create misunderstanding as to its real purpose. One of the services which modern institutions of arbitration have rendered, aided by arbitration laws and the courts in interpreting these laws, has been the restoration of arbitration as a quasi-judicial process and the placing of conciliation and mediation in their proper perspective as bargaining processes without benefit of legal enforcement.

It was also inevitable, with the development of law and the establishment of courts and with the emergence of a profession of law, that arbitration, in this period of confusion, should have experienced a very considerable eclipse. As disputants became more involved in litigation, they neglected to exercise their own powers of self-regulation. Due to the absence of any contemporaneously organized arbitration machinery or established rules of procedure, it became far easier for parties in dispute to litigate than to arbitrate.

During this period of partial eclipse, arbitration laws did little to encourage arbitration. In theory these laws were intended to confer upon parties in dispute the legal right to arbitration and to bring the courts to their aid in enforcing their arbitration agreements and awards. But both the common and early statutory laws imposed technical requirements which, if not observed, could render the agreement non-enforceable and the award void. For example, failure to file a submission with the court, or to have it made an order of the court, could have this effect. Other requirements, such as that of beginning suit before arbitration, made it necessary for parties in dispute to conform to various court regulations before they could proceed with their arbitration. Under these restrictions, arbitration inevitably fell into disuse, except in instances where parties were content to rely upon good faith, without recourse to legal aid.

But none of these early handicaps explains the obscure and humble role played by arbitration in early American history; or why a people, so bent upon freedom, self-discipline, and self-regulation, should have ignored arbitration, which so embodies these qualities.

Except for its adoption by a few trade and commercial organizations and its use in the settlement of some differences over colonial rights and boundaries and in the collection of debts, arbitration does not appear to have struck deep roots in early American life. It did not become an integral part of the early social and economic development of the country nor a recognized institution of any consequence and its impact was negligible upon the growth of justice in the country. Arbitration literature of this early period is exceedingly sparse and inquirers are therefore handicapped in examining the somewhat vague course taken by arbitration and the causes of its inaction. Such record as exists, appears generally in court decisions, rendered in the course of controversy over the process of arbitration, rather than in its normal usage by individuals and trade groups.

It is probable that this situation was due somewhat to the attitude of Americans toward discord and dispute. They were complacently accepted phenomena, to be settled by force or by litigation, if need be. America was a rich country, full of adventure and could afford a considerable volume of disputes at a high cost of settlement. As disputes were regarded as an inevitable and healthful process in the development of a new country, the prospect that they might sometime become a menace to society was not of immediate concern. Since in trade and commerce the margin of profit was then sufficient to allow for a very considerable waste, the attribute of economy was not an attraction to arbitration. In industrial relations, parity of power between employers and employees had not reached the point of encouraging arbitration.

It is also probable that this early American attitude toward disputes also failed to give arbitration any outstanding advocates. Without such leadership, so conspicuous in other advancing fields of endeavor, arbitration could not present an effective challenge to the fast growing volume of disputes.[1]

Prior to World War I, America had its great judges, scientists, authors, artists and other leaders, but arbitration could claim no such distinction. No monuments had been dedicated to its achievements, no awards had been made for distinguished service, and symbols of its advancement were difficult to find. Arbitration seems always to have been a homeless, friendless wanderer among men and nations, remembered only in periods of acute distress when it was often too late for it to be of service.

Although arbitration had found a foothold in chambers of commerce as early as 1768 in New York, 1794 in New Haven, and 1801 in Philadelphia, the examples thus set had not resulted in its general acceptance by other chambers of commerce; and even when established it was not generally used because little effort was made to educate the public in its use. Of the thousands of trade associations in operation in 1927, only a comparatively small number of them knew about or used arbitration.[2] Financial and commodity exchanges that had found arbitration practical in New York achieved only a limited application in similar exchanges throughout the country. Collective bargaining agreements had not come into general use, although a few pioneer organizations, such as the building trades, printing, and clothing industries had quite generally used arbitration and had thereby blazed a new trail.

Therefore the only clear record of development was still to be found in the court decisions interpreting such common law and statutory provisions as were applicable to arbitration. Through these decisions, certain principles and policies of immense significance to the future development of arbitration had been established.[3] But they offered no clear view of the normal history, develop-

[1] See Chapter XXV for Distinguished Service Awards, 1926-1947.

[2] For historical development of commercial arbitration through business organizations, see *Year Book on Commercial Arbitration in the United States*, published by the Oxford University Press for the American Arbitration Association in 1927.

[3] As the legal history has been so ably set forth in *Commercial Arbitrations and Awards* by Wesley A. Sturges and less technically in *The Code of Arbitration*

ment or progress of arbitration in the United States; nor of its relation to public welfare; nor did they portray arbitration as an institution having a definite impact upon the economic life of the country.

The historical pattern as traced through early American history, through the scant records that are available, was therefore, tolerance of the inevitability of disputes, indifference to their cost, acceptance of a prodigious amount of litigation, and an almost total absence of organization that would make arbitration readily accessible to the people. Education in the knowledge or use of arbitration was unheard of, nor was there source material available, nor had teachers thought of instruction in the subject.

Generally speaking, unawareness was the phenomenon of this early period. Americans were unaware of the contribution that arbitration could make to their national economy, or of the service that arbitration could render in the advancement of goodwill, good faith, confidence and co-operation in its commercial relations. They were also unaware of the latent power of arbitration for advancing international peace and security through world trade. The era had not yet arrived for resumption by the individual of the exercise of his natural right of self-regulation in matters of dispute, a right he had been steadily relegating to rigid processes of law. Nor had there emerged any outstanding leadership to change the historical pattern that seemed destined to follow a medieval design of negation, if not subjugation.

Practice and Procedure and in *Arbitration in Action* by Frances Kellor, there is no need to set them forth in a record not concerned primarily with the legal aspects of arbitration.

CHAPTER II

The Pattern Changes in America

«««« »»»»

THE new era in American arbitration began in 1920. It was characterized by the modernizing of arbitration law, systematic planning, organization of machinery, the cultivation of a spirit of arbitration, and the construction of foundations of knowledge. Its incentive came from World War I and the resolve to avoid future wars insofar as the settlement or control of disputes through arbitration could accomplish that end.

In thus changing the historical pattern, Americans had before them some invaluable lessons in previous undertakings. One of these lessons arose out of the Conferences of 1899 and 1907 which had laboriously established the Permanent Court of Arbitration at The Hague. The Conventions there adopted carefully defined the processes of inquiry, mediation, and arbitration, set up rules of procedure for each process, and provided machinery for their administration. High hopes were held that this Court might prove an instrumentality for the prevention of future wars. But one fundamental omission was made. No provision was made for cultivating the spirit of arbitration, or for educating either governments or their people in the knowledge and use of arbitration. So, the first World War came without the Court's having functioned in the settlement of major issues.

A similar mistake was made in the next great international adventure when the League of Nations was organized. It also provided for arbitration and committed its members in principle. It went further and established the first Permanent Court of International Justice with ample machinery for its operation. But the League also failed to cultivate the spirit of arbitration or to teach nations or peoples its use either in their home affairs or in international relations. So, the second World War came, without the League or the Court having been able to settle differences among states.[1]

In the meantime, a third experiment had been tried. Over a period of half a century, the American Republics, acting through a central organization, known as the Pan American Union, were pursuing a different course. They were binding the Republics together in peace through a network of conventions, agreements, arrangements, and undertakings which established the central principle of settlement of disputes through amicable processes, including arbitration.[2] Not only were these agreements consummated, but the Pan American Union unceasingly, through many different educational and scientific undertakings, cultivated the spirit of arbitration and educated governments in the use of pacific processes of settlement.[3] This experiment held these Republics together under the stress of international war and the strain of threatened wars among themselves. This experiment furnished both the inspiration and the hope for a new era in American arbitration and for a change in the historical pattern.

The event that was to precipitate this change in pattern, like so many inconspicuous events that later prove momentous, gave no indication of its significance either to American life or to international peace and security. It was, on the contrary, the rather drab event of enacting a modern arbitration law in 1920 in the State of New York—the first of its kind in the United States.[4] This law

[1] Frances Kellor and Antonia Hatvany, *Security Against War*, I, *International Controversy and the Machinery for Peace*; II, *International Courts and the Outlawry of War*. (New York, Macmillan & Co., 1924.)

[2] For a summary, see *The Basic Principles of the Inter-American System*. (Pan American Union [1943].)

[3] Among these treaties and agreements were the Gondra Treaty of 1923, which sought to avoid or prevent conflicts; followed in 1929 by a General Convention of Inter-American Conciliation, a General Treaty of Inter-American Arbitration, and an additional Protocol of Progressive Arbitration; then by an Anti-War Treaty of Non-Aggression and Conciliation in 1933. In 1936, there appears a scientific note, namely a Convention for the Maintenance, Preservation, and Reestablishment of Peace; and a Convention to Co-ordinate, Extend, and Assure the Fulfillment of the Existing Treaties between the American States. The same year, 1936, also witnessed an Inter-American Treaty on Good Offices and Mediation and one on the Prevention of Controversies.

[4] The enactment of this law was due largely to the initiative taken by the New York State Bar Association, and to the support given by the Chamber of Commerce of the State of New York and other commercial organizations. The publication of *Commercial Arbitration and the Law* by Julius Henry Cohen in 1918 was influential in obtaining the law.

possessed the unusual features of looking forward instead of backward, and of enabling parties in dispute to control future disputes as well as to settle existing disputes. Although similar features had existed in British and Scottish laws for many generations, it proved to be a revolutionary step in the Americas as it had not been in other countries.

Under the provisions of this new law, agreements to submit to arbitration future disputes arising out of the contract containing such agreements, were made legally valid, enforceable, and irrevocable save as any other contract is revocable. Hitherto only existing disputes had enjoyed such legal protection. Furthermore, this law closed the courts to parties to arbitration agreements until they had complied with their arbitration agreements and it brought to the aid of the parties the powers of the court in enforcing agreements and awards by authorizing them to appoint arbitrators or otherwise expedite arbitration upon default of one of the parties.[5]

Little was it dreamed in 1920 that under this and subsequent laws of a similar nature, arbitration clauses in contracts would become the foundation stones of wide flung systems of arbitration.[6]

The enactment of this law might, however, have proved no more significant in the United States than had similar laws in other countries, but for the fact that it led to the organization of the first permanent independent institution of arbitration.

This new institution was organized in 1922 as the Arbitration Society of America. It offered arbitration a normal, active career of its own, with its own headquarters and personnel. It made possible the organization of systems of tribunals administered by an independent and responsible institution. It freed arbitration from commodity and geographical limitations to serve all of the people all of the time.

This change in pattern from indifference and casualness to scientific organization was effected not only by a new type of organiza-

[5] For a full description of the provisions of this law and its application, see *Suggestions for the Practice of Commercial Arbitration in the United States*, published for the American Arbitration Association in 1928 by Oxford University Press.

[6] This law was followed by the enactment in 1925 of the U.S. Arbitration Act and by similar statutory laws in the states of Arizona, California, Connecticut, Louisiana, Massachusetts, Michigan, New Hampshire, New Jersey, New York, Ohio, Oregon, Pennsylvania, Rhode Island, Washington, and Wisconsin.

tion but by the adoption of different methods for the advancement of arbitration. Under a distinguished leadership, this institution put on an educational campaign that carried arbitration to the people in a new way throughout the country.

Under this stimulus, arbitration made front page headlines in the press. It went out to luncheon and to dinner; receptions were held in its honor, and forums were dedicated to its exposition. It became the subject of conference, debate, and instruction. It frequented exclusive clubs and found its way into homes, churches, schools and theatres. It passed the exclusive portals of law offices, banks, and corporation board rooms. It came out of dry law books, where only the difficulties were recorded, and found a place in general as well as special periodicals, books, and pamphlets. Sometimes arbitration wore evening clothes; at other times it appeared in overalls, or in a professor's gown; but always it aroused curiosity and interest.

Nowhere in the world had arbitration ever had such an audience as when sixty members of the New York Judiciary sat down to dinner in its honor, followed by a conference at which more than four hundred business and professional men discussed its future.[7]

But, other experiments were to come. One morning the *Arbitration News* made its appearance—and the first arbitration publication was born. Arbitration had become news, for the things that were done and said about it were spotlighted and its leaders became known to the public. Along with *Arbitration News,* "Learn to Arbitrate" became the slogan of the new Arbitration Society, and a stamp bearing this slogan made its appearance.

A highlight of the Society's endeavor to make arbitration better known, occurred in 1923, when May 7-12 was made "Arbitration Week." Charles L. Bernheimer, Chairman of the Arbitration Committee of the Chamber of Commerce of the State of New York, arranged a program in which more than fifty trade and commercial organizations participated. The educational work carried on during that week marked a sharp departure from the traditional treatment of arbitration.

During its first year and a half, the Society recorded the distribution of 158,000 pieces of literature at 1,200 meetings, confer-

[7] At the home of Mr. and Mrs. Vincent Astor, February 28, 1923.

ences or gatherings where arbitration was discussed. It received 600 applications for information or for the settlement of disputes. And during its lifetime, from 1922-26, there were enacted modern arbitration laws in Massachusetts and New Jersey. The Society was also instrumental in effecting the enactment of the United States Arbitration Law in 1925, applicable to interstate commerce and foreign trade transactions.

The influence of the Society spread in many directions. Trade and commercial organizations began to furbish their own facilities and services for their own groups and to participate in making this broader pattern of arbitration a reality. For example, in 1923, Will H. Hays, soon to become a Director of the Society, established an arbitration system in the Film Boards of Trade for the motion picture industry. A report on this system, set forth in the *Congressional Record*, was instrumental in furthering the enactment of the United States Arbitration Act.

Not less significant was the new leadership developed by the Society. It brought business men, lawyers, economists, teachers, and professional men together in a common endeavor. It found staunch and distinguished advocates to champion the cause of arbitration, not solely as judges in disputes, but for its general advancement. These advocates changed the passive role of arbitration to one of action and gave it a new prestige. No longer was it submerged in contracts or limited to resolutions and endorsements, nor to having its failures publicized in law books. On the contrary, arbitration sought the people; it besieged their conscience to recognize its usefulness in the control of future disputes. It stormed the American's complacency over the social consequences of discord and disputes. It confronted men in their trade press; it challenged their attention at meetings; it stared at them from cartoons and haunted their conference tables.

During the four years of its existence, from 1922-26, this new Society substantially changed the pattern of arbitration. It brought arbitration out of its austere juridical area into the limelight as an instrumentality which people themselves could use generally for the voluntary settlement of many kinds of differences. It made arbitration procedures readily accessible to the people through the establishment and operation of a commercial arbitration tribunal.

It created a new leadership through panels of arbitrators and trade groups. It directed public attention to a hitherto drab and obscure subject. It flung a challenge of self-regulation to private enterprise. It opened the eyes of lawyers to a new practice in arbitration tribunals. It envisioned the dawn of a new profession by starting a panel of arbitrators and beginning their education. It brought arbitration to the people in a simple yet dramatic way and stimulated their faith in this age-old method of solving differences and maintaining friendships. It introduced into the American way of life a new institution for building and maintaining good faith, goodwill, and confidence in human relations.

All of this was the contribution of a single leader, Moses H. Grossman, and the devoted group of men who comprised the Society's first Board of Directors and their associates of the bar, bench, business, education, and the professions. It was, therefore, representative of people from all walks of life, participating in a new concept of arbitration.

Having experienced this change from indifference to approval, from a passive role to action, and from obscurity to public acclaim, arbitration could never again become a forgotten way of American life and was destined to find its way eventually upon a broad international highway.

CHAPTER III

The American Arbitration Association Arrives

«««« »»»»

THE young and lusty Arbitration Society of America, with its new ideas and challenging program, was not destined to see the realization of its national plans, nor to have any part in their international application. Its activities proved too disturbing of the old concepts to go unchallenged. In 1925, when the Society was but three years old, that challenge was issued by a new organization, sponsored by that keeper of arbitration tradition since 1768—the Chamber of Commerce of the State of New York. This new organization was the Arbitration Foundation, headed by Charles L. Bernheimer, then Chairman of the Arbitration Committee of the Chamber.

The more conservative purpose of the Foundation was to spread the use of arbitration through study and the dissemination of knowledge concerning it, to co-operate with other organizations, to coordinate law and arbitration practice, to improve arbitration law and to furnish advice and provide facilities and funds for the furtherance of the great causes of arbitration, mediation, and conciliation.

Although these were worthy purposes, they were without the public appeal that the Society was making. Also, the Foundation lacked the democratic approach to the people. While the Society was bent upon taking arbitration to the people, the Foundation was primarily interested in the more conservative processes of research and co-ordination and improvement of arbitration practice. Furthermore, the methods of financing the two organizations differed. The Foundation relied chiefly upon an insurance fund payable upon the death of Mr. Bernheimer and upon substantial contributions, while the Society was interested in building a membership organization that would include many people and institutions, large and small.

The real difficulty, however, was that an Arbitration Foundation was ahead of its time. Just as the leaders in the Society saw so clearly that arbitration must be set free to serve mankind, that it must have a home of its own, and from that home, taken to the doorsteps and housetops of the common people, and that it must have leadership and a clarion call, so the organizers of the Foundation, looking into the future, foresaw that the time would come when a foundation would become necessary to furnish the wherewithal to make the American concept of arbitration available to many people in many countries and to carry its message of goodwill and co-operation throughout the world.

But what neither organization envisaged were the long days of preparedness that would be required before either objective could be achieved. What neither master builder foresaw was that he would pass from the scene before the necessary steps of the long journey were completed.[1]

So deep-rooted were the differences between the champions of the new, and the preservers of the old order, that arbitration, the reconciler of differences, was likely to be split into factions. In the one group, lawyers, professional men, small traders, and the average citizen combined to support the new order; in the other group, substantial business interests combined to continue commercial arbitration very much as it had come down through the ages.

The conflict, however, was not without its benefits. It set men thinking seriously about arbitration and the place it should hold in American life. It brought different types of minds to consider future problems. It inspired a new type of leadership and captured the imagination of hitherto indifferent segments of society. And, finally, this conflict brought together seven wise men who not only met this crisis, but planned for American arbitration a brilliant future of a type hitherto unknown in the world.

In 1925, by mutual consent, the Society and the Foundation each appointed a committee of three men to resolve their differences and

[1] Moses H. Grossman, founder of the Society, died in 1942 and Charles L. Bernheimer, organizer of the Foundation, died in 1944. At that time, the insurance fund accumulated by the Foundation passed to the Chamber of Commerce of the State of New York.

conflicting interests.[2] These six representatives chose Lucius R. Eastman (business man and lawyer), and President of the Merchants' Association of the City of New York, as their Chairman. Together, they spent the better part of a year in reconciling the differences, co-ordinating the various projects, and formulating a combined program.

This Committee recommended that the two pioneering organizations should be consolidated in a new organization that embodied the vision and plans of both organizations, and that the new organization should accord to the two leaders and their adherents positions of leadership in the new organization.

In 1926 these recommendations were accepted by the Society and the Foundation, and both passed out of existence in name and function when the American Arbitration Association was created. The new Association was authorized by order of Supreme Court of the State of New York, under the Membership Corporation Law, on January 29, 1926, upon the foundation of the combined charters. The members of the Committee became its first Board of Directors, with Anson W. Burchard, then President of the International General Electric Corporation, as the first President of the Association.

The new Association received a rich inheritance in ideas and plans from both consolidating organizations. From the Society came memberships, a Commercial Arbitration Tribunal, a Panel of Arbitrators, and a progressive educational program. From the bar, the Association drew the distinguished and enthusiastic leadership that had helped to create the Society. From the Foundation came the conservative business leadership that was to prove of inestimable value in charting the future course of the new Association.

Honorary Presidents were nominated by the consolidating organizations: Charles Evans Hughes and Charles L. Bernheimer by the Foundation; and Herbert Hoover, Newton D. Baker, and Moses H. Grossman by the Society. These were the first Honorary Presidents of the new Association. The new Association also appointed several vice presidents.[3]

[2] The Foundation appointed John F. Fowler, James H. Post, and Anson W. Burchard, all business men. The Society appointed Henry Ives Cobb (architect), Felix M. Warburg (banker), and Frank H. Sommer (then Dean of the New York University Law School).

[3] For list, see Ch. XXV, p. 186.

While both the Foundation and the Society had been national in name and scope, neither had attained a national status; the former because its program did not materialize, and the latter because it found New York an absorbing place of action in itself. The Tribunal, Panel, Directorate and educational work of the Society were, therefore, largely representative of the great city of its birth. Such immediate problems as relieving the congestion of Supreme Court calendars, then three years in arrears, and of adjusting the many differences of a complex New York commercial society, absorbed both the resources and time of the Society.

The new Association immediately reached out through the country for its builders and for the expansion of its facilities. Outstanding was the organization of a Board of 520 industrial Vice Chairmen.[4] These men were chosen from every branch of industry throughout the nation. They organized meetings, wrote for their trade press, addressed conventions, recommended arbitration clauses, and carried arbitration to all of the trade corners of America.

Not less influential were the 200 or more national and regional trade and commercial organizations which became affiliated with the new Association in its educational activities.[5] This relationship resulted also in a wide improvement in the practice of arbitration within their own groups. At a dinner tendered the Association in 1936 by some of these groups, on the occasion of its tenth anniversary, many of these organizations recorded the progress made by them through their affiliation with the Association.

Lawyers had been outstanding in building the Society and continued their interest and co-operation with the new Association. Judges and lawyers served on the Board of Directors and also on the various committees; they became members of the Association; they strengthened its organization and determined many of the policies that were eventually incorporated in the procedure for its Tribunals. They served as arbitrators, or appeared in Tribunals on behalf of clients. They put arbitration clauses in contracts and were instrumental in securing better arbitration laws. They wrote on arbitration for law reviews, lectured in law schools, and conducted conferences and debates in law associations. They functioned actively

[4] For members, see Ch. XXV, p. 186.
[5] For members, see Ch. XXV, p. 199

in the new Association through a Special Committee of Lawyers and an Arbitration Law Committee.[6] The Arbitration Committee, acting under the Rules, has always been composed of lawyers. Later, the Panel of Arbitrators for the Accident Claims Tribunal was composed entirely of lawyers.

Lawyers, through the organization of Arbitration Committees in the Association of the Bar of the City of New York and the New York County Lawyers' Association, were also highly instrumental in the later improvement of the New York arbitration law.

From an unexpected source came a new type of arbitration builder. These were bankers whose active interest was first set in motion by the endorsement of modern arbitration laws by the American Bankers' Association, and augmented later by the interest taken in educational work by the American Institute of Banking. They became members of panels and of committees and were authors of articles on finance and credit in relation to arbitration. The bankers assumed a new responsibility for solving disputes, many of which had found their way to their desks in the normal course of business.

So, also, accountants, through their various national organizations, particularly the American Society of Certified Public Accountants, brought to the Association the talent of the accounting profession.

These men and organizations brought arbitration to public notice and thus reached deeply into the social and economic life of the nation. For the first time, a national consciousness that arbitration was an American way of life became apparent.

Members of the first Panels of the Association must be included among its builders, for through their fair and disinterested service they helped greatly to give the Association prestige and to build confidence in its activities. It is impossible to pay sufficiently high tribute to the men who have served quietly and conscientiously as arbitrators, without benefit of public acclaim or personal reward, in the many cases submitted to arbitration. They are the real founders of a continuing belief in arbitration; and they are the source of the phenomenal development of the Association. They are the practical builders of good faith, goodwill, tolerance, co-operation,

[6] For members, see Ch. XXV, p. 204

and confidence. They are the best exponents and advocates of arbitration, for they speak with the authority of experience.

Any account of the real builders of the Association would be incomplete, were no mention made of the parties in dispute who early in its history submitted their differences to arbitration in the Commercial Arbitration Tribunal. Parties who had gone through the experience of an arbitration supplied the Association with a laboratory in which it could experiment and thereby improve its own services and facilities. They brought their problems and helped in the discovery of basic principles for the solution of new problems. They have kept the Association alert to new opportunities for service.

Also, the Association counts as builders the many makers of contracts who used its clauses and services in the early days. It was through their faith in arbitration and willingness to use clauses and submit controversies, that arbitration took root in new areas of industrial and economic life at home and abroad.

The beliefs and activities of these many founders have been directed and co-ordinated by the successive Boards of Directors who have carried out the policies and plans formulated in the early history of the Association. It is these consecutive Boards of Directors and officers that have carried the Association through to its present status.[7]

If there are master builders in a cause so richly endowed with founders, members of the staff of the Society and later of the new Association are entitled to that distinction, for they, unfailingly and with fidelity, carried out the ideals, principles and policies laid down in the charter.[8]

To the business men, engineers, lawyers, accountants, credit men, purchasing agents and countless others, the Association owes its vision and enthusiasm. Trade and commercial groups and their leaders have furnished valuable experience and technical advice. To members of Panels, the reputation of the Association for fearless and fair dealing in the actual settlement of disputes is largely

[7] For membership of the various Boards that have participated in building the American Arbitration Association and its related systems, see Ch. XXV.

[8] Those serving faithfully throughout the early years of the Association were J. Noble Braden, Antonia Hatvany, George A. Little and Joseph Mayper.

due. From parties who have submitted their disputes to arbitration, has come the laboratory out of which have resulted the improvement in techniques. To its early contributors and members, may be attributed its present sound financial condition.

To all of these men and organizations, Americans owe the prestige of creating the first independent institution of arbitration as a fundamental part of the social and economic life of the country and later of the Western Hemisphere.

CHAPTER IV

The American Concept of Organized Arbitration

«««« »»»»

WITH the completion of a new institution of arbitration, the American Arbitration Association was ready to construct a national system for economic peace and security in domestic affairs and to use this system for international peace and security. The Association was ready to apply, through arbitration, the principle that impartial and swift justice is a permanent attribute of any system of arbitration. It was prepared to test its belief that until people of their own accord, and through their own efforts, learn to arbitrate their differences within the range of their own activities and experiences, governments will not be much inclined amicably to solve their differences. It was soon to take the educational measures necessary to bring its belief in arbitration into actual practice and to stimulate public interest and opinion in support of the general acceptance of arbitration.

But first the Association had to provide ways and means through a national system of tribunals, for the greater development of individual responsibility in the settlement of disputes and for the encouragement of self-reliance in doing so. It fully believed that this individual responsibility could be organized without impairment of the voluntary right to arbitrate and that a system of arbitration could become an integral part of the social and economic structure of the nation.

What the Association did not, in its enthusiasm, realize was the tremendous amount of preliminary work that had to be done to establish a national system, before it could hope to become instrumental in world affairs, and that many years must pass in organization, administration and experimentation before its ultimate international vision came to be realized.[1]

While there was to be no change in arbitration as the voluntary act of the parties in dispute, nor any restriction upon their right to choose their own judges nor any infringement upon their right to define their own controversy or fix the jurisdiction of the arbitrator and determine their own procedure, there was to be a very important change in the establishment of a system of arbitration within which parties might find accommodations to exercise these rights.

The idea of a national system of arbitration was in itself a departure from the fixed pattern. Its organization required an independently created institution of arbitration that would be free from alliances with any other organization and that would not be concerned with fixed economic theories or the advocacy of other causes. The American Arbitration Association was this kind of an institution; for whatever economic views might be held by its directors, members of committees or affiliated trade groups, these in no way were reflected in the organization of the system of commercial arbitration which the Association established. The function of the Association was to provide, in the form of Tribunals, facilities and services which parties could use at their discretion and of their own free will. These facilities and services were not to be determined by commodity groups nor to be limited by geographical limitations within the United States and its territories. The Association was to be the administrator of the system under established Rules that governed all Tribunals.

The idea of a system of arbitration, operated economically and competently for the convenience or benefit of parties in dispute and in the public interest under uniform rules of procedure and under identical facilities and services, indicated a profound change in the American attitude toward arbitration.

The old concept that economic society should continue to bear the extravagant waste and pay the heavy cost of trade disputes, was giving way to public concern over this *laissez-faire* attitude. The hitherto accepted thinking that parties must wait for a dispute to arise and run its ruinous course before applying arbitration was

[1] See Ch. XXII, p. 157.

becoming an outworn procedure in favor of anticipating and providing in advance for the settlement of future disputes. The old theory that arbitration was to be judged by the number of disputes that were submitted or settled rather than by the number it prevented, was receiving little credence in the new institution. The old practice of avoiding rules of procedure, resulting in loopholes through which the courts could upset awards, was giving way to procedures that would be litigation proof and would thus bring credit rather than discredit upon arbitration through the elimination of uncertainties and delays. The old practice of appointing arbitrators and leaving them to blunder along under a vague definition of their powers and without procedural guidance, appeared susceptible to vast improvement. Nor was the selection of arbitrators to be left to chance, if the parties could be persuaded to appoint impartial persons from scientifically organized panels whose members were held in readiness for their choice.

This change in philosophy substituted prevention for cure, foresight for hindsight, planned references by way of clauses for casual submissions of existing disputes, and scientific organization for the historic disorder.

The organization of a system also changed the attitude toward arbitration. A system developed arbitration as a normal process of civilization, having its own standards, rules of procedure and administrative services, together with research and educational facilities. The record was to be written in terms of its general acceptance and use by the people rather than exclusively in terms of litigation under arbitration laws. A practice of arbitration, such as existed in other professions, was made possible by the organization of arbitration.

These changes in organization, in philosophy and in attitude, required substantial changes in the kind of machinery that was needed to give them reality and acceptance by the people. Hitherto localized by geographical or trade limitations, arbitration was to be made national. Hitherto characterized by wide differences in procedure, the process was to acquire uniformity. Hitherto relatively inaccessible, arbitration was to be taken to the people. Hitherto enmeshed in legal technicalities, arbitration was to be made simple and attractive. Hitherto, parties who had refrained from using arbitration for fear of unfamiliar detail, were to have impartial and competent administrators to take care of such detail.

The newly formed Association was institutionalizing arbitration by giving it a central administrative organization, facilities for research and education, a laboratory for experiment, and a national system of tribunals. Its organization was non-profit-making, non-political, and unofficial, created by the trade, commercial, professional, and economic interests within the framework of private business enterprise in the United States. It was a voluntary organization, dependent upon private interest and support, and without official funds, representation, or direction. The institution was national in scope, and operated through its own established machinery and through co-operating financial, commercial and trade organizations.

As finally organized, the Association was equipped to study, organize, and publish information and knowledge concerning arbitration and to conduct research and education in its own name. It was competent to establish and administer the machinery of arbitration and to provide parties in dispute with facilities and services, panels of arbitrators and administrative services. It had authority to suggest arbitration clauses that would call its services into action when needed. Finally, it was competent to plan a future course of arbitration development for the benefit of individuals and the nation and of international trade relations.

Organized arbitration also changed the assembling of arbitrators. Small consideration had been given to standard qualifications for arbitrators or to recording their performance in office. The Association, as part of its organization, established a national panel, with a membership based upon well-defined qualifications. It set standards for the office, issued instructions and provided training for the duties of that office.[2]

The participation of parties in a system of arbitration also underwent changes. Generally, they had selected their own arbitrators and conducted their own proceeding in comparative ignorance of rules, laws, court decisions, or other safeguards. In some vague manner, parties were supposed to meet the legal requirements for making a valid arbitration agreement and for obtaining a valid

[2] See Ch. XIV, p. 104.

award, without special knowledge of legal requirements. This casual attitude had often resulted in the non-enforcement of agreements and the setting aside of awards to a degree that was discouraging.

The Association believed that parties not only needed the guidance of well-prepared rules and assembled knowledge of laws and decisions, but that a very considerable part of the detail of conducting a proceeding might readily be turned over to an administrator of their own choice, without in any way impinging upon or restricting any of the fundamental rights of the parties.[3] This belief the Association put into effect in its Rules of Procedure for Tribunals.[4]

During its evolution through the centuries, arbitration, which in fact is the final decision of an arbitrator based upon the facts of the matter voluntarily submitted by the parties who agree to abide by the decision, had become identified with bargaining processes of mediation and conciliation. Out of this identification had grown the belief that arbitration was a species of compromise and therefore it was unnecessary to prepare for arbitration on the basis of obtaining justice. This belief was immediately dispelled under the concept of organized arbitration which the Association put into effect. All of its Panel members were instructed to act as arbitrators and not as mediators or conciliators, under Rules that made no provision for any proceeding not of a quasi-judicial character. While parties were always free to settle and withdraw from arbitration any matter they had submitted, at any time before the award was made, Panel arbitrators were not authorized to participate in these settlements nor to make suggestions to the parties. Through these provisions in the Rules for its Tribunals, the Association established a practice of arbitration under arbitration laws and in conformity with arbitration tradition. It is through adherence to this standard that lawyers have come so generally to practice arbitration in tribunals.[5]

Another change in the traditional pattern, brought about by organized arbitration, was in the perspective. Contracting parties,

[3] See Ch. XV, p. 111.

[4] For text of Rules, see Annex I, p. 219.

[5] In 1938, in 70 per cent of the commercial matters submitted to arbitration, lawyers represented clients; in 1946, it was 82 per cent. In 1942, in 84 per cent of the labor matters submitted to arbitration, lawyers represented clients; in 1947, it was 96.1 per cent.

hitherto content to wait for a dispute to arise, began to include arbitration clauses in their contracts with a view to avoiding future delays in settlement or resort to litigation. In proportion as facilities and services became available through systems of arbitration, the frequency of these clauses appeared. It was the assurance that an arbitration could be held with speed, economy, and justice that encouraged its use. Soon, industrial groups were adopting these clauses generally for their members, thereby greatly stabilizing a practice of arbitration through assurance of the use of Tribunals. There was to emerge eventually a quite considerable fabric of security against the waste and costs of disputes through the wide adoption of these clauses in contracts.

The American concept of arbitration was unique in that it provided for a central independent institution that operated systems of tribunals and that also carried on the research and experimentation that made these tribunals responsive to the social and economic needs of American commercial and industrial life. This concept was unusual in that it systematically encouraged individuals in self-regulation and in the control of their disputes within the framework of free enterprise and business institutions. It accustomed individuals and groups of individuals to the use of systems that provided them with uniform and competent facilities and services anywhere in the United States.

Through the organization of arbitration the Association has changed much of public indifference toward the waste and futility of unsettled disputes and inculcated the idea of the prevention and control of disputes. It started new thinking about disputes which led to a change from a defeatist philosophy to one of enlightened mastery. It made arbitration easy and natural and dispelled much of the fear of the unknown caused by entrusting the settlement of disputes to untrained arbitrators. It clarified the confusion between compromise processes and judicial determination wherein awards were legally enforceable as judgments of the court. And, finally, organized arbitration changed the perspective from the past to the future and away from cure to prevention.

Some of these practices, viewpoints, and achievements had characterized earlier arbitrations in other countries. The contribution of the Association was unique in that they were integrated systematically and logically in a process that was made available to the people of an entire country who were encouraged through education, precept and example to participate in the new American concept of organized arbitration. It was the people and not a privileged few who have made these systems into public institutions of worth to the United States.

CHAPTER V

The Association as a National Institution

«««« »»»»

AMERICANS have the distinction of having organized the first national arbitration institution. By this is meant they were the first to separate the practice of arbitration from other economic or social institutions. They conceived the idea of its complete independence from agencies created for other purposes. They set arbitration upon a path of its own where it must depend upon itself for organization, administration and financing.[1]

The Association was first organized as a commercial arbitration institution for the convenience generally of American business. As certain principles and policies were adopted and followed in its organization, for which no precedent existed, and as the Association is encouraging the organization of similar institutions in other countries,[2] it may be of interest briefly to examine the kind of institution which the Americans designed.

The Association is a non-profit membership corporation operating under a New York State Charter. It is empowered under that Charter to create and maintain and administer facilities for arbitration; it may carry on research and educational work; it may suggest improvements in arbitration law; it may make experiments in arbitration practice; and it may create a science of arbitration if that

[1] The Institute of Arbitrators in London was organized in 1915. This is, however, primarily an organization for training and supplying arbitrators and not an institution in the sense used by Americans.

[2] From information received in November of 1947, it seems likely that China will be the second country to organize a National Arbitration Association to co-operate with the American Arbitration Association in the settlement of Chinese-American trade disputes. (See also Ch. XXI, p. 152 for pending negotiations for a Chinese-American Trade Arbitration Commission.)

seems a practical objective. All of its resources are directed toward these ends.

It is a voluntary organization engaged in developing the voluntary resources of the country for the settlement or control of economic disputes. Because of its quasi-judicial functions, neither the Association nor its personnel is identified with other organizations or activities. None of its officers or staff may profit financially from any of the activities of the Association.

The Association is governed by a Board of Directors representing the public, trade, commercial, professional, and labor interests of the United States. These Directors, in classes with terms expiring in four-year periods, are chosen at an annual meeting held in January in the manner provided in the by-laws.[3] Its officers consist of a President, First Vice-President who is the executive officer, and several Vice Presidents in charge of different activities; a Chairman and a Vice-Chairman of the Board; a Chairman of the Executive Committee; a Chairman of the Arbitration Committee; a Secretary; and a Treasurer. These officers are elected by the Board of Directors following the annual meeting. An Executive Committee of fifteen members administers the affairs of the Association.

The income of the Association is derived from the following sources: (1) grants or contributions for research and education; (2) fees from parties for the administration of their arbitration in Tribunals; (3) and memberships for the general maintenance of the organization and the development of its activities. For the administration of any special system as, for example, that of the Motion Picture Industry or the Fur Industry or the Aviation Industry, the Association receives grants of funds which are expended for that purpose. The Association has no endowment and receives no government funds or subsidies. It pays no dividends.

The Association maintains administrative offices on the eleventh floor of the Time and Life Building, 9 Rockefeller Plaza, New York. These headquarters include administrative offices, hearing rooms, and adequate research facilities. They are the publication office of *The Arbitration Journal*. They are also the offices of the Inter-American Commercial Arbitration Commission and of the Canadian-American Commercial Arbitration Commission and of other inter-

[3] For members of previous and present Boards of Directors, see Ch. XXV, p. 184.

national arbitration systems with which the Association is identified.

The Association functions from its central headquarters through thirty branch offices staffed by clerks and, when necessary, by a secretary. From these branch offices, arbitrations are administered, literature is distributed, and arbitration is cultivated within that area by means of co-operating commercial and trade organizations or through individuals or social agencies.

Central headquarters maintain a research and information bureau where literature is prepared for general distribution or use of branch offices, where conferences are held, and where problems or policies presented by Tribunals or otherwise are considered, solved, and are integrated in the organization and its activities.

These headquarters are the administrative offices for national and special panels of arbitrators. One is the National Commercial Panel, from which arbitrators may be selected to hear and determine any kind of commercial or civil dispute in any part of the country. Its members are commercial peace officers of the nation. They are busy men engaged in regular pursuits who, upon request of the parties, lay aside their regular duties and act as judges to settle the matter in dispute. The other is the National Labor Panel from which arbitrators may be selected to hear and determine disputes between management and labor.

Members of Special Panels are usually appointed upon the request of a business group to perform services for their members under Rules set up for that particular industry. Illustrations are afforded by the Motion Picture Panel of approximately 1,200 men, the Air Transport Panel of about 150 members, the Accident Claims Panel of approximately 300 lawyers, and the Fur Industry Panel of 100 members. As a rule, the industrial group specifies the number required and their distribution at points where disputes are likely to arise.

Central headquarters is responsible for the drafting of Rules and the development of systems of arbitration, although the Arbitration Law Committee considers amendments to arbitration laws and the drafting of arbitration clauses.

The administration of tribunals is centered in a Tribunals Department with a Tribunals Vice President in charge. All matters submitted to arbitration are handled by this Department. Neither the parties nor their records are identified with the other activities of the Association. This separation of functions has proceeded upon the theory that an arbitration is the private affair of the parties, and that a Tribunal set up for their convenience is their Tribunal. None of the officers or staff members, not engaged in Tribunal work, is authorized to function in a proceeding. Under this policy the judicial determination of a dispute by an arbitrator is not subject to control or direction of the Association other than through the Rules of Procedure which are administered by the Tribunals Vice President and his staff.

The executive functions of the Association are performed by executive officers under the By-Laws; the judicial functions of Tribunals are performed by members of Panels under Rules of Procedure. Parties are thus left in full control of their arbitration proceeding, subject only to the rules they adopt and to the prevailing arbitration law.

In accordance with this practice, it has always been the policy of the Association never to act as arbitrator. Every matter submitted in a Tribunal is always determined by a member of the Panel chosen by the parties. Only when a party defaults does the Association appoint the arbitrator. Parties may, of course, choose arbitrators who are not members of the Panel but they cannot authorize the Association to act as arbitrator. If so designated, the Association follows its customary practice of submitting names of members of its Panel.

It is the function, however, of the executive branch of the Association to set the standard qualifications for arbitrators and to maintain quotas, to keep the Rules of Procedure up to date, to set administrative fees for services rendered to the parties and to receive and disburse all funds deposited by parties in the course of their arbitration. It is also the function of the executive staff to train arbitrators, to provide them with literature, and to keep them informed concerning the duties of their office. But once a Panel member enters upon his judicial duties as arbitrator, he is subject only to the Rules which the parties have adopted.

This first arbitration institution is a staff and line organization. It does not operate through local committees nor through subsidiaries. Its branch offices are primarily Tribunals headquarters. While it had Advisory Committees as, for example, on labor, and on arbitration law, and from time to time appoints special committees, these are not concerned with the actual settlement of disputes nor with the administration of a Tribunal.

The Association, as an incorporated, educational, and scientific organization, assumes full and direct responsibility for all activities carried on in its name and for the integrity of its arbitration proceedings conducted under its Rules in its Tribunals.

CHAPTER VI

The Problem of Financing Arbitration

«««« »»»»

WHEN arbitration was organized as an independent institution, a new problem in financing was presented. Previously, arbitration had been carried as a part of the activities of trade, commercial, or financial organizations and was supported by these organizations. The maintenance of facilities and services was part of their annual budgetary expense.

When casual arbitrations were arranged between parties, or by their counsel, outside of established machinery, the cost was paid by the parties to the arbitration and that was the end of their responsibility. It was also customary for arbitrators to fix their fees and assess their expenses in the award. Sometimes the parties agreed to the rate of fees and expenses, in advance of the arbitration; in other instances, they might receive a "surprise" in the award.

Where facilities and services were provided for members of trade organizations, or by chambers of commerce, it was usual to charge a small case or administrative fee, the amount being ordinarily set in the Rules. But this amount was not intended to cover maintenance of permanent facilities but only the actual cost of a particular arbitration. The maintenance cost was usually absorbed in the general expenses of the organization, including the services of its executives.

Under this arrangement, arbitration was usually the stepchild of the organization and rarely received sufficient funds to allow it to be more than a static element in the organization that was usually concerned with many other purposes. Rarely was educational work undertaken or consideration given to the public implications of arbitration.

In commodity exchanges, however, where disputes were concerned chiefly with questions of quality, facilities for this purpose were maintained in concrete form and with more adequate funds.

With the organization of systems of arbitration, not sponsored by any particular trade or commercial organization, the new problem of financing became acute. The American Arbitration Association had to supply this need by becoming a financing organization, not only for its central office activities but for the maintenance of tribunal facilities and services.

Through its early experience, the Association arrived at the basic conclusion that a system of arbitration can not be successfully established unless there is a sponsoring organization that is willing and able to finance its maintenance and operation. This conclusion was amply demonstrated in the building of the Inter-American Commercial Arbitration System which the Association was able to finance in its initial stages.

It is pertinent here to examine the basic costs of establishing and maintaining systems of arbitration.

In practically every instance there are studies to be made, for only systems based upon knowledge have a chance of survival. As will appear in later chapters, such studies preceded the establishment of the American, Inter-American, and Canadian-American Systems.[1]

The cost of establishing and maintaining Panels of Arbitrators is very considerable. A later description of these Panels indicates some of the items of cost.[2] The actual upkeep of a Panel, once it is established, is a continuing one if parties are to be assured of available competent and impartial arbitrators.

The preparation of rules and clauses is not something that can be done once and then be forgotten. New conditions, current court decisions, or changes in laws require constant examination of rules. Starting with one standard clause, the Association now has at least a dozen clauses that are in current use. These have been made necessary by trade conditions, government regulations, or other

[1] See Ch. VII, XVII, and XVIII.
[2] See Ch. XIV, p. 104.

factors that require special types of clauses. A constant analysis of these changes must be made if American business men are to find arbitration a satisfactory proceeding when a dispute arises.

Standards are expensive to maintain. They do not just grow. They must be formulated on the basis of practical experience. They must be explained to the parties in order to obtain their acceptance of them. They must be transmitted to arbitrators. They must be put into manuals of instruction for tribunal clerks. They may relate to arbitration generally as, for example, the maintenance of the voluntary principle of arbitration, or they may concern ethical conduct by arbitrators in office for which a Code of Ethics is prepared. Experts are necessary if these standards are to be really effective in a practice of arbitration.

The minimum requirements of an institution of arbitration appear to be: the maintenance of a central headquarters, together with staffs for Tribunals administration, research and education; the selection and upkeep of Panels of arbitrators; the maintenance of facilities and services for conducting arbitrations; the promulgation and distribution of rules of procedure; the assembling of a knowledge of court decisions; a repository for records; and publications devoted to the advancement of the knowledge and practice of arbitration. These minimum requirements are basic in the sense that they must be maintained irrespective of the number or kind of disputes to be submitted to arbitration; for, should their initiation await the submission of specific matters to arbitration, it might well be frustrated.

It is, however, the use of arbitration clauses that creates a heavy burden of expense. Whenever a clause is used in a contract that names the Rules of the Association, or of any system affiliated with it, the user of that clause assumes that, should he have a dispute, facilities and services will be available to him for its settlement. For the actual service rendered in that arbitration, he is willing to pay the administrative fee set forth in the Rules. This covers preliminary arrangements, the cost of a hearing room, the time of a clerk, and the processing of his arbitration.

But the difficulty is that parties as a rule brook no delay. They want a qualified arbitrator, a hearing room, a clerk, and service at once. The preliminary cost of having this machinery available and in good working order so it can function immediately is not one that parties are ordinarily willing to finance. Nor are administrative fees sufficiently high or constant to meet this cost, for reasons that appear later. Consequently, in the establishment of any system, the sponsoring organization must be prepared to finance the basic cost of maintenance of permanent machinery so as to meet the requirements of clause users.

While an institution of arbitration must, therefore, be prepared to render service through maintained machinery in some relative degree to the prevalence of clauses that name its Rules, the preponderance of private settlements prevailing under these clauses reduces the income from arbitrations. Even when matters are submitted to a tribunal, in at least one-half of them, the matter is settled by the parties in the course of the proceeding and the matter is withdrawn before the hearing or award. In such instances, parties expect a return of a portion of the administrative fee in the belief that it is they, and not the Association, who have effected the settlement.

This tendency, while of the greatest benefit to the parties, and in the public interest, constitutes a problem in financing—so much so that the Association has, in a number of instances where a group uses its clause, preferred to have an annual administrative fee in lieu of "case fees," as constituting a more stable source of income for the maintenance of facilities.

A second principle of financing, therefore, is that parties should not be encouraged to use clauses recommended by an organization, and referring to its Rules, unless that organization is in a position to maintain basic machinery or can, through arrangements with other organizations, make their machinery available to such clause users. Such has been the objective of the Association in entering into arrangements with chambers of commerce in foreign countries under which their facilities, as well as those of the Association, become available.

As the use of systems progressed, a third principle of financing emerged. It was discovered that parties to arbitrations cannot be expected to pay the total cost of maintaining a system of arbitration because many amounts in controversy are small, or the parties are poor. Arbitration should not be denied them because of these circumstances. It will be denied them if costs are put too high. It is against public policy to let any dispute go unsettled which parties are willing to arbitrate, for often as not that seemingly trivial or unimportant dispute may cause acute repercussions. For example, a dispute involving one employee in a small plant may precipitate strikes of high magnitude in unexpected quarters. Furthermore, some opponents of arbitration may try to defeat the usefulness of arbitration by insisting upon high costs as a means of curtailing its usefulness. The Association is, therefore, in favor of keeping the costs of arbitration within financial limits so it can be used by any disputants.

The true function of arbitration is to enable parties to settle their dispute. Whether they do this by an award or by themselves during the course of a proceeding is immaterial, for in either instance arbitration has performed its true service. But the very efficiency of arbitration defeats it as an income producer. As settlements by the parties increase with the effectiveness of arbitration clauses not too much reliance can be placed upon case fees as a predictable source of income for maintaining a system.

Organized arbitration processes are comparatively new. Parties are not yet accustomed to the use of rules and forms and to the clerical routine which an arbitration must take, if a fair and just award is to result—an award which will stand the procedural scrutiny of the court, should its annulment be asked by a party. Parties are not even familiar with the amount of work and care that is involved in the submission of a list drawn from the Panel, for their acceptance or rejection. Therefore, until much more educational work is done and the parties become more familiar with the working of a system, administrative fees cannot be put on a basis to cover fully the cost of maintenance. The effect would be not to increase the income from arbitration cases but to deter parties from arbitrating.

Furthermore, a system of arbitration is not organized solely in the interest of parties in dispute. It is organized to find ways and means of avoiding disputes; to broaden the scope of arbitration; to influence the cultural and social life of a nation in the direction of co-operation, and to promote confidence and goodwill among its people; and to advance unity and understanding through the reduction of conflict. Arbitration is organized to protect society generally from the risks and hazards of unnecessary disputes and to reduce their cost and waste to civilization. One of its functions in a democratic society is to encourage self-regulation and self-discipline within a framework of individual initiative and private enterprise.

Parties engaged in the settlement of an annoying or critical dispute cannot be expected to consider the benefits of arbitration to society. Nor do they necessarily command the resources nor have they the inclination to use them for such broad purposes. They have profits or commodities at stake for which they are contending. To assess fees upon the basis of public welfare would appear to them to be both impractical and inopportune.

Arbitration, also, has another limitation that affects adversely its income. One of the great producers of income is advertising. This is a privilege denied to arbitration. The records of a court are public and litigation is constantly being publicized in the press. Not so arbitration. Its hearings and records are private and though the case may be filled with human interest, the record is rarely available to influence others to arbitrate. If using the press to advertise the merits of arbitration in some of its famous cases were permissible, there would doubtless be an increase in the volume of arbitrations and in income from this source.

Where an arbitral institution combines general research and educational activities in the advancement of arbitration generally with the operation of systems of tribunals where justice is administered, it suffers another handicap in that its sources of income cannot be such as to carry any implication of influence or control over the decisions of arbitrators. The separation of its general from its tribunal functions must be so absolute that memberships or contributions bear no relation to an arbitrator's consideration of the issue before him.

If then, systems of arbitration are not to be supported by economic organizations of which they were formerly a part, or from fees from arbitrations, how shall they be financed, not only in their initial stages of organization but in their permanent maintenance.

The American Arbitration Association does not claim to have solved this problem but it has at least financed the American systems and been able to project international systems through initial support.

Of first importance are memberships. These not only supply a stable source of income but they provide a democratic form of financing in which many persons or organizations of all kinds participate. Members also constitute an educational body for the advancement of arbitration. The Association now has American members who support the American systems and Inter-American members whose dues are allocated to the maintenance of the Inter-American System. Whether it will prove feasible to have international memberships for the support of international systems has not yet been determined. Memberships comprise more than 25 per cent of the budget of the Association for 1947. As memberships take persistent and hard educational work to obtain, too much reliance cannot be placed upon them for starting new systems.

Administrative fees, even when a considerable volume of arbitrations is assured, are a not entirely reliable source of income. They comprised about 40 per cent of the 1947 budget of the Association. They are usually obtainable only after a system is established and has won the confidence of contracting parties. They cannot be relied upon to finance new systems, particularly international systems, where the expense is increased by distance, languages, and differences in laws, trade practices, and regulations.

There remain contributions as a source of financing. It is unquestionably true but for contributions from persons and organizations interested in the public advantages of arbitration, the American Arbitration Association could not have survived the first few years of its existence. Nor could it have acquired the basic knowledge to construct a sound system, nor could it have maintained a sufficient central organization to plan and develop systems of arbitration. It is axiomatic that any new system that is projected must depend upon voluntary contributions not only to start it but to maintain it for a considerable time.

As to the source of such contributions, the Association has adopted a policy which may not be pertinent to the financing of international systems but which is essential to the American systems.

The Association believes that voluntary arbitration in the economic field is the act of private individuals; that it is their self-regulation and individual effort that should be encouraged, and that, therefore, systems that encourage or apply voluntary arbitration among contracting parties, should be privately financed. The Association has not, therefore, sought government funds, except for research in the Inter-American field from the Office of the Coordinator of Inter-American Affairs.

The Association also believes, while contributions for research and educational purposes may be of sizable amounts, that contributions for its general work should be for smaller amounts and be widely distributed. There never has been, and the Association intends there shall not be, any question that its policies or the decisions of its arbitrators are influenced by any of its sources of income, nor by the size of any contribution.

The Association is of the further opinion that industry should bear the burden of maintaining commercial and labor systems of arbitration and that an equitable apportionment of the basic cost and maintenance should be made among the leading branches of industry. It believes also that unions should pay a proportionate cost of maintenance of labor systems. Were this basic cost to be apportioned and assessed each year, systems of arbitration would not only be more effective but could expand their facilities and services and better serve the public interest.

The problem of financing systems of arbitration during a World War was presented to the Association in 1940. By reason of the resort to force and regimentation that prevails during a War, arbitration usually diminishes. This is particularly true in commercial relations, when governments of necessity carry on much of the trade. In the second World War, this diminution was only partly true. First, United States Government corporations used arbitration clauses in contracts as did also foreign purchasing commissions and agencies; and inter-American trade was kept free from disputes by arbitration, so commercial arbitration was carried on by governments as well as by private traders.

In labor relations, arbitration assumed an important role in preventing strikes and in expediting war production through the prompt settlement of disputes. Its use was greatly advanced by the National War Labor Board and by the activities of the Association. In order to expedite war service use of arbitration and to provide for its financing, a War Service Committee was appointed during that period. Under the Presidency of C. V. Whitney in 1940-41, and later, this Committee enabled the Association to carry its systems without impairing their efficiency and to be of very real service during the war.[3]

For the development of international systems of arbitration so each country may have its own national association of arbitration and so adequate facilities and services and educational work may be carried on as a foundation for international peace and security, the problem is peculiarly difficult.

An example was recently afforded by an undertaking to finance a Central Bureau of the recently organized International Commercial Arbitration Committee in Paris, France. Four subjects of study were approved and assigned to the co-operating organizations.[4] Each co-operating organization undertook to finance out of its own funds the study it accepted, but no agreement could be reached as to financing the Central Bureau and for the time being, co-ordination of the studies must proceed without funds.

Would governments be the best instrumentalities to finance systems of arbitration? The Seventh International Conference of American States and the Pan American Union thought not when they created an Inter-American Commercial Arbitration System, for they made no appropriation and specifically provided that the System should be independent of official control. The Soviet thinks otherwise, for all of its functions are state financed. The Court of Arbitration of the International Chamber of Commerce and the Western Hemisphere systems are supported by private funds contributed by business men.

It would seem that the only solution of the problem lies in the creation of an International Arbitration Foundation with sufficient funds to establish, maintain and co-ordinate systems of arbitration. Such a fund would be expended in the study of arbitration laws and practice in different countries, in the organization of national associations of arbitration, and in the establishment and maintenance of facilities and services in important trade centers. It would be used also to co-ordinate national systems as a part of international systems, and to carry on educational work in institutions of learning

[3] For members of War Service Committee, see Ch. XXV, p. 209.

[4] 1. Unification of the Law on Arbitration and the Enforcement of Arbitral Awards. 2. Co-ordination of Arbitration Systems. 3. Arbitration between Governments and Individuals. 4. Arbitration Education.

and through public instruction in the knowledge and practice of arbitration. A part of such a fund should be devoted to the maintenance of panels of arbitrators and to their training for the office. The need for periodic international conferences on arbitration is already apparent, as are more adequate and representative publications. Without some such fund, international systems are likely to develop slowly and haphazardly, and often without due preparation as to policies and organization, and may thus fail to advance either the practice or prestige of arbitration.

CHAPTER VII

Adventures in Research and Education

«««« »»»»

THE publicity campaign, begun by the Arbitration Society of America, challenged public interest and greatly stimulated curiosity about arbitration. The new Association was hard pressed to supply the information or answer the many questions this campaign had aroused. It found itself faced with a very considerable task of research and with a very real problem of both technical and general education. The field was so vast and the opportunities were so great, and the funds for such work were so limited, that it was difficult to chart a constructive course. Fortunately, grants from John D. Rockefeller, Jr. continued over a number of years. Michael Friedsam, Frederick Brown and others enabled the Association to undertake certain fundamental studies which it believed were indispensable to the founding of sound systems of arbitration in the United States and in other countries.[1]

As the Association was inexperienced in research, it was fortunate in obtaining the advice and assistance of members of a Research Council.[2]

The first step in this program of research and education seemed to require the assembling of a knowledge of the history, status, and progress of commercial arbitration in the United States. The Association, therefore, early in 1927, instituted an inquiry into the history and current use of arbitration by trade, commercial, and financial organizations in the United States. The results of this inquiry were published in 1927. They were both revealing and

[1] For recent developments in international arbitration research, see Ch. XXII, p. 161.

[2] For members, see Ch. XXV, p. 204.

encouraging. They showed more than 300 organizations—some national, others regional or local—that were committed to the principle of arbitration or that had arbitration facilities and services for their members, or communities.[3] This publication presented for the first time in any country an account of the normal practice of arbitration outside of courts and in commercial organizations. It made available to all organizations, the rules, practice, experience, and progress of each of them. By thus revealing the principles, policies, standards, and practical use of arbitration for the entire country, it placed at the disposal of the Association essential information that was of real assistance in the later organization of its national system. This study brought these trade, commercial, and financial organizations and their leaders into close co-operation with the Association and was widely distributed through the Research Council.

A similar dearth of information existed in the field of arbitration laws and in the assembly of court decisions interpreting these laws. Not since 1872, when Morse had compiled them, had this kind of information been available in the United States.

The Association believed it could not proceed wisely with proposals to advance modern principles of arbitration without a fuller knowledge of the existing laws. A study was, therefore, initiated under the direction of Dr. Wesley A. Sturges, then professor of law, and now dean, of the Yale Law School. This study resulted in bringing up to date the practice under common and statutory law, together with leading decisions and gave business and the bar the reference book they so much needed.[4]

These two comprehensive studies of tribunal and court practice of arbitration were followed by the publication of a *Code of Arbitration Practice and Procedure* for use in the Tribunals of the Association. It combined tribunal and court practice in a practical guide.[5] This Code had been preceded by *Suggestions for the Practice of*

[3] *Year Book on Commercial Arbitration in the United States*, published for the American Arbitration Association by the Oxford University Press (1927).

[4] *Commercial Arbitrations and Awards* by Wesley A. Sturges, Vernon Law Book Company, (1930).

[5] *Code of Arbitration Practice and Procedure of the American Arbitration Tribunal* (1931), 284 pp. Published by Commerce Clearing House, Inc. for the American Arbitration Association.

Commercial Arbitration in the United States—a publication largely devoted to the application and interpretation of the New York Arbitration Law.[6]

Both the *Code* and *Suggestions* dealt with the practical problems of how to make submissions and clauses, how to initiate proceedings under Rules, how to select arbitrators, and how to conduct proceedings and regulate costs. They referred to a number of decisions from which leading arbitration principles had been derived. They contained a series of twenty-eight forms which had been devised for convenient use under the Rules. They comprised the first manuals on commercial arbitration.

An undertaking to keep the *Code* up to date, particularly with reference to decisions and awards and news of the advance of arbitration, was made through the issuance of a monthly Bulletin, called the *American Arbitration Service*. This was the first loose-leaf service for commercial arbitration, a form of publication now common for labor arbitrations. Later reporting of decisions appeared in the *Arbitration Journal* which continues to be the only publication in which current court decisions on the entire subject of arbitration are assembled. Accompanying these publications was an up-to-date bibliography on commercial arbitration.

In accordance with the authorization in its Charter, the Association prepared a Draft State Arbitration Act. This draft incorporated the principles of the New York State and Federal Arbitration Laws. It was placed at the disposal of organizations interested in the improvement of arbitration law. In addition to the modern arbitration laws in effect in New York, Massachusetts and New Jersey, prior to the organization of the Association, the Draft Act was instrumental in obtaining modern arbitration laws in the states of Arizona, California, Connecticut, Louisiana, Michigan, New Hampshire, Ohio, Oregon, Pennsylvania, Rhode Island, Washington, and Wisconsin.

In the preparation of the Draft Act, as well as in the constant improvement of arbitration law, the enactment of new laws and in the amendment of present laws and in appearances of the Associa-

[6] *Suggestions for the Practice of Commercial Arbitration in the United States* (1928), 247 pp. Published by the Oxford University Press for the American Arbitration Association.

tion as *amicus curiæ* on important issues before the courts, the Association has had invaluable co-operation from its Arbitration Law Committee.[7]

A more ambitious research project was launched early in 1927. Upon examination of the existing information, it was found that no history of commercial arbitration in the United States had ever been written. The Association began such a history through special grants for scholarships. So far as is known, these were the first arbitration scholarships. This history was planned upon the basis of state surveys. An outline for the study was prepared for each state and included Alabama, California, Connecticut, District of Columbia, Illinois, Maryland, Massachusetts, New Jersey, Ohio, Oregon, Pennsylvania, Texas, Virginia, and Washington.

Supplementing these state studies were special surveys. The American Society of Certified Public Accountants, through the interest of Homer A. Dunn, Chairman of its Arbitration Committee, financed and assisted in the direction of some of these studies. Another study on the use of arbitration in inter-trade relations, particularly in the distribution field, was initiated and financed by A. Lincoln Filene, a member of the Board of the Association. Still another was a study of arbitration in banking, initiated by the late Thomas B. Paton, General Counsel of the American Bankers Association, under the auspices of the American Institute of Banking.

In 1941, the data assembled through these various studies and surveys was brought together in *Arbitration in Action* as a guide to the practice of commercial arbitration.[8]

With the enactment of the New York State Arbitration Law of 1920 and of the United States Arbitration Law of 1925, foreign trade arbitrations were attracted in increasing number and variety to the United States. Through the inclusion of arbitration clauses in foreign trade contracts, requests came to the Association for information about the laws and practice of arbitration in other countries. As in commercial arbitration in the United States, it was found that the information requested was not available.

The Association, therefore, instituted and helped to finance studies

[7] For members of the Committee, see Ch. XXV, p. 204.

[8] Frances Kellor, *Arbitration in Action*, published for the American Arbitration Association by Harper & Brothers, (1941).

of arbitration in other countries. The first project was carried out in co-operation with the International Chamber of Commerce. Funds were made available for the survey by the International General Electric Company in honor of Anson W. Burchard, former President of that Company and first President of the Association.

These studies covered the arbitration law and practice in Belgium, France, Germany, Great Britain, Italy, the Netherlands, and Switzerland. The brochures, subsequently published, were in effect the first manuals on the practice of arbitration in other countries and were distributed in the United States as well as in other countries. Another project was the translation and publication in English in 1928 of Volume I of the International Year Book on Civil and Commercial Arbitration, edited by Dr. Arthur Nussbaum. It provided essential information upon the law and practice in many European countries.[9]

In the planning and preparation of these publications, the Association had the advice and counsel of members of an Editorial Council of which the late John H. Finley was Chairman.[10]

One thing was lacking in this program of research and publications. There was no way of keeping information up to date and constantly before the public. In 1926, the Arbitration Society of America had endeavored to solve this problem by publishing the *Arbitration News*. This was discontinued for financial reasons when the new Association was organized. Ten years later the Association began the publication of a quarterly *Arbitration Journal*. It was published first under the joint auspices of the Association, the Chamber of Commerce of the State of New York, and the Inter-American Commercial Arbitration Commission. It appeared under a rather impressive personnel, having an Editorial Board, a Law Review Committee, a Joint Advisory Board representing the three sponsoring organizations, and a Business Advisory Committee.[11]

For its foreign news, and articles, the *Journal* relied upon an initial group of 29 collaborators located in different countries outside of the Western Hemisphere. This staff of collaborators was

[9] *International Year Book on Civil and Commercial Arbitration*, published by the Oxford University Press, for the American Arbitration Association (1928).

[10] For members, see Ch. XXV, p. 208.

[11] For members of Editorial Boards and Committees, see Ch. XXV, p. 208.

later increased to 65,[12] from the following countries: Australia, Belgium, Bermuda, British West Indies, Burma, Canada, Chile, China, Colombia, Costa Rica, Cuba, Denmark, France, Great Britain, Hungary, India, Ireland, Italy, Japan, Mexico, The Netherlands, Newfoundland, New Zealand, Panama, Paraguay, Roumania, Southern Rhodesia, South Africa, Sweden, Switzerland, and Venezuela.

In his introduction to the first issue of the Journal, Mr. Eastman, the Chairman of the Board of the Association, said:

"The *Arbitration Journal* is the logical next step in the organization of knowledge. It undertakes to 'hive off' a sphere of knowledge, hitherto undifferentiated from the field of law in which arbitration has been submerged and from the atmosphere of courts which has long penetrated its practice. It seeks to obtain a new focus and to paint new pictures of a somewhat hitherto drab existence and to bring to bear upon the whole subject a closer observation and a more discriminating judgment.

"In a specialized publication such as this it is possible to present, in attractive detail and in systematic form, various experiments and to incorporate the results of research and of special studies. It is possible to encourage exploration of the past and to assemble current information and to provide for its exchange in all countries. There is afforded the opportunity to follow not only the adventure of ideas but to present some of the adventurers. In this way, human knowledge will be extended and the pattern of the science will begin to take form, lifting arbitration from its narrow sphere of law, from its attributes of a panacea, and making it the servant of man's welfare and progress.

"Let us be more specific: By opening the archives of history, the accumulated general knowledge of the centuries becomes common knowledge. By recording current history, the simultaneous action of men and nations takes on a coherence and a prominence that gives to the subject the authoritative voice to which it has long been entitled. By maximizing knowledge, that is, by correlating it in one place, its significance to the welfare and progress of men assumes a new and more intelligible importance. By analyzing and discussing the subject, as a whole and the relation of its parts, chaotic thinking is reduced to order, ignorance is dispelled and prejudices allayed."

[12] For personnel of collaborators, see Ch. XXV, p. 208.

During the war, when much of the research and publications had to be suspended,[13] the Association published the *Arbitration Magazine*. This was an illustrated periodical, designed to aid the war effort and to keep arbitration more constantly in the public mind. With the resumption of the publication of the *Arbitration Journal*, the *Arbitration Magazine* was discontinued.

Although these studies and publications furnish much needed source material for instruction in commercial arbitration, such instruction has been neither uniform nor extensive. Outside of the instruction given at the New York University Law School by Dr. Walter J. Derenberg, at the Yale Law School by Dean Wesley A. Sturges and his staff and at the Harvard Graduate School of Business Administration by the late Dr. Nathan Isaacs, the teaching of commercial arbitration has not greatly advanced. In 1945-46, considerable progress was made in the training of teachers through New York State Teachers Colleges; and through an "In-Service Course," carried on under the joint auspices of the Associate Superintendent of New York City Schools and the Association in 1945.

Preparations for carrying instruction forward in a more methodical way are now being made. Under a fund established as the R. Emerson Swart Memorial Research Fund, the Association will publish in 1948, a textbook on arbitration and in 1949, a survey and program for education in arbitration. It will then be possible, with this additional source material to propose courses of instruction generally in American and foreign institutions of learning.

Research and instruction have become quite general in labor relations, and to an increasing degree they include arbitration. Systematic education in this field is well on its way, as the following illustrations indicate:

The National Industrial Conference Board, the American Management Association, the Society for the Advancement of Management, and various personnel conferences have devoted meetings or arranged round table conferences for the presentation and discussion of labor arbitration, practice and procedure, and clauses used in collective bargaining agreements. One of the earliest practice arbitrations was

[13] The *Arbitration Journal* suspended publication during the war and was resumed in 1945 as *The International Arbitration Journal*, and as *The Arbitration Journal* (New Series) in 1946.

presented by Panel Members and the staff of the Association to a meeting held by the National Industrial Conference Board in 1942. The Textile Workers Union (C.I.O.), and the United Steelworkers of America (C.I.O.), have also introduced lectures on arbitration. In a five-and-one-half-day conference held by the Textile Workers Union, at Black Mountain College in North Carolina, one half-day was devoted to arbitration and at the Steelworkers' Institutes held throughout the country, arbitration was discussed.

Perhaps the most thorough presentation has been made during the past two summers at the Institute held at Pennsylvania State College in co-operation with the College and the Steelworkers and at which the Tribunals Vice President of the Association, J. Noble Braden, lectured on the use of arbitration in labor disputes and conducted a practice arbitration in which members of the Steelworkers' Union participated representing both labor and management. Institutions of learning also realized the importance of this trend and a number of them now include courses in arbitration in their departments of management. It is believed that the first full course is that given by the Graduate School of Business Administration of New York University, in which Mr. Braden is the lecturer. A course is also presented at the School of Business at Columbia University and Professor Paul Brissenden, one-time vice chairman of the National War Labor Board in the New York area, is the instructor. Lectures on arbitration have also been included in connection with courses on labor relations and industrial management in many other institutions throughout the country.

CHAPTER VIII

Towards a Science of Arbitration

«««« »»»»

WHEN the Association was organized in 1926, a century and a half had elapsed since the first arbitration tribunal had been established by the Chamber of Commerce of the State of New York in the United States to dispose of commercial disputes affecting the welfare of certain residents of New York. The six gentlemen who met every Tuesday or oftener to adjust such differences as the parties in dispute agreed to leave to their judgment, could have had no premonition that they were constructing the rudiments of a science of arbitration.[1] They could have had no idea that by giving arbitration an independent existence in a commercial organization, they were setting it on a new course.[2]

In its progress towards a science, arbitration was to experience the full meaning of the old Chinese proverb that a journey of a thousand miles begins with the first step. Many indeed were the steps to be taken over that century and a half; many were the obstructions, delays, and difficulties to be overcome; high were the prejudices and skepticisms to mount before the course set in 1768 was to achieve organization befitting a science.[3]

[1] The six men chosen to make arbitration history were: Theopy Bache, James Jauncey, Robert Murray, Samuel Ver Plank, Miles Sherbrooke and Jacob Walton, of the Committee of the Chamber of Commerce of New York (1768).

[2] In the New York Public Library records, it is indicated that from July 1779 to November 1, 1792, 230 cases came before this Committee.

[3] For a historical survey of the development in New York, see *Report of the Special Committee on Commercial Arbitration*, Chamber of Commerce of the State of New York, of February 2, 1911, and *Annual Report of the Committee on Arbitration*, of May 6, 1943. For Case Records, see *Arbitration Records of the Chamber of Commerce of the State of New York 1779-1792*, printed from the

In 1926, the Association faced the challenge: arbitration was to continue either within the narrow confines of arbitration law and trade groups, or it was to be free to serve mankind whenever and wherever it was needed. It was either to be made accessible to all the people or to remain the privilege of the few. It was either to be cloistered in high places or be taken into the homes, workshops, offices, and schools of the nation. It was either to have an active role in the affairs of the nation or to remain in seclusion.

The American Arbitration Association could continue the work of the Society by facilitating the settlement of a few cases each year submitted casually by contestants for their special benefit; or it could begin the construction of a science that might one day help to bring peace and tranquillity within the nation and security against war.

The Association chose the latter course and thereby laid out for itself a stupendous task. It had no idea what kind of a science would meet the tests of force so well organized as the science of war. It had still less idea how the constructive elements of goodwill, good faith, and co-operation could be systematically stimulated to combat the destructive forces then at work in the economic life of America and throughout the world. It was under no illusion that the few cases hitherto submitted to arbitration, or the few that might follow, would create any marked change in the well-being of the nation or would influence international affairs.

The Association, by reason of its choice of the broader concept, became a laboratory for the study of arbitration and for the formulation of the policies and principles that were later to form the beginning of a science of arbitration. As other adventurers in the organization of knowledge had done, the Association called to its aid research and educational experts. This was the first time that research had been applied generally to the subject matter of arbitration or that a body of men distinguished as leaders in other sciences had been called into consultation.[4]

The idea that arbitration could be organized as a science was

---

original manuscripts in the New York Public Library. See also *The Earliest American Tribunal*, by Charles T. Gwynne, in *The Arbitration Journal*, Vol. I, (1937), p. 117.

[4] For members of Research Council see Ch. XXV, p. 204.

based upon the following assumptions: *First*, that men and nations preferred amicable ways of settling their disputes, and that there was latent a high degree of confidence, good faith, goodwill and co-operation that could be released by methodical organization, to facilitate this power of self-regulation. *Second*, that the promise to settle amicably differences or disputes that might arise in the future out of human relationships, if made at the time a contractual relationship was established, offered the best basis for the new science. *Third*, if this promise could be embodied generally in the contractual relations of human beings, it would provide a foundation upon which to build a stable and effective science of amicable settlement and the eventual control over disputes. *Fourth*, the science would be both corrective and preventive in its application. While the Association was interested in the settlement of existing disputes, it was even more interested in building a structure of economic contracts that contained arbitration provisions which would eventually control differences and disputes and thus lessen the prevalence of conflict.

How was a science of arbitration to differ from the prevalent use of arbitration? It was necessary first to define its purposes and a plan of organization.

The subject matter of a science of arbitration is human conflict. This results in differences or disputes that threaten the peace, security, and happiness of those immediately concerned, and of the community of which they are a part, or of communities or states in relation to each other.

The purpose of a science of arbitration is to devise and apply in a systematic way measures of prevention, control, and settlement so differences and disputes will not affect adversely or disastrously the welfare of individuals and communities or their amicable relation to one another.

The elements of such a science have now been fairly well established. Indispensable is arbitration law, which gives legal validity to any contract to arbitrate and which provides for the enforcement of awards. Such law should carefully differentiate between the powers of the court when legal sanctions are sought and powers of the parties and arbitrators in the normal process of arbitration wherein legal sanctions need not necessarily be invoked. In the

United States, unfortunately, there cannot be one law, for there are forty-eight state laws which must be unified before this element becomes stable and dependable. The progress made under the United States Arbitration Act and fifteen modern state laws offers encouragement for the further development of this essential element.

The acceptance of arbitration law as a foundation narrows the application of the science, for only the arbitration of disputes which may be made the subject of contract may receive legal sanctions. This does not, however, exclude the wider range of human relations if the parties in dispute are willing to abide by their arbitration agreements and awards in good faith, or if economic organizations or other agencies apply the pressure of public opinion in the interests of the community.

Arbitration laws lay down certain principles or establish certain requirements that must be observed if the courts are to give legal enforcement to agreements or awards. While they give stability to arbitration, they do not provide the framework of a science. For that an institution of arbitration is required that will plan and develop systems of arbitration, that will conduct the research necessary to its understanding, that will make experiments for its advancement, and that will establish procedures and machinery for its practice.

The broad function of such an institution is to combine into a workable system all of the indispensable elements that will make arbitration effective in achieving its purposes and that will utilize the self-regulative powers of the people individually and collectively through organization for the control or settlement of controversy.

The establishment of a practice of arbitration under arbitration law or through co-operating trade and commercial organizations is a necessary element in organizing a science of arbitration. For this purpose systems of arbitration must be established. These must provide the facilities and services which parties require for the processing of a dispute through an arbitration proceeding. This machinery is not only mechanical in the sense of providing physical conveniences and rules. It must have competent administrators and qualified arbitrators to perform the functions described in the subsequent chapters on the practice of arbitration.

The organization of a science of arbitration is something more than the development and unification of arbitration law and the provision of systems of facilities and services. It is within its province constantly to study the different types of controversy and the different forms of contract in order to reduce conflict in human relations. It is within its province to make experiments and devise new ways of meeting different kinds or sources of conflict. It is within its province to increase the degree of acceptance of arbitration by convincing parties and the public of its benefits to mankind; and to encourage the use of arbitration clauses as a means of controlling future disputes or of avoiding conflict. The selection, distribution, and training of arbitrators for the duties of their office is also a function of such a science. So, also, is the teaching of arbitration. How many of these different elements or activities have been combined in the beginning of such a science is illustrated in Part II on the practice of American arbitration.

The acceptance of organized arbitration as a science of the amicable settlement or control of disputes implies that it will at some time include a recognized profession and that its practice should be initially developed by those interested in the maintenance of its principles and policies.

In the practice of law, there are two component parts—the institution of the courts and their organization, administration and personnel and the members of the bar who practice in these institutions. So in a properly organized science of arbitration, there are tribunals, their organization, administration, and personnel and parties to arbitration agreements, with or without counsel, who practice arbitration in these tribunals.

Here the similarity ends, for in the practice of law, there is a body of both substantive and procedural law to guide judges and members of the bar who in their juridical capacities operate within the framework of an established judicial system. While this body of law is complex and often contradictory, it is nevertheless a basic factor around which a profession can be organized. For the practice of law there are established schools and courses of instruction and members of the profession must qualify under regular examinations, first as lawyers and as judges. Also, the legal profession has a network of well-organized bar associations which are ever zealous to uphold the standards of their profession and to advance its prestige and welfare.

Arbitration possesses little of this basic structure or advantage and the question is to what extent these must be systematically developed as a foundation for the organization of a profession of arbitration. As originally conceived, arbitration was a friendly service rendered by a disinterested person, without compensation, upon the invitation of parties in dispute. As used in the modern complex economic world, it has had to acquire machinery, procedures, and procedural laws and rules to be serviceable to the larger needs of society.

Two approaches have been made to this subject—one in London and the other in New York. Under British procedural law, and under the machinery established in chambers of commerce, exchanges, and trade bodies, there has accumulated over a period of many generations, if not centuries, an experience and tradition which afforded a background for the organization of a London Institute of Arbitrators.

The purposes of the Institute, as stated in its Memorandum on Organization, are primarily to train men in the duties of the office of arbitrator, to promote and hold examinations in arbitral law and procedure and to grant certificates of qualification to men who qualify thereunder and to provide instructions, information, and guides for the use of such qualified persons. The purpose is also to establish canons of ethics for members and to eliminate abuses regarding excessive fees, partisanship, and other unethical practices. It is also to foster among arbitrators and members of Panels a solidarity and community of interest which will advance the science of arbitration, promote reforms and facilitate the administration of justice through co-operation with juridical institutions.

The Institute also deemed essential to such a profession, arrangements for affording means of communication between arbitrators in different fields of activity and to effect an exchange of views, practice, and experience, and for holding meetings and conferences and by other educational means to increase the dignity, prestige, and confidence which should attach to the office of arbitrator.

In order to give effect to these purposes, the Institute established five classes of membership and qualifications therefor; it established a list of approved public arbitrators and specified the qualifications for membership. In addition, it could appoint examiners to inquire into the qualifications of a candidate and to conduct examinations. It established a schedule of fees which it recommended for such arbitrators and it provided Arbitration Committee Rules of Procedure. Members thereby became public approved arbitrators.

In advancing a profession of arbitration as part of a science of arbitration, the Institute has held practice arbitrations which have taken a proceeding through all the steps from its beginning to the making of an award; it has held examinations covering the law of contract, law of arbitration and procedure and evidence in arbitration, and it has facilitated the preparation and publication of handbooks on procedure and evidence and simple guides on the common sense of arbitration.

In approaching this subject, as previously indicated, the Institute possessed the advantages of an excellent arbitration law, an established practice of arbitration over many centuries in commodity exchanges, chambers of commerce, and other British organizations and had the benefit of a long line of court decisions which had established principles and policies which could be readily incorporated in building a profession of arbitration. The British had an approved national policy of arbitration which could be readily understood and into which all arbitration developments could be fitted. This policy included the acceptance of arbitration clauses in contracts which for half a century have been legally valid and enforceable, thereby stabilizing a practice of arbitration.

In the United States, the idea of organizing a profession of arbitration had to be approached quite differently. There was no adequate law but rather a diversity of arbitration laws; there was no established machinery comparable to that in London; there was no general acceptance of organized arbitration as an American policy; there was no body of arbitrators trained in the fundamentals of arbitration law or practice, and there was opposition to the concept of organized arbitration, a circumstance fought through and to a considerable degree eliminated, over centuries of practice in England.

Consequently, the improvement of arbitration law, the creation of an institution of arbitration comparable to the London Court of Arbitration, the establishment of a qualified body of arbitrators on a national basis seemed to be prerequisite to the consideration of including arbitrators as members of a profession. Furthermore, the ancient tradition of honorary rather than paid service predominated in trade and commercial organizations in the United States and the body of men interested in arbitration fees was relatively small. On the contrary, in England, compensation had long been recognized as the customary practice on the theory that a "laborer was worthy of his hire."

In the United States, the concept of a profession of arbitration includes not only arbitrators who are the judges in arbitration proceedings, but also the parties and their counsel who are the practitioners, and also the administrators. All of them have a place in a profession of arbitration.

In 1934, the Association drafted a plan for an American Institute of Arbitrators which was to take the initiative in organizing such a profession. The time for its development did not seem opportune, with the intervening war years and economic changes. In 1947 its scope was broadened to a Research Institute for the Advancement of a Science of Arbitration, now in process of organization, to include the training of arbitrators, parties, and administrators in a practice of arbitration.

In the meantime, the idea of arbitration as a profession had received stimulus during the war in labor arbitrations. It was facilitated by the National War Labor Board and the Division of Conciliation of the U. S. Department of Labor. As arbitrators appointed by these government agencies usually received compensation, a new body of paid arbitrators came into existence for labor arbitrations. With the coming of peace, some of the members of this group of arbitrators, whose services were no longer needed in the war effort, organized in 1947 a National Academy of Arbitrators. Other organizations also became interested. In order to co-ordinate these efforts, the American Arbitration Association called a conference of the interested organizations and as a result, a conference board representative of these groups is in process of formation.

The organization of a science of arbitration is essential for other reasons: *First*, it is necessary to the survival of arbitration itself as an institution and as a practice. *Second*, it furnishes a systematic process for the reduction of conflict and for the control and settlement of individual disputes. *Third*, it possesses great potential power for the avoidance of war. International relations since World War II have clearly indicated that procedural disputes can delay peace settlements to the point of engendering war, or threats of war, and that the absence of organized procedures and machinery prolongs these disputes. It has been made regrettably clear that unorganized arbitration, without including promises to arbitrate future disputes, and without procedures and machinery that can be readily invoked, is impotent to prevent or settle controversies that contain threats of war.

It is equally certain, except in trade relations, that the preventive power of arbitration has not been fully tried. Where it has been tried, as among American Republics, pacific settlement of disputes has held these Republics together under the strain of two World Wars. But people and nations are only on the threshold of calling upon their immense reserves of goodwill, good faith, confidence, and co-operation in a systematic organized way for the amelioration of conflict and for the prevention of disputes before they erupt into threats of war.

A Research Institute for the Advancement of a Science of Arbitration that would give direction to the orderly development of such a science, that would arouse public opinion on its behalf, and that would offer a further challenge to the scientific minds that are now so deeply engaged in the advancement of international peace and security, is an important development in the process of organizing arbitration as a science.

Part II

THE PRACTICE OF AMERICAN ARBITRATION

CHAPTER IX

The General Practice of Arbitration

«««« »»»»

ALTHOUGH arbitration has been in use for many centuries, resort to it had been occasional rather than regular, except in certain commodity exchanges and trade groups. No general practice had been developed as part of a national policy.

By a general practice of arbitration, the Association had in mind not only the processing of arbitrations in tribunals under Rules of Procedure, but also the larger aspects of increasing the frequency of arbitrations, of improving its techniques so as to give better arbitrations, of advancing modern arbitration laws, and of taking the risks out of arbitration itself. It had in mind also making studies and experiments, holding conferences, and advancing instruction with a view to establishing a well-organized science of arbitration.

The general practice of arbitration is distinguished from its casual or occasional use, first by the establishment of permanently accessible facilities and services known as the machinery of arbitration. This machinery and its operation or administration is called a system of arbitration because it is available generally for the settlement of all kinds of disputes; it is not bound by territorial, commodity, or membership limitations, and it has uniformity in its administration and procedures. A system is also characterized by having panels of arbitrators available in any locality and selected on a basis of qualifications which gives them recognized competence for their office.

A general practice of arbitration can become a reality only in countries where arbitration law makes agreements to arbitrate future, as well as existing, disputes, legally valid, enforceable, and irrevocable. It only becomes a reality when contracting parties avail themselves of the benefits of these laws by using arbitration clauses in their contracts; and do so sufficiently regularly to insure a permanent and high degree of use. Finally, it becomes a reality when references to arbitration take place with frequency within the established systems.

This is true because the casual or occasional reference to arbitration that occurs after a dispute has arisen is usually so difficult to arrange, and the proceeding is so haphazard, that references to arbitration possess neither the uniformity nor the frequency that is characteristic of arbitrations that arise out of clauses in contracts.

Furthermore, a general practice of arbitration tends to eliminate the somewhat artificial barriers that have been erected within the concept of arbitration, particularly in the tendency to separate commercial and labor arbitrations. The Association found in establishing a general practice in its systems that both were amenable to similar rules, standards of administration, and to methods of selecting arbitrators and of conducting proceedings, and that, therefore, collective bargaining agreements and commercial contracts could be integrated under one general practice. Such an arrangement is obviously of great convenience to corporations that are parties to both kinds of contracts. It is equally beneficial to unions that have collective bargaining agreements with many different corporations to find that they have a uniform practice. The Textile industry, for example, which uses the voluntary labor arbitration system of the Association in many of its collective bargaining agreements, is thus assured of the application of similar standards, procedures, and safeguards in the selection of arbitrators in all localities where an arbitration is called for.

The general practice of arbitration is also characterized by impartial, impersonal administrators under Rules that prescribe their duties and define their powers. While there are some who consider that rules perhaps unduly restrain the arbitrator or direct a proceeding, the Association would be unwilling to operate a system without Rules of Procedure to govern tribunal proceedings with a high degree of uniformity. Whatever may be lost in freedom of action is more than compensated for by the assurance that both the arbitration agreement and the award, when processed under Rules, are generally found to be legally valid and enforceable.[1]

The function of Rules is an important one, especially when a general practice develops under the use of arbitration clauses in standard or uniform commercial contracts, or under collective bargaining agreements where a standard type of agreement is used by the same union with many different employers.

It is a function of rules to implement or supplement the provisions of arbitration law so they are put concretely into operation in a tribunal without the parties finding it necessary to incorporate them in a clause or submission. When persons of different minds and experience undertake to write clauses and put rules into them, essential things are often forgotten or changes are made which increase ambiguity, thus creating disputes over the procedure before the actual arbitration of the dispute itself can be held.

Rules prescribe the steps to be taken in processing a case, as among the parties, arbitrators and administrator, thus avoiding duplication, conflict, or confusion as to what each participant should do in processing a case.[2]

Rules avoid frustration of arbitration through delays or attempted evasions by providing time limitations and by prescribing the steps to be taken under default by either arbitrators or parties. The filling of vacancies, for example, created by the withdrawal or disqualification of an arbitrator, is a chief cause of delays or frustrations unless a method for filling the vacancy is provided. Putting before the arbitrators a specific claim, arising out of a general arbitration clause in a contract, causes the parties no end of trouble unless a method has been provided for doing so.

Rules provide for contingencies that parties usually ignore, in the belief that they will never arise. It is the function of Rules to anticipate these contingencies. For example, when parties fail or are unable to agree upon the locality where their arbitration shall be held, how and when that issue will be decided is problematical, unless Rules provide a method.

Rules protect the arbitrator from an expansion of his judicial

[1] The record of the arbitrations, held under the Rules of the Association, show less than 6 per cent of the awards have been attacked in court and in less than 1 per cent have the attacks been sustained.

[2] For allocation of powers and duties, see Chap. X, p. 76.

powers beyond what he contemplated when he accepted the appointment. They also protect the parties from the assumption by arbitrators of authority or powers which the parties do not intend to confer upon the arbitrators. For example, the presentation of new claims under a general clause after the arbitration has been initiated upon a specific issue, must be made in a way not to impose unexpected duties upon the arbitrator.

Rules protect the public from unsettled disputes. This is particularly true of labor disputes where reference to arbitration is often overshadowed by the threat of a strike. By avoiding delays and expediting settlements, Rules facilitate settlements of disputes that might otherwise end in public disaster.

Rules are also indispensable to the administration of justice. Rules that provide a method for private investigations, for the presentation of all pertinent and material evidence in the presence of the parties and for exchange of all information and documents pertaining to a proceeding among parties, offer examples of the way in which justice is facilitated under a practice of arbitration.

The construction of Rules and their constant adaptation and improvement is a necessity. Definite principles obtain in the making of such Rules, for they must be applicable, under many different statutes as well as common law, and to many different kinds of controversy.

An arbitration system differs also from unorganized arbitration in that it is administered by persons or organizations having no personal interest in any specific arbitrator and without regard to any particular arbitration. This concerns primarily the creation, maintenance, and management of the general machinery and facilities by officers of the Association in accordance with policies and directives which they have approved. Authority is derived from the charter of the Association, under which the Association is organized and operates.

The administration of a specific tribunal is quite different from the general management of a system. Its powers are not discretionary with the administrator. They are fixed in the Rules. A tribunal is created by the parties in dispute and is, in one sense of the word, their own personal property, for it comes into being with the reference of a specific matter to arbitration and is dissolved with the making of an award or with the withdrawal of that matter. A tribunal, thus created, is not available to any other parties. The administration of a tribunal is, therefore, entrusted to a clerk who acts as assistant to the parties and to the arbitrators. His general duties are prescribed in the Rules or by stipulation of the parties. While his duties are fairly uniform, they may be varied at the will of the parties according to their requirements. The Association is responsible for the faithful performance of the duties of a clerk as set forth in the Rules but its consent to their variation is not necessary, unless they are impossible of performance or in conflict with established principles. For example, if a clerk is called upon to perform judicial functions, the policy of the Association would prevent him from doing so.

The authority, therefore, for administering a tribunal is derived from the parties and requires their specific consent by their adoption of the Rules of the Association or by their amendment and the authority is co-extensive only with the life of the tribunal. The service performed by the administrator, as set forth in the Rules, is in the nature of a contract between the Association and the specific parties only for that proceeding.

Systems of arbitration, as established by the Association for the practice of arbitration may be either general or special. A general practice includes all kinds of controversies and all kinds of parties. The Commercial Arbitration, the Voluntary Labor Arbitration, and the International Commercial Arbitration Systems, subsequently described, are illustrations of systems in which a general practice prevails. The Motion Picture, Fur, Air Transport, and Accident Claims Tribunals offer illustrations of a special practice. These Tribunals use the Commercial Arbitration system as their base in that its concepts, principles, and organization constitute a framework within which these special Tribunals operate. The administrative personnel is, generally speaking, the same for all of them.

Systems of arbitration offer to lawyers the opportunity to engage in the general practice of arbitration. Systems provide the necessary scope, stability, and procedure that make arbitration acceptable to lawyers representing their clients in a proceeding. They carry assurance that if lawyers recommend or include arbitration clauses in contracts which they draw, that facilities and services and machinery for a quasi-judicial practice will be available.

Lawyers also participate in what may be called the larger aspects of the practice of arbitration outside of tribunals. They are members of Panels and frequently serve as arbitrators at the request of parties, particularly in matters where questions of law are involved. They serve frequently as the third arbitrator where the other two are trade experts. In the Accident Claims Tribunal all arbitrators are drawn from a special panel of lawyers. Lawyers participate through membership on the Board of Directors and through Special Committees. To an Arbitration Law Committee is entrusted the consideration of amendments to laws, problems of legal construction, and policies in relation to the law and court decisions. A Special Committee of Lawyers has directed the work of the Accident Claims Tribunal since its organization in 1933. The Arbitration Committee which functions under the Rules is composed of lawyers. Many of the leading bar associations have Arbitration Committees which study and improve arbitration law and procedures and take a leading part in educating members of the bar in arbitration. Lawyers also take a leading part in advancing a practice of arbitration through Rules of Procedure, manuals of instruction, and Codes of Ethics which they assist in formulating.

Lawyers are taking a leading position in the development of a practice of arbitration through education. They teach arbitration in law and business schools;[3] write articles; make addresses; supervise studies; and, in general, cultivate a broad field of knowledge.[4] Much of the research necessary to the development of arbitration is of a legal nature and is under the direction of members of the bar.

Lawyers as judges are called upon to interpret the arbitration laws, to construe arbitration agreements, to appoint arbitrators and to examine awards for procedural defects. The practice in courts and in tribunals may be synchronized in a manner to become

[3] Notably in the New York University Law School, under the direction of Dean Frank H. Sommer and Walter J. Derenberg; and in the Harvard Graduate School of Business Administration under the able direction of the late Dr. Nathan Isaacs and in the Yale Law School under Dean Wesley A. Sturges.

[4] Illustrations are offered by *Pennsylvania Law Review*, Vol. 83, No. 2 (December, 1934), and *New York University Law Quarterly Review*, Vol. 17, No. 4, (May, 1940).

mutually constructive rather than destructive. For example, when the making of an arbitration agreement is in issue, parties are encouraged under the Rules to refer this issue at once to the courts for a determination and arbitrators suspend proceedings while the matter is being decided. On the other hand, rules are so meticulously drawn and applied that in technical matters of compliance with the law, resort to the court need hardly ever be had, nor need awards be challenged on these grounds.

In the expansion of the use of arbitration clauses, which have made a continuous practice of arbitration possible, lawyers make a significant contribution, for it is upon their recommendation that businessmen adopt them and it is their legal training that produces good clauses. As counsel to corporations and trade groups and business enterprises, it is generally the lawyer who determines whether clauses will be used and in what form.

The Association has, in fact, opened to lawyers a general practice that is lucrative to them and of benefit to their clients, for they are the gainers in the saving of time and in the lowering of their own overhead costs.

A general practice of arbitration also differs from the casual use of arbitration under submissions of existing disputes in that it is organized according to definite principles. As to general principles, some of these are laid down in arbitration laws while others appear in the Rules. But, generally speaking, these principles recognize the rights of parties in dispute to settle their own differences, to choose their own judges for that purpose, and to conduct their own proceedings. They recognize the rights of parties to be represented by counsel in these proceedings. They recognize the right of parties to foresee and forestall the effects of possible disputes through agreements to arbitrate future disputes. It is the exercise of these rights through organized facilities and routine procedure that makes a general practice of arbitration by parties to contracts both feasible and attractive, not only occasionally but continuously.

A general practice of arbitration is also characterized by an ethical content or standards which obtain generally in all arbitrations. These pertain to parties, arbitrators and administrators. They are derived not only from rules and laws and decisions interpreting such laws but also from practical experience in the processing of arbitrations in tribunals.

Examples of ethical standards that pertain to parties are the following: They are expected to lay aside the tactics of litigation in an arbitration tribunal; and to treat each other with the courtesy that becomes an amicable proceeding. They are expected to assemble in an orderly way and to present expeditiously and competently their evidence and witnesses. They are expected to expedite their proceeding by performing promptly their own duties and to consent to adjournments of hearings only for good and sufficient reasons.

Illustrations, taken from the Code of Ethics formulated by the Association, indicate some of the standards that apply to arbitrators.[5]

The Arbitrator should decline an appointment when he has:

(1) Any personal, financial, or close family relation, or close business relation, such as partner or agent, to any of the parties.

(2) Any probable pecuniary interest in the outcome of the controversy.

(3) Any private understanding with, or obligation to, any party respecting the subject matter in controversy or making of an award.

(4) Any personal bias or prejudice in favor of, or against, any of the parties.

The Arbitrator should avoid:

(1) Acting as a conciliator. The duty of an Arbitrator is not to facilitate a compromise but to reach a fair decision and to make a just award.

(2) Acting as an advocate or agent for either party. His duty is not to argue or defend the case but to hear and decide it according to his best understanding.

(3) Delegating his duties or authority. Each Arbitrator is personally responsible and is obligated to perform the full duties of his office.

(4) Appearing to have a bias. The Arbitrator should not express opinions or views concerning the parties or the controversy before or after the award is made.

[5] See Annex III Text of Code.

The Arbitrator should remember:

(1) That time is money and he should use his best efforts to expedite the proceeding by being on time, by taking few adjournments and by observing all time limitations imposed by the Rules or otherwise.

(2) That arbitration is a low-cost proceeding and he should keep down the costs by not incurring any unusual or unnecessary expense and by expediting hearings.

(3) That an arbitration is not a litigation and he should keep it free from technicalities or legal formalities and the spirit of litigation. Upon him devolves the responsibility for keeping the arbitration free from animosity, recriminations, and conduct tending to impair the goodwill of the proceeding.

(4) That he is chosen to decide the issue impartially and fairly and not to act as counsel for either party, or to give legal advice or to aid one party more than another in their presentation of their case.

The making of an award is the final culmination of a proceeding. It, therefore, occupies a place of high importance in the practice of arbitration. So much so that in its Code of Ethics, the Association has included as standards for making an award the following:

(1) It should not go beyond the terms of the arbitration agreement.

(2) It should be a complete adjudication of every matter submitted by the parties.

(3) It should observe each and every condition set forth in the arbitration agreement.

(4) It should be rendered within the time limit, if any, specified in the arbitration agreement.

(5) It should be certain and definite and final in its terms.

(6) It should reserve to the arbitrators no duties to be performed after the award is made.

(7) The award should be made in clear and simple language, technical expressions of law being avoided. The award should be so phrased that its terms are possible of performance.

(8) It is clearly the duty of the Arbitrator not to give any inkling of what his decision is to be before the hearing is closed and the award is made; nor to indicate the nature of his

> thinking. This rule of conduct is most important, for nothing so discourages the presentation of full and conclusive evidence as for a party to get the idea that the Arbitrator's mind is made up or that he is no longer interested in taking evidence.

The administrator is also governed by ethical concepts that do not necessarily appear in the Rules. For example, its personnel must be as impartial and disinterested in any arbitration as is the arbitrator. Its personnel may not express any opinion of a decision, nor give out information concerning the proceeding except to those authorized to receive it. Clerks may not be present at deliberations of arbitrators as that could be construed as participating in the making of a decision. They may not release records or awards except on request of the parties or by their written authorization. They may not accept gratuities or favors from parties or arbitrators. They may not become members of other organizations if such association might indicate a line of interest that might create a question as to their disinterestedness. Such, for example, would be their identification with either management or union organizations.

A general practice of arbitration is, however, something more than machinery and procedures for the settlement of disputes or the control of controversy through their regular submission to arbitration. It involves the larger aspects of the study of controversy, so the general practice may be extended to new areas of conflict. It requires the constant improvement of techniques in order that better arbitrations may result. It necessitates the training of arbitrators and of administrators and other arbitration personnel. It must undertake experiments and discoveries that will take the risks out of arbitration for parties and the public. It arranges conferences for the exchange of opinion and information and for the formulation of standards of ethical conduct. It envisages the organization of a profession of arbitration as one means of advancing a general practice. Without these accompanying activities, a general practice of arbitration exercised only in tribunals tends to become narrow and to solidify.

An illustration is afforded by the necessity for taking the risks out of arbitration. Without the safeguards of a well organized practice in tribunals, accompanied by research, experiment, and education, the risks of arbitration are considerable. To the parties, they involve the likelihood of arbitrating under biased arbitrators, high costs, delays, and the frustration or annulment of awards. To the public, they may mean the miscarriage of justice or increase in controversies that remain unsettled. To arbitration itself, these risks mean loss of prestige and of private and public confidence. So the responsibility for reducing risks is definitely involved in a general practice of arbitration.

In the following chapters, the practice under different systems and in different types of tribunals is described.

CHAPTER X

Civil and Commercial Arbitration

«««« »»»»

THE American Commercial Arbitration System is established to provide parties to civil and commercial controversies with facilities and services for the prompt settlement of these controversies. The proceeding, beginning with the initiation of the arbitration and ending with the rendering of the award, or other settlement of the controversy, takes place in the Commercial Arbitration Tribunal under Rules of Procedure formulated by the Association. These Tribunals are created out of the permanent machinery maintained by the Association. Practice in these Tribunals is briefly described as follows:

In the construction of its Rules of Procedure, the Association has embodied certain fundamental principles as being necessary to a sound practice: (1) They are drawn in accord with the mandatory provisions of arbitration law such as, for example, the arbitrator must receive all pertinent and material evidence. (2) They implement the arbitration law when its provisions are permissive or vague, as for example, the requirement for impartiality by providing for a means of insuring it. (3) They supplement the law when it fails to provide for essential steps in a proceeding, as for example, by establishing time limitations. (4) They furnish a complete procedure, so the arbitration may proceed smoothly from its initiation to the making and delivery of an award. (5) They allocate duties and powers among parties, arbitrators, and administrators so each enjoys full rights without infringement upon those of the others in performing their duties. (6) They provide a method of appointing arbitrators when the parties fail, neglect, or refuse to do so. (7) They are sufficiently elastic to permit amendment in special cases where the provisions are inadequate or inapplicable. (8) They are non-technical in terms and are made attractive and intelligible to users, through forms, manuals, and guides. (9) They are made attractive to parties in that their provisions are set forth in simple language, are arranged to apply progressively to each step in a proceeding, and are accompanied by forms and instructions that relieve the parties of detail.

These Rules offer to each party practicing arbitration in a tribunal the same advantages and services and similar opportunities for self-regulation, by providing: (1) A competent method by which all parties may institute their proceedings under a submission; (2) An equally competent method by which they may do so under a clause in a contract by requesting the initiating party to state clearly his claim or dispute and by permitting the defending party to file an answering statement or counterclaim; (3) A way of fixing the locality of the arbitration, if and when the parties fail, or are unable to agree upon, a mutually acceptable place; (4) A method of determining the number of arbitrators should the parties fail to agree thereon; (5) A method of appointing impartial arbitrators from Panels and of safeguarding parties from evident bias disclosed during a proceeding; (6) A method by which parties retain their right to appoint arbitrators in their own way, in preference to a choice from Panels; (7) A fixing of time limitations for appointments of arbitrators so the arbitration will not be unduly delayed or be frustrated; (8) A method of filling vacancies in the office of arbitrator; (9) A procedure for selecting the time and place of the hearing; (10) A way of giving notice to a party in sufficient time so that the other party may be represented by counsel; (11) A provision for selecting impartial stenographers for taking the record, when so authorized by the parties, or for selecting an impartial interpreter, if one is required; (12) A method for determining who may attend hearings, and when adjournments may be taken and for what cause; (13) An orderly presentation of the case by each party and for the taking of evidence orally or by affidavit; (14) A proceeding for making independent inquiries and investigations with the consent of, or in the presence of, the parties; (15) A means for the conservation of property pending the rendering of an award;

(16) A way of closing or reopening of hearings; (17) A method for extensions of time by parties or by the arbitrator or, in the event of a deadlock, by the administrator; (18) A method of serving notices; (19) A way by which parties may make new or different Rules when such are needed; (20) A way of interpreting the Rules when differences over their meaning arise; (21) A procedure by means of written documents when oral hearings are waived; (22) A definite fixing of a time period within which the award shall be made; (23) A method for the signing and delivery of the award.[1]

It is, however, by the allocation of the duties, powers, and rights of all of the participants in a proceeding that an effective practice is established. These participants are the parties, arbitrators, and administrators. An analysis of the Commercial Arbitration Rules offers an example of such an allocation:

To the parties is assigned the responsibility of: (1) Determining the matter they will submit to arbitration; (2) filing their claim in the manner provided in the Rules for instituting their arbitration proceeding; (3) Notifying each other under a clause of their intention to arbitrate, filing an answering statement, and sending copies thereof to each other; (4) determining the locality of the arbitration; (5) designating the number of arbitrators; (6) selecting arbitrators either directly within the time limits set or from lists drawn from a Panel; (7) specifying the kind of arbitrators required; (8) passing upon circumstances that might constitute bias; (9) bringing charges of bias for removal of an arbitrator before the administrator; (10) filling of vacancies; (11) notification of name of counsel to the other party, with copy to the administrator; (12) authorization of the taking of stenographic record and deposit of funds therefor; (13) authorization to call interpreters; (14) authorization of adjournments of hearings or suspension of proceedings; (15) presentation of case, including evidence and exhibits, summations, arguments and briefs; (16) request for issuance of

[1] The Rules, adopted in 1927 and as amended in 1944, are those in effect as of January 1, 1947. To the late Philip G. Phillips of the Harvard Graduate School of Business Administration and former Legal Research Assistant of the American Arbitration Association, and to Dr. Walter J. Derenberg, former Legal Research Assistant and lecturer at New York University School of Law, the Association owes a great debt for the excellence of its Rules, attested by the very few appeals taken under them to the courts for annulment of awards.

subpoenas where law authorizes the arbitrator to do so; (17) request to have evidence submitted by affidavit; (18) authorization of inspections or investigations outside of hearings with notice of intention to be present; (19) consent to conservation of property during a proceeding; (20) authorization to close hearings by notice that no further evidence or witnesses will be presented; (21) application for reopening of a hearing; (22) waiver of right of objection when there is knowledge that Rules are not being complied with; (23) extensions of time; (24) consent to serving of notices; (25) acceptance of delivery of award; (26) compliance with terms of the award; (27) payment of administrative fee as provided for in the Rules; (28) authorization of expenses before they are contracted for and make advance deposits therefor; (29) payment of arbitrators' fees when agreed upon; (30) interpret, amend, or change Rules by mutual agreement with administrator prior to submission of claim or during a proceeding.

From this analysis it appears that the parties retain quite full control of their proceeding at all strategic points and in all important functions.

To the arbitrator is entrusted the power and duty of making a final decision in the matter referred to him by the parties. In the course of arriving at this decision, he is assigned the following duties and powers: (1) Notify the administrator before acceptance of the office of any circumstances that might constitute a suspicion of bias. (2) Accept appointment by written notice thereof. (3) Appoint other arbitrators within prescribed time, if so authorized by the parties. (4) Set the time and place of the hearing. (5) Determine who may be present at hearings. (6) Require the retirement of witnesses during a hearing, if he deems it necessary. (7) Take adjournments for good cause shown. (8) Take oath of office. (9) Require witnesses to testify under oath. (10) Take procedural decisions. (11) Open the hearing by receiving submission and statement of claim and by the recording of a minute indicating that all entitled to be present are present. (12) Conduct the hearing by receiving all pertinent and material evidence and hearing witnesses and receiving exhibits. (13) Judge of the relevancy of evidence. (14) Receive and consider evidence by affidavit. (15) Make inspections and investigations and set the time therefor and issue notices thereof to parties. (16) conserve property direct upon authorization of the parties. (17) Close or reopen hearings. (18) Receive documentary evidence in absence of oral hearing. (19) Assess fees and expenses in the award in favor of any party. (20) deliver signed award to clerk, duly executed, for transmission to parties within the time prescribed in the Rules or agreement.

To the arbitrator is thus reserved full control of all matters that affect, or are directly involved in, the performance of his judicial functions.

The duties and responsibilities of the administrator fall under two classifications: *First*, the duties that are universally and regularly performed by each clerk of a tribunal; and, *second*, those irregularly performed from time to time by the administrator not acting through a clerk.

A summary of the duties that are ordinarily performed as a routine matter in all tribunals by clerks assigned to them indicates both the nature and scope of their services and the extent to which partics are relieved of necessary, but technical and uninteresting detail: (1) Answering inquiries concerning a proposed arbitration and furnishing the forms necessary to its initiation. (2) Obtaining the agreement of the parties to adopt the Rules if the contract does not provide for arbitration under the Rules. (3) Receiving from the party initiating the arbitration and filing the Submission Agreement or the Demand for Arbitration made under a future dispute clause. (4) Directing the attention of the initiating party to any failure to comply with the provisions of the Rules regarding the initiating of the arbitration. (5) Advising the defending party of the filing of the Submission or the Demand, and in the case of the Demand of his right to file an answering statement. (6) Ascertaining whether the parties have agreed upon the locality of the arbitration and, if not, securing their statements as to their selection of a locale and notifying the administrator that it is required to make a designation. (7) Receiving and filing the answering statement of the complaining party and checking to ascertain if the initiating party has received a copy of the answering statement. (8) Receiving the administrative fee from the initiating party and billing the defending party for the fee due from him. (9) Estimating whether any deposit will be required for special expenses such as the taking of the minutes of the hearing, and billing the parties for a deposit to establish a trust fund for such purposes. (10) Receiving and filing a copy of any amendment to the claim or answer and ascertaining that the other party has received a copy thereof. (11) Ascertaining whether the parties have designated the number of arbitrators and if they have not, ascertaining if they can agree upon the number. (12) Receiving notice of any compensation to be paid arbitrators by the voluntary action of the parties and keeping a record thereof. (13) Keeping a record of all disbursements from funds deposited by the parties for expenses in order that an itemized statement may be rendered to the parties at the close of the proceeding.

In the appointment of arbitrators, a clerk renders the following services: (1) He ascertains from the arbitration agreement the method designated for the appointment of arbitrators and notifies the parties if action is required from them. (2) Notifies parties of the time limits set in the agreement, or prevailing in the Rules for making appointments. (3) Notifies the parties when the time has expired; and if not extended and the appointment has not been made, advises the administrator of its duty to make the appointment. (4) If lists from Panels are required, the clerk ascertains the wishes of the parties and he or the administrator draws the names accordingly, has them typed on the proper form and mails them simultaneously to the parties. (5) Calls their attention to the time set for the return of such list and from the returned lists computes the order of selection. (6) Gets in touch with the persons chosen and obtains their consent to serve and notifies the parties of their acceptance. (7) If, however, no names remain on the mutual lists or the persons selected are not available, by agreement of the parties, the clerk submits a second list, drawn from the Panel in the same way. If the parties do not mutually request a second list, the clerk notifies the administrator to make the appointment. (8) If lists are not returned within the time limit, he proceeds with the appointment from the lists submitted, as, in the absence of objection from the parties, all names submitted are deemed to be acceptable. (9) Sends out all notices to arbitrators of their appointment and receives their signed acceptance. (10) In consultation with parties, counsel and arbitrators, he arranges the details for the time and place for the hearing and at the direction of the arbitrators, he notifies them thereof in writing. (11) Should any arbitrator have doubts as to his own qualifications, he communicates with the clerk who brings the matter to the attention of the parties and obtains from them their decision as to the continuance of the arbitrator. He then notifies the arbitrator of the decision. (12) Advises the administrator or the parties of withdrawals or vacancies created in the office of arbitrator, so the vacancy may be filled in the same manner as the original appointment was made. (13) Keeps the administrator advised of any irregularities that require its attention.

In the conduct of a hearing, a clerk renders the following services: (1) Attends all hearings, but not the meetings of the arbitrators. (2) Upon request of a party, he makes the necessary arrangements for obtaining stenographic or interpreter service. (3) Secures deposits for such purposes and transmits them to central headquarters for deposit in a trust fund. (4) Makes a record of all adjournments and sends out notices for subsequent hearings. (5) Whenever an oath is required, he sees that the oath is administered to the arbitrator or witnesses by a qualified person. (6) Keeps the minutes of the proceeding, including a record of the presence of the arbitrators, names and addresses of parties, counsel, and witnesses, and of the receipt of all exhibits offered by parties or counsel. (7) Receives requests for subpoenas, prepares the forms for the arbitrators and forwards them to the party requesting them, for service. (8) Receives briefs of counsel or other documents intended for the arbitrators but not submitted at the hearing and transmits them to the arbitrators and ascertains if opposing counsel have copies thereof. (9) If the arbitrators desire to make an investigation outside of the hearing, they request the clerk to obtain the consent of the parties in writing and to arrange the time and place and notify the parties so they may be present. (10) At the request of the arbitrators, the clerk may assist in obtaining the consent of the parties to the conservation of property, pending the rendering of the award. (11) Notes in writing in the record the date of the closing of the hearing. (12) Receives the application for the reopening of a hearing, transmits it to the arbitrator and notifies the parties of the ruling of the arbitrator. (13) Keeps a record of all waivers and extensions of time and full files of all proceedings.

In relation to the award, a clerk may be called upon to: (1) Notify the arbitrator of the time fixed within which the award must be made. (2) Receive the text of the award for typing upon the standard form. (3) Arrange to have the signature of the arbitrator affixed to the award. (4) Transmit the award to the parties or their counsel. (5) Furnish certified *facsimiles* of all documents, upon the written request of a party. (6) Ascertain if the award has been complied with or whether a motion has been made to vacate it and with what result, thus completing the record.

As distinguished from these routine services, performed by clerks assigned to tribunals, the administrator, through its Arbitration Committee or responsible officials, is authorized under the Rules to perform other duties. These are not of a routine nature and are called for only in emergencies. They may be performed in such degree and manner as the situation calls for. If the parties and the arbitrators exercise all of their rights and powers, the administrator need take no action; but if the parties, for example, fail to select the locality for their arbitration, or fail to agree upon the number of arbitrators, then the administrator is empowered to act.

The circumstances under which the administrator may act directly indicate the precision with which its powers are limited in the Rules:

(1) The administrator may designate the locality of the arbitration when the parties fail or neglect to do so. (2) It may determine the number of arbitrators when the parties fail to agree. (3) It may name the arbitrators when the parties cannot agree upon names submitted from lists or when they fail to make an appointment in the manner they have agreed upon within the time limitations fixed in their contract or set by the Rules. (4) It may determine charges of bias against a Panel arbitrator. (5) It may vacate the office of arbitrator for failure or neglect or refusal to perform services and direct that the vacancy be filled. (6) It may extend periods of time, except those fixed for making the award. (7) It may approve of arrangements for the compensation of Panel members which arrangements must be made through the administrator and not directly by the arbitrator with the parties. (8) It may interpret the Rules that are to be applied by the administrator, and the Rules relating to the powers and duties of arbitrators only when there is more than one arbitrator and they are unable to agree.

To the question of whether it is necessary to have procedural services so meticulously defined and so minutely carried out, the answer is that the Rules have grown out of experience, and each provision has been carefully considered and then recommended by the Arbitration Law Committee of the Association. Practice under the Rules has also justified their provisions; for the references to courts challenging proceedings have been infrequent under awards rendered pursuant to these Rules. Nor have delays, except by mutual consent of the parties which takes them out of time limitations established under the Rules, frustrated arbitrations as so often occurs in arbitrations conducted without rules.

The process of referring a commercial dispute to arbitration is quite simple. A party to an arbitration agreement notifies the Association of his intention to arbitrate and files a copy of the arbitration agreement. The Association then puts its Rules into effect, arbitrators are chosen and the time and place of hearings are arranged. All of the detail in making such arrangements is attended to by the administrator. On the day of the hearing the parties appear before the arbitrators with their witnesses and proofs and are heard. When all of the proofs are in and all witnesses have been heard, the arbitrators arrive at their decision and prepare their award, sign and transmit it to the Association, which then sends it to the parties. Because many details are taken care of, parties find commercial arbitration easy and satisfactory, expeditious and inexpensive, and the public is less and less plagued by unsettled controversies.

CHAPTER XI

Labor Arbitration

«««« »»»»

The Voluntary Labor Arbitration System was established by the Association in 1937. Since its organization in 1926, the Association had been arbitrating what were in effect labor disputes under the standard contracts of the Actors' Equity Association—a member of the A. F. of L. and from time to time it was called upon to open its tribunal for the settlement of other labor disputes. The Association did not, however, organize a Labor Arbitration Tribunal and publicize its use for the settlement of labor disputes.

With the expansion of collective bargaining agreements, following the enactment of the National Industrial Recovery Act in 1933, requests for labor arbitration facilities and services became frequent. As the Association was frequently referred to in these agreements, it became necessary to establish a separate system for labor arbitration. This was done without changing substantially the foundations, principles, and policies already adopted for civil and commercial arbitration.

Through these earlier experiences, the Association was aware that it would be dealing with social and economic problems of a far wider scope than in commercial arbitration. It realized that, in this new venture, arbitration would be less concerned with questions of interpreting and applying contracts than with issues arising out of complex and sensitive human relations. The parties would not be casual contractors, buyers and sellers, or manufacturers and distributors of commodities, where questions of quality, prices, time of delivery, commercial customs, and regulations predominated.

On the contrary, parties to labor controversies would be concerned with quite different matters and a long-term relationship. While the dispute might deal with the dismissal of one person, or the seniority rights of one man, or the alleged violation of the agreement might concern a few persons, the settlement itself might affect all of the members of the union of which the party was a member, or might eventually affect the operation of an entire industry or service. Non-settlement, or delayed settlement, or the failure to obtain a friendly settlement, might precipitate a work stoppage, not only in one but other related industries. As the public had a vital and often immediate interest in labor disputes, their settlement often assumed an importance not indicated by the immediate issue.

The establishment in 1937 of a Voluntary Labor Arbitration Tribunal presented new questions of policy to the Association. Of first importance was the inclusion of bargaining processes in the procedure of the new Tribunal. There were advocates of continuing to mix bargaining with judicial processes and there were others in favor of their separation. As finally adopted, the policy was to confine the functions of the new system to the quasi-judicial process of arbitration, thereby excluding the administration of mediation or conciliation proceedings.

There were several reasons for this decision. Conciliation is the act of a third party bringing together the two parties in dispute for negotiation and for settlement of the dispute.

Mediation is the process whereby the third party not only brings the two parties together but actively participates in the negotiation, generally consulting with each of the parties separately and, by persuasion, effecting a compromise acceptable to both. Conciliation and mediation are often merged into a single process.

Arbitration, on the other hand, is a judicial process. The arbitrator is a judge. The parties agree to accept his decision as final and binding. The parties are required to submit evidence, and each is permitted to cross-examine the evidence of the other. Upon the evidence submitted the arbitrator makes his award.

From this differentiation it is apparent that an arbitrator cannot be a conciliator at one stage in the proceeding and then become a mediator, and then change into a judge. An orderly proceeding for the presentation of evidence, calling of witnesses, and receipt of exhibits pertains only to an arbitration. For example, when there is a threatened strike or lockout, the conciliator or mediator has the immediate responsibility, not of administering justice, but of avoiding that disaster. He must be prepared to make reasonable suggestions with a view to compromising. He must meet informally with the parties and become part of the bargaining process. He must undertake to obtain the best possible terms as a basis for maintaining industrial peace. There are no rules of procedure to guide him, for each situation differs from the other. Mediators are not clothed with authority to make binding decisions. When the mediator has reconciled the views and demands of the parties to the point of continuing the relations of management and labor, his task is done. In that process he may have made suggestions or expressed views which might affect adversely the degree of impartiality required in an arbitrator acting as judge.

In considering these duties of mediators and conciliators, the Association was of the opinion that conciliation and mediation were processes of settlement that should be fully tried and exhausted by management and labor, and that arbitration should be the last resort. When and if these grievance procedures failed, the matter should then be submitted to a judge having had no previous connection with the settlement on the basis of conciliation and mediation.

For these reasons, bargaining processes were excluded from the Labor Tribunal.

A second question of policy concerned compromise decisions. In labor arbitrations, settlement is so much desired in the public interest, that a compromise decision is often sought. Should labor arbitrators conform to the principle obtaining in commercial arbitrations that justice and not compromise was the objective of the arbitrator? The Association concluded that insofar as arbitration was held for the purpose of obtaining a fair, just and binding decision, compromise decisions should no more obtain in labor than in commercial arbitration. Members of its panel of arbitrators were so instructed. This policy does not prevent parties from settling their own disputes in the course of an arbitration and withdrawing from the proceeding. It only means that it is neither the duty nor the function of arbitrators to facilitate such action, nor to make compromise decisions. For experience has indicated that compromises which do not embody justice settle issues only partially, whereas arbitration is intended finally to dispose of them.

The Association also found that the encouragement of compromise decisions aroused opposition to arbitration on the ground that the preparation of a case and the careful presentation of the issue often prove useless in a compromise proceeding. This proved discouraging, particularly to lawyers who expected to appear in a Tribunal and plead the merits of their case on behalf of a client, only to find themselves involved in a bargaining procedure. To this arrangement whereby compromise decisions are not encouraged, the Association attributes somewhat the increase in the participation of lawyers in arbitration.

Another question of policy was presented by the character of the national commercial panel. For the membership on this panel certain standards had been established. Obviously men chosen for their experience, standing and ability in commercial affairs were not necessarily the best qualified for the settlement of labor relations. The Association therefore undertook as rapidly as possible to establish qualifications for members of a labor panel and to set up a separate panel for this purpose.

A perplexing question also arose with reference to rules of procedure. Custom has predisposed both management and labor to the settlement of labor disputes without rules of procedure. They were accustomed to informality and irregularity and time-consuming processes; they were afraid that the introduction of rules would lead to rigidity of proceedings. They were unaware of the function of rules in preserving the rights of parties and of allocating duties in a manner to encourage greater freedom.

Notwithstanding the prejudice against rules, the Association approved of rules of procedure for its Labor Tribunal and accepted only matters submitted under these rules. While they differ from the Commercial Arbitration Rules in certain particulars that make them better adapted to labor proceedings, they nevertheless establish the routine which the Association considers essential to the efficient conduct of an arbitration proceeding.[1]

The Association had also established in its Commercial Arbitration Rules a schedule of administrative fees based upon the number of

[1] For Rules, see Annex I, p. 219.

hearings and the amount of the claim. These fees, which are payable to the Association for its administrative services, use of hearing rooms, attendance of clerks and other services, were deemed too high and might thereby exclude from arbitration small companies or unions. Also the nature of the disputes,—involving personal relations rather than monetary claims—did not lend themselves to the method of fixing administrative fees in Commercial Tribunals. Therefore a modest sum of $25 from each party for the first hearing, and $15, from each party for each subsequent hearing,—was fixed in the Rules. While this does not pay the cost of maintenance of the Labor Tribunal, sums are allocated from the general funds in sufficient amount to cover the difference.

For ethical as well as practical reasons the Association also deemed it advisable to create separate divisions of Commercial and Labor Tribunals under the general administration of the Tribunals Department. By this separation, corporations processing commercial disputes in no way come into contact with the processing of labor disputes except through their separate submission under collective bargaining agreements; and the efficiency of administration is increased by having a separate personnel in charge of each system.

The Association took one further step in changing its policies. Originally created for commercial arbitration, the Board of Directors necessarily consisted of business and professional men. With the establishment of the Labor Tribunal union labor representatives were invited to serve on the Board, and on the Executive Committee and an Advisory Labor Council was appointed.[2]

On the other hand, no changes in policy were made with respect to the voluntary nature of arbitration, to which principle the Association has steadily adhered. Nor was any change made in the method of selecting arbitrators, for the Association adhered to its principle of encouraging parties to choose their own arbitrators.

No substantial change could, however, be effected in the so-called "umpire" practice which has so long prevailed in labor arbitrations. Under this practice, each party appoints an arbitrator, presumably more or less friendly to his claim, and only the additional or third arbitrator is completely impartial. For this reason the Labor Arbitration Rules do not empower the administrator to declare vacant

[2] For members of Council, see Ch. XXV, p. 209.

the office of arbitrator on a charge of bias when it appears in an arbitrator appointed by a party; but the power may be exercised when a panel member is serving as the impartial or third arbitrator and is charged by a party with bias.

Labor arbitrations also presented another problem in the subject matter to be presented. In commercial arbitration there is usually one well defined issue or claim, and occasionally a counterclaim. Labor matters submited to arbitration may involve several grievances of different kinds: dismissals for various causes, questions of seniority or increase in wages involving time studies. There is frequently no gauge as to what grievances may be submitted and in what number. In one instance there were close to half a hundred. The question is often presented as to whether one arbitrator shall hear them all or whether each shall be assigned to a separate arbitrator. In the latter instance, the cost is considerably higher. The policy of the Association is to schedule as many issues as possible arising out of each collective bargaining agreement before one arbitrator, and to find the person best qualified to dispose of them. This is a policy of public interest in that it restores more swiftly amicable relations between management and labor. The parties in their collective bargaining agreements may, however, determine otherwise and such determination is binding upon the administrator.

Quite recently the Association has been besieged with requests for the publication of awards rendered in its Labor Tribunal. It has, however, continued the policy of privacy that prevails in commercial arbitrations. The Association regards all awards, even when they are fraught with very considerable public interest and consequential public effect, as the property of the parties who submitted the question to arbitration. The Rules guarantee privacy of the proceedings and of the records, including the award. While parties are, therefore, free to release or publish an award, neither the Association nor the arbitrator may do so without the specific written authorization of the parties.

The responsibility, therefore, rests with the parties. Experiments made by the Association to obtain written consents have proved so negative as not to encourage the Association in changing its policy. It is evident from the returns that privacy is one of the most highly regarded attributes of arbitration.

Another policy concerns the fees of arbitrators. While the Association retains its policy of providing arbitrators from its Labor Panel on an honorary basis, a practice of paying labor arbitrators was encouraged during the war by the National War Labor Board and by the Conciliation Service of the U. S. Department of Labor. Under this practice arbitrators could fix their own fees. Subsequently the National War Labor Board recommended that the fees vary from $25—$100 per diem; but it was only a suggestion and not a regulation.

The Association has followed a quite different policy for members of its Panel. Where a fee is to be paid, the arrangement must be made by the parties through the Association and prior to the first hearing and must specify whether it is only for hearings, including the preparation of the award, or whether that is to be reckoned in addition. The arrangement must be approved in writing by the parties. The Association has set its own standard at a minimum of $25 and a maximum of $100 per day. If through arrangements with the parties, members of Panels are inclined to charge higher rates, the frequency of their service may be diminished, through non-selection from the lists. Panel members who consent to serve only on a fee basis are expected to serve on an honorary basis in arbitrations where the parties are unable to pay fees.

Under the Rules, the parties are required to pay the traveling and other special expenses of the arbitrator and tribunal clerk and to make a deposit in advance to cover estimated expenditures. At the close of the proceeding, an itemized accounting is made, checked by the tribunal clerk, and then rechecked by the central office accounting department. When the statement has been audited and approved, an accounting is rendered to each party from the central office.

Under this system, the Association has received and disposed of many hundreds of labor disputes;[3] it has greatly increased the acceptance of its standard labor arbitration clauses in collective

[3] The principles obtaining in the making of the Rules (p. 74), the advantages and services provided under Rules (p. 75), and the allocation of powers and duties of parties, arbitrators, and administrators fixed in the Rules (p. 76), set forth for Commercial Rules, are applicable to labor arbitrations and should be read in conjunction with this Chapter. (See also Annex I for text of Rules.)

bargaining agreements;[4] and it has provided technical and general education in labor arbitrations. *The Arbitration Journal* not only carries in each issue a section on Labor Arbitration but reports court decisions relating to labor arbitrations.

While parties may use any clause they agree upon, the advantage of using a standard clause is that it obviates the necessity for entering into stipulations subsequently in order to supply the essential elements that are frequently overlooked and that make the processing of a case difficult, if not impossible. An adequate clause is especially necessary if the parties intend to enter judgment upon the award. So frequently has this situation arisen that early in 1937 the Association issued a "Warning on Clauses in Labor Contracts" in which it drew the attention of management and labor to certain essentials that should be included in all clauses in order to have them fully disclose the intentions of the makers of collective bargaining agreements.[5]

The activities of the labor tribunal are not confined to disputes arising under collective bargaining agreements. The Association is sometimes called upon to name an arbitrator without processing the dispute under its Rules. This service it performs, but advises the Panel arbitrator that he accepts without administrative services or the protection of rules in the performance of his duties. The Association is also called upon from time to time to recommend members of its Panel as a permanent arbitrator or as impartial chairman in an industry. This service it also performs.

The Association has also been called upon by parties to supervise an election to determine the bargaining unit. This responsibility it exercises through an arbitrator approved or selected by the parties. The Association offers three methods of performing this service: (1) By a comparison of records; (2) by balloting by mail; and (3) by holding a ballot box election at the plant in question, or at a convenient locality agreed upon by the parties.[6]

[4] For text of clauses, see Annex II, p. 234.

[5] See *A Guide to Labor Arbitration Clauses* issued by the American Arbitration Association in 1947. This Guide contains a number of clauses with suggestions as to their application.

[6] For a description of these alternate procedures, together with the forms, see *Memorandum on Voluntary Determination of Collective Bargaining Agency,* obtainable from the American Arbitration Association.

Another service the Association has been called upon to render, by invitation of American corporations employing labor in other countries, is the conducting of labor arbitrations in those countries, under its Labor Arbitration Rules and its administration. This service was undertaken in Canada at the suggestion of American corporations which operate plants in both the United States and Canada and who desired to use similar provisions and facilities in all of their collective bargaining agreements. With the consent of the Canadian authorities, such arbitrations have been carried on and the awards rendered have been observed.

The Association, through these various activities, has made the settlement of labor disputes a part of the new American pattern, *first*, by providing a national tribunal that operates in the same manner for all disputes in accordance with the principles and policies found advantageous for arbitration generally; *second*, by separating bargaining from judicial processes; *third*, by creating a Labor Panel whose members have qualifications adapted to the settlement of labor disputes and by installing competent methods of upkeep of such a Panel; *fourth*, by retaining all of the democratic processes that reserve full rights of action to the parties; *fifth*, by the regulation of costs; and *sixth*, by the use of Rules that encourage an orderly proceeding.

The policy of combining commercial and labor arbitration systems under a single administration has many advantages, although operating as separate tribunals. The experience gained in one system is often of value to the other. The fact that similar standards and procedures are applied makes it unnecessary for a corporation or group having both commercial and labor contracts to go to a separate institution for similar service. An experienced administrator renders competent service of a routine kind in both kinds of arbitration. The combination places at the disposal of each system the research and educational facilities of the Association as well as its basic machinery distributed over the United States. The combination makes possible the inauguration of an American pattern, such as exists in no other country.

Arbitration thus moves forward steadily and constructively to public advantage in all areas of disputes.

CHAPTER XII

Practice Under the Motion Picture Consent Decree

«««« »»»»

IN 1940, there occurred one of the events that made arbitration history and that also diversified the American pattern of arbitration. This event was the signing of a court decree to which the United States Government and five major motion picture distributing companies were parties.

As has been noted earlier, one of the accomplishments of the Society was the adoption of arbitration by the Film Boards of Trade in 1923. Arbitration was provided by the Boards for disputes between distributors and exhibitors involving the licensing of motion pictures. In an endeavor to secure standard trade practices, the distributing companies had adopted a uniform contract which all exhibitors were required to accept, and in a further endeavor to secure uniformity and to meet the difficulties of enforcing arbitration agreements and awards in the forty-eight states the companies had further arranged for an exchange of information regarding performance of contracts and awards which was reflected in the credit position established for the exhibitors. In 1930, the U. S. Supreme Court held that this concerted action of the distributors was a violation of the anti-trust laws and, in effect, compulsory arbitration, and, accordingly, the arbitration system of the Film Boards of Trade ended.[1]

Another action was brought in 1938 and threatened with a long and expensive suit by the United States Government for alleged violation of the Sherman Anti-Trust Law, five of the leading motion picture distributors (Paramount Pictures, Inc.; Loew's, Inc.; RKO-

[1] *U. S. v. Paramount Famous Lasky Corporation*, 282 *U. S.* 30.

Radio Pictures, Inc.; Warner Bros. Pictures, Inc.; and Twentieth Century-Fox Film Corp.) entered into an agreement with the United States Department of Justice under which they voluntarily consented to correct some of the practices in the licensing of films for exhibition and the Government agreed to suspend the suit for a period of three years.

In 1945 the suit was reopened and the Court was asked by the Government to direct the motion picture distributors to divorce themselves of the ownership of the motion picture theatres. The matter is now pending before the United States Supreme Court.

Although this experiment may be discontinued by reason of the present decision of the lower court and by subsequent action by the United States Supreme Court, it possesses so many unique features that historically it comprises a part of the American pattern. It is for this reason that the special practice under this Decree is recounted somewhat in detail and from the viewpoint of its differentiation from the general practice.

This agreement, when approved by the United States District Court, became the Consent Decree under which a practice of arbitration was instituted. In several respects this Decree established a new type of arbitration.

Hitherto, parties to arbitration obtained their rights to a legally enforceable agreement and award from the Legislature in the form of an arbitration law. In this instance, arbitration law was superseded by a mutually acceptable court decree giving the court issuing the Decree direct power to enforce the submission to arbitration and any award rendered thereunder, against the consenting distributors by retaining supervision under the Decree.

There was also a change in the form of making the agreement. The parties were the defending distributor companies and the plaintiff Government. The beneficiaries were the exhibitors who were not parties to the Decree, but who might voluntarily invoke its provisions. While its use was voluntary with the exhibitors, the distributors consented to be bound to arbitrate when the exhibitors exercised their voluntary right. It also permitted intervention by a third party. Any exhibitor who believed his rights might be affected by the determination of the claim of a complaining exhibitor was given the right to appear and become a party to the arbitration.

There was also a change in that the Decree was in fact a Code of Fair Trade Practice for the industry, for it contained prohibitions against certain practices and commanded the performance of other acts for the benefit of the trade. The arbitration provisions were confined to a determination of the violation of the acts committed or to a failure to perform those commanded. Accusations were brought before a Motion Picture Arbitration Tribunal upon complaint of an exhibitor as the aggrieved party.

The most fundamental change was in the establishment of a system of arbitration by agreement of the Government and business interests. It was established in two ways: by provisions in the Consent Decree and through rules of procedure agreed to by the parties and approved by the court.

The system itself was established in accordance with the following provisions in the Decree: (1) An arbitration system for the settlement of claims and controversies submissible under the Decree shall be administered by an impartial administrator. (2) A tribunal shall be established and maintained by the administrator in each city in the United States in which three or more distributors maintain exchanges (a map showing the territory over which each tribunal had jurisdiction and called an arbitration district was officially filed as part of the Rules). (3) The administrator shall maintain and establish a panel of not less than ten persons for each tribunal. (4) Each tribunal shall have suitable offices and personnel, including a clerk. (5) No person having any financial interest in or any previous or present connection with the production, distribution, or exhibition of motion pictures, or who has any interest in any motion picture theatre, may be appointed a member of a Panel. (6) The cost of installing and operating the system shall be paid by the distributor defendants and shall be fixed annually by a Budget Committee. (7) The Budget Committee shall consist of three members, one to be appointed by the administrator, one by the distributor defendants, and the chairman to be the Chairman of the Appeal Board. (8) An Appeal Board of three members, appointed by the court, shall have power to determine appeals from awards made in arbitration tribunals. (9) Each arbitrator shall be selected and the proceeding shall be conducted in the manner prescribed in the Rules of Arbitration. (10) Such Rules may be amended or added to by the administrator with the approval of a majority of the Appeal Board upon notice to the Government and distributor defendants and after an opportunity for a hearing on the proposed changes. (11) The expenses of the system are to be paid from a fund derived from filing fees and monies contributed by the distributor defendants in proportionate amounts to be fixed in accordance with their respective annual gross receipts. (12) An arbitration proceeding is instituted in the manner prescribed in the Rules, upon condition that the person instituting the proceeding file a demand for arbitration and submission with the clerk of the Tribunal in the form prescribed by the administrator, and stating in the demand, the substance of the complaint and an undertaking in the submission to abide by and comply with the award. (13) Provision is made for persons, not direct parties to the dispute but whose interests are affected, to file a declaration of intervention and submission with the clerk in like manner and thereby become an intervening party to the proceeding. (14) Representatives of the Department of Justice, duly authorized in writing, are permitted reasonable access to all records of Tribunals or of the Appeal Board.

The American Arbitration Association was named administrator of the system and in accordance with the foregoing specifications, it established 31 offices in the prescribed areas, selected and trained a personnel for them, and appointed a Panel of approximately a thousand men to serve as arbitrators in Motion Picture Tribunals. The administrator also assisted in the establishment of headquarters for the Appeal Board.

The following practice was established for the 31 Tribunals by the Rules of Procedure approved by the Court: (1) An arbitration is initiated by the filing of a demand for arbitration and a submission and the payment of a filing fee of $10 to the clerk. (2) The demand has to be signed by the complainant and must set forth the name and address of each theatre involved, name and address of each exhibitor and distributor against whom the complaint is made or of those whose interest may be affected by the award, and a brief statement of the claim and relief sought. (3) The clerk is required to deliver a copy to each defending party and to each other exhibitor and distributor named in the demand. (4) Within seven days thereafter each party receiving a copy of the demand may sign and file with a clerk a list giving the name and address of each exhibitor or distributor not named in the demand whose business or property it believed may be affected. The clerk is required to send a copy of the demand to each person so named. (5) Persons so named may intervene prior to the commencement of the first hearing and thereby become parties upon filing a declaration of intention and a submission and upon payment of the $10 filing fee. (6) One arbitrator mutually satisfactory to all parties is appointed from a list chosen from the Panel and such list is submitted to each party within a period of not less than fifteen nor more than seventeen days after the filing of the demand. Parties may indicate their preference on the list. If not returned within a period of seven days, all names on the unreturned list are deemed acceptable. When the lists are received, the clerk appoints one arbitrator from the names remaining on the lists and in their order of preference. If no name remains, the administrator appoints one arbitrator from members of the Panel whose names were not submitted. As an alternative to this method, the parties, by written agreement, may unanimously appoint a member of the Panel as arbitrator. (7) Prior to the date of an award becoming final, the administrator, upon proof that an arbitrator is disqualified by reason of an interest in the arbitration, as prohibited in the Decree, may revoke the appointment and declare the office vacant and the award, if any, is vacated. Such application must be made immediately upon discovery of the fact and five days' notice thereof must be given to all parties. (8) The administrator may revoke the appointment should an arbitrator neglect, fail or refuse to perform the duties of his office. (9) The arbitrator fixes the time and place of the hearing, usually at the office of the Tribunal in the designated district and the clerk delivers notice thereof to all of the parties at least five days prior to the date set. (10) The procedure at hearings is similar to that in commercial arbitration proceedings, as are also the provisions for closing and reopening a hearing.[2] (11) When a party defaults or withdraws from a proceeding after the arbitrator is appointed, the matter proceeds to an award, unless all of the parties consent to a dismissal. A defaulting or withdrawing party may not further participate in the proceeding but is bound by the award. (12) The powers of

[2] See Annex I, Sect. V and VI, p. 224.

arbitrators with respect to subject matter are prescribed in the Decree and are limited thereto. (13) Awards must be filed with the clerk within a period of thirty days from the date of closing the hearings or from the date fixed by the arbitrator for the filing of briefs. (14) The arbitrator may assess costs against a losing party or apportion them among the parties. Costs include filing fees and the arbitrator's fee. (15) The administrator is authorized to fix for each arbitration district the arbitrator's fee on a per diem basis, not to exceed $50. A per diem is determined as each day or part thereof that the arbitrator attends a hearing or makes an inspection. In order to encourage arbitration the fee was fixed at $10 per diem. (16) Any expense involved in an inspection is borne equally by the parties. After the award is made, the arbitrator is paid his fee out of sums deposited by the parties. Any undisbursed funds are returned to the parties. (17) The clerk transmits to each party a copy of the award, duly signed and executed, together with the opinion of the arbitrator. (18) The clerk may make arrangements for the taking of a stenographic record, when requested by one or more of the parties. Any party desiring a transcript pays the cost thereof but in the event that such party did not pay the cost of taking the record, it reimburses the other parties for its share of the cost, if later such party requires a copy of the transcript. Three copies of a transcript of the record must be filed with the clerk of the Tribunal in order for an appeal to be taken. (19) Extensions of time may be taken by agreement of the parties, and except the time set for making the award, the arbitrator may extend the time upon written application of a party and upon five days' notice to all other parties.

The practice of arbitration before the Appeal Board is governed by special Rules which include: (1) The party or parties file a notice of appeal, pay an appeal fee of $25, and file three copies of the transcript of the hearings. (2) The clerk of a tribunal then files a copy of the notice of appeal with the clerk of the Appeal Board and when the transcript is received, files three copies with the Appeal Board, together with the demand, declarations and submissions of intervening parties, notice of appointment and signed acceptance of the arbitrator, clerk's record of hearing, exhibits, and award. (3) Each party is entitled to file a brief within thirty days or a reply brief within forty days after filing the notice of appeal. (4) Consideration of the appeal is based upon these documents, unless by written agreement of all parties a request for an oral hearing is made or unless the Appeal Board upon its own initiative directs a hearing. Oral arguments are heard, only in New York at a time and place fixed by the Board. (5) All members of the Board pass upon all appeals, and the concurrence of two is necessary for a decision, except in extensions of time where one member may act, upon written application of a party and upon five days' notice thereof to all parties. (6) In its decision, the Appeal Board may affirm, modify, correct, or reverse an award, including provisions for costs; or it may remand the matter to the Tribunal for rehearing or further action in accordance with the decision of the Board. (7) The Appeal Board may assess the cost of the stenographic record or transcript thereof against the losing party, or apportion it among the parties, as it deems proper. (8) Unless the Appeal Board remands the matter or reopens the hearing, its decision is final within ten days after it is filed with the clerk of the Tribunal. (9) Within this ten-day period, the Appeal Board may reopen a proceeding for the purpose of correcting inadvertent errors. In such an instance, the corrected decision becomes final and binding when it is filed with the clerk of a Tribunal. (10) Access to the records of the Tribunals or of the Appeal Board are not permitted to any person not a party except that all awards, decisions, and opinions, whether made by a Tribunal or the Appeal Board, may be made public. It is customary to print decisions of the Appeal Board.

In accordance with the practice instituted under these Rules the Association as the administrator provides the necessary forms and manuals of instruction for clerks of Tribunals. These manuals cover separately the financial system and the proceedings. What was doubtless the first school of arbitration was conducted by the administrator when clerks were brought to headquarters for training.

A separate department for the administration of this System was set up in the Association under the immediate supervision of an Administrative Council which considered problems of organization and policy.

The Motion Picture Arbitration System is administered as an integral part of the Association's national commercial arbitration system in that the machinery, experience, facilities, and services of that system constitute the foundation upon which Motion Picture Tribunals are operated. It is an independent system in that the Decree and Rules control the practice and its permanence is dependent upon the Decree or such other authority as the industry itself may establish. It conforms to the American pattern in the principles and policies set forth in the Association's Commercial Arbitration Rules.

Whether or not the system becomes permanent, it has been demonstrated that it is feasible for Government and business to co-operate in maintaining good relations among the component parts of an industry; and that for the welfare of a country co-operation, rather than prosecution, may produce the greatest benefit.

This system has worked effectively, *first*, in the disposal of claims under the Decree; *second*, in the reduction of friction and disagreement; and, *third*, in inducing voluntary settlements, thereby keeping down the number of arbitrations. As in other industries, the presence of facilities and services and the will to arbitrate have actually resulted in a low rate of arbitrations as against the thousands that were expected.

Of this system, Judges Augustus N. Hand, Henry W. Goddard, and John Bright, the statutory court designated to try the anti-trust suit in 1945, when the continuance of the Arbitration System was under consideration, said, in a Memorandum Opinion:[3]

> "These tribunals have dealt with trade disputes, particularly those as to clearances and runs, with rare efficiency, as both government counsel and counsel for other parties have conceded. . . . We strongly recommend that some such system be continued in order to avoid cumbersome and dilatory court litigation and to preserve the practical advantages of the tribunals created by the Consent Decree."

[3] *United States* v. *Paramount Pictures*, 70 F. Supp. 53 (1947), on p. 76.

CHAPTER XIII

Special Practice in Accident Claims Tribunals

«««« »»»»

THE quite different origin of the Accident Claims Tribunal, established by the Association in 1933, offers an illustration of the wide range of practice in different types of tribunals which may take place within the framework of organized arbitration. It indicates another use to which arbitration may be put and the interest taken in such experiments and their benefit to public welfare.

Arbitration as a method of relieving court calendars and of expediting the administration of justice, began in the New York City Board of Municipal Justices in 1917. In that year it adopted rules of procedure which provided that the parties could agree to substitute arbitration for trial by filing a consent to arbitrate with the clerk of the court where the case was pending. The arbitrator selected by the parties, or appointed by the court, made his award in writing and filed it with the court where it was then entered as a judgment.

Arbitration applied under these simple rules did not, however, take deep root and did not, therefore, afford the anticipated relief. *First*, consent of the parties was difficult to obtain, as both plaintiff and defendants were reluctant to try what seemed to them a new method of settlement; *second*, counsel for both parties were generally opposed to exchanging a jury for an arbitrator; *third*, some of the justices themselves were indifferent to this method of reducing the court's delays. But more generally responsible for the failure was the fact that arbitration was usually suggested on the call of the calendar when the matter was about to come to trial, by which time much of the goodwill necessary to arbitrate had been dissipated through negotiations for settlement. Also, the lack of organized effort or systematization of the proceeding, or of educational work, contributed to inaction under this first experiment.

It was evident that, without the interest of the business men, particularly in the automobile industry since a very considerable number of the accidents involved were automobile accidents, and of men in the casualty insurance field, little progress would be made. In 1927 the Association called the first conference on this subject. It was the sense of the conference, over which Alfred H. Swayne, Vice President of General Motors presided, that business shared with the bar the responsibility for providing a remedy. The Conference appointed a Committee on Arbitration and Automobile Accident Claims to inquire into the matter. They were the originators of the plan which was later approved by the Claim Department of the National Bureau of Casualty and Surety Underwriters, the Board of Municipal Justices, the New York State Department of Insurance,[1] the Automobile Merchants Association[2] and a Special Committee of Lawyers.[3] This cooperation resulted in the organization of a special Tribunal in New York City by the Association in October, 1933.

A Special Panel of Arbitrators, consisting only of lawyers, was appointed and a special clerk was assigned to the Accident Claims Arbitration Tribunal. Arrangements were made first with President Justice Lauer, and later with President Justice Bissell, for arbitrations to be held in this Tribunal under the Rules adopted in 1917 by the Board of Municipal Justices for settlement in the courts, so as to make the entry of judgment upon the award more expeditious. Forty-five insurance companies agreed to submit cases to arbitration upon the condition that the Association would undertake to obtain the consent of the claimants.[4]

The procedure for obtaining consent was the following: When a case was filed by an insurance company for arbitration, notice was

[1] Of which George S. Van Schaick was Superintendent, later succeeded by Louis H. Pink, who continued the initial co-operation.

[2] Under the direction of Lee J. Eastman and Harry G. Bragg, this Association rendered valuable assistance in establishing the Tribunal and in securing the interest of the automobile companies.

[3] For members of this Committee, see Ch. XXV, p. 207.

[4] For list of insurance companies, which submitted cases, see Ch. XXV, p. 207.

sent to the President Justice of the filing of the claim, together with the names of the complaining parties and of their counsel. He then sent a letter to the counsel for the claimant, urging consent to arbitration. At the same time, the clerk of the Accident Claims Arbitration Tribunal contacted counsel for the claimant and advised him of the willingness of the insurance company to arbitrate the claim. He described the functioning of the Tribunal and availability of lawyer-arbitrators and requested the co-operation of the lawyer in obtaining the consent of his client.

By agreement with President Justice Bissell, the insurance companies filing the case paid a filing fee when the matter was submitted to an arbitrator and the Association shared the balance of the cost of maintaining and operating the Tribunal. To the claimant this arbitration was without cost. When consent was obtained in writing, the clerk proceeded with the arrangements for a hearing after the Association had appointed an arbitrator from the Special Panel of Lawyers set up for that purpose. When consent was not obtainable, the matter proceeded to trial in court in the usual way.

Practice under Municipal Court Rules was supplemented by the Commercial Arbitration Rules, in that the general requirements of arbitration law were observed, and the principles and policies governing that procedure were applied, thus taking advantage of the additional safeguards provided in these Rules. The administrator, the Association, was thus able to place its existing machinery, personnel, and services at the disposal of the new Tribunal.

The originators of this plan were not solely concerned with obtaining settlements in the interest of the parties, much as that was needed in many instances. It was realized that persons injured, often through no fault of their own, and unable to obtain just and prompt compensation or a hearing of their grievance, are predisposed to become detractors of the American form of government and critical of the courts. Under such circumstances, they may become centers of disaffection from which proceed illwill and attacks upon American institutions. It seemed, therefore, that in the interests of public welfare, the prompt disposal of accident claims was desirable. For these reasons it was not so important that the matter should proceed to formal arbitration and result in awards, as that the introduction of arbitration should be instrumental in bringing about a friendly settlement in as prompt a manner as possible, thus maintaining a high level of goodwill in the community.[5]

Whether this experiment will be expanded into a national system remains to be seen. During the war, restrictions on travel greatly reduced the number of accident claims, enabling courts to catch up with their calendars. Since then, the rise in accidents has been quite phenomenal. Plans have been in the making for extending the facilities to other cities, but until a more satisfactory method of financing is found, these plans are being held in abeyance.

Other plans have been under consideration for expediting the settlement of accident claims. One insurance company proposed to use an arbitration clause in its policies but it did not meet with favorable consideration from other companies. There was also under discussion the use of coupons under which agreements to arbitrate might be entered into at the time of the accident.

In the public interest, the prompt settlement of accident claims is imperative, for the human elements of suffering and privation involved lend themselves to misrepresentations of American justice if settlements are too long delayed.

Whether or not arbitration will play a greater or lesser part in solving the problems created primarily by highway accidents, the experiment of maintaining an Accident Claims Tribunal has proven that it is practical to apply arbitration to the relief of injured persons or to the settlement of claims for property damage.

[5] During the period, 1933-1937, 14,411 claims were referred for arbitration in the Accident Claims Arbitration Tribunal, resulting in many awards and settlements after consent of the complaining party was obtained.

CHAPTER XIV

Panel Arbitrators Keynote American Arbitration

«««« »»»»

AMERICAN arbitration is particularly distinguished by its Panels of arbitrators. While Panels had long been maintained in commercial and trade organizations, the distinction of creating a National Panel, representative of all industry, belongs to the American Arbitration Association.

The Panel arbitrator is a permanently selected person of known qualifications who is generally available for Tribunal service. He is the indispensable factor in a system of arbitration. It has been found that the fact of a Panel arbitrator's known availability and qualifications is often the determining element in inducing parties to submit their dispute to arbitration or to use a clause in a contract.

By the performance of an arbitrator, arbitration succeeds or fails, its prestige is advanced or diminished and its future use encouraged or disparaged. Therefore, the selection of Panel members, their qualifications and training, and their conduct in office, are factors of major importance in systems of arbitration.

Certain qualifications established by both law and practice over the centuries have made the task of selection easier. They concern expertness in the field of controversy, impartiality and freedom from bias, absence of fraud and corruption, and right conduct in office. They also concern the amity, justice, speed, and economy with which the arbitrator conducts a proceeding.

In an undertaking to fix a somewhat uniform basis of selection for membership on its National Panel, the Association finally arrived at the following standard requirements as best calculated to obtain men suitable for service as a commercial arbitrator:

(1) He must have achieved success in his own profession, trade or calling; otherwise he would not be acceptable as an expert in a controversy arising in that field of activity. (2) He must be a person of high standing in his own community; otherwise he would not inspire the confidence of the parties. (3) He must have a judicial temperament; otherwise he would not be sufficiently patient and probing at hearings to obtain the essential facts and to weigh evidence. (4) He must be a person of integrity; otherwise he would not rest his judgment upon the facts and the evidence adduced before him, nor observe carefully the terms of his appointment. (5) He must have been disciplined in human and public affairs; otherwise he would not show the tolerance and understanding necessary to the evaluation of the human elements in a dispute. (6) He must have sufficient leisure and financial income from his own calling to enable him to act upon an honorary basis in the rendering of a public service; and he must consider his office as one of public significance and responsibility. (7) He should be identified with some public activity and take an interest in public affairs.

The establishment of these standards appears to have been the first attempt in America to obtain arbitrators having somewhat uniform qualifications for their office.

The problem of how to find men possessing these qualifications and who were willing to accept membership on a Panel, where service was not remunerated, was then presented. A plan was, therefore, developed for obtaining nominations, in the localities where arbitrations were likely to be held, from persons and organizations in the best position to know suitable nominees.

As finally adopted, the plan was to obtain nominations of men having the above-named qualifications, from business and trade organizations, banks, credit organizations,[1] law and other professional bodies and from social, civic, economic, educational, and religious organizations in the community. When these nominations were received, the nominee was sent a qualification sheet requiring such personal information as he was willing to supply in answer to the questions asked. On the basis of the nominee's record and the

[1] For example, such business organizations as Dun and Bradstreet, the Equitable Life Assurance Society, National Association of Credit Men, and members of the ATAE, through their various members, branches or agencies, contributed their services in checking the records of proposed members of Panels.

nominator's recommendation, together with such other inquiries as the Association wished to make, the appointment was either confirmed or not approved.

According to the special aptitudes, revealed by nominators or by nominees in their qualifications sheets, Panel members were separated into categories. As finally established, these covered more than a hundred different callings, including all of the important trade divisions, together with separate categories for bankers, lawyers, engineers, educators, accountants, and other specialists. As the establishment of new commercial enterprises, such as plastics, required experts, other categories were added. By this method, the Association has available at all times the best known experts or leaders in the category to which they are assigned.

Before members of Panels are called into active service as arbitrators, they must pass a test of selection by the parties. This test is applied by submitting to the parties identical lists of names drawn from the Panel for their approval or rejection. The parties have a period of seven days in which to apply their own methods of determining the adaptability and fitness of the proposed arbitrator. They need disclose no reasons for their rejection, but it is binding upon the Association not to appoint a rejected person.

In the selection of these names from the Panel, parties have a voice. They specify the locality where the arbitration is to be held, thus giving preference to members in that locality. They may specify the kind of qualifications, thus indicating the particular type of expert the settlement of their dispute requires. Any preferences or directives, expressed by the parties, are considered by the Association in drawing up the lists.

Under this method of selection, where each party approves or rejects names submitted and marks those retained in the order of preference, the judgment of the parties and any special knowledge they possess is brought to bear upon the appointment.

In an effort to appoint the members of its Panel who are impartial, the Association also calls upon the person chosen for assistance. In the notice of appointment, and before returning his acceptance, the prospective arbitrator is asked to disclose any circumstances or facts which he believes might create a presumption of bias toward either party or toward the subject matter. When such facts or circumstances are disclosed, they are transmitted to the parties who may then accept or reject the arbitrator. If they accept him, the circumstance is waived, but if either party objects, the appointment is withdrawn by the administrator.

These screenings, through qualifications for membership on the Panel, by parties from lists, and by arbitrators of their own qualifications, may still be insufficient to assure complete impartiality. It sometimes occurs that in the actual process of arbitration, unforeseen circumstances arise that either create a suspicion of bias or give positive evidence of it.

If during a proceeding an allegation of bias is made by a party, the administrator is empowered to hear the charge and, if satisfied that bias exists, it may vacate the office. A successor is chosen in the same manner as the original appointment was made.

Under administered systems of arbitration, a clerk is always present at all hearings. Any situation that may develop which indicates an impairment of confidence in the Panel arbitrator's impartiality or conduct, or if any violation of the Rules which insure such impartiality appears, the clerk advises the administrator. It may then confer with the parties as to the situation and arrange for a waiver or a withdrawal.

There are in reality nine techniques for checking the qualifications and performance of Panel arbitrators: (1) Nominations for the Panel. (2) Submission of record by the Panel member before his appointment. (3) Provision in the Rules which prohibit the serving of any Panel member having an interest in the controversy or in the parties. (4) By parties checking qualifications of persons whose names are submitted to them on lists. (5) Arbitrators chosen from list, before accepting appointment, checking up their own record and interests as possibly constituting a suspicion of bias. (6) Vacating the office of arbitrators who show bias during a proceeding. (7) The presence of a clerk in Tribunals to observe the performance of arbitrators while in office. (8) Recording the quality of service rendered by arbitrators. (9) Obtaining the opinion of parties as to their evaluation of the services of Panel arbitrators.

Although the above methods of checking arbitrators applies to labor arbitrators, the qualifications of labor Panel arbitrators are less readily established. In the first place, many arbitration laws that set standards for conduct in office are not applicable to labor arbitrations and there is not the wide range of court decisions to assist in formulating standards. Nor has the idea of impartial arbitrators been so generally accepted as in commercial arbitrations. There still predominates the practice of each party appointing an arbitrator, under which method the third person alone may be disinterested. Furthermore, there still prevails the idea that in labor arbitrations, involving as they do continuing relationships between management and employees, the processes of mediation should not be so definitely excluded as they are in commercial arbitrations. Therefore, a type of person who possesses unusual qualities of patience, persuasion, and adjustment is often favored as an arbitrator. Also, since the same arbitrator is called upon more frequently than in commercial arbitrations and, therefore, may be more often rejected, the standards set for original appointments may not always continue under these circumstances. Furthermore, while the economic views and experience of commercial arbitrators are generally an advantage in commercial arbitration, they may prove a detriment in labor arbitration. Generally speaking, men experienced in human relations or interested in social service or public affairs have the desired qualifications.

Such considerations as these have led the Association to place emphasis upon performance in office. Through the adoption of Codes of Ethics, applicable to both labor and commercial arbitrations, screening through performance is rendered more accurate.[1]

By reason of the standards which determine selection for the Panel and appointment to office, and conduct in office, the commercial and labor Panel arbitrator has become in effect an approved arbitrator and is in a different position from the casual arbitrator. He belongs to a select company and is part of a system of which he is the keynoter.

Panel arbitrators also occupy a distinguished position of leadership in their own community. They have become leaders in arbitration. They write, speak and confer on arbitration matters. They advance the use of arbitration clauses in their own business contracts and collective bargaining agreements. They perform a valuable service as critics, as their practical suggestions, obtained through

[1] For text of Code of Ethics, see Annex III, p. 235.

experience, lead to many improvements. They advance good business and labor relations by being always ready to assist in the settlement of disputes. They constitute a body of peace officers, in a country where free enterprise has need of them.

The Panel also offers an opportunity for training and education, for co-ordinated action according to established standards, and for a method of discipline under acceptable rules. A Panel makes possible the keynoting of a system of arbitration through specific service to parties in dispute and thus performs an immensely important public service.

CHAPTER XV

Administrators of Arbitration Systems

«««« »»»»

WHEN the Association established systems of arbitration for the actual settlement of specific disputes submitted by parties in its Tribunal under its Rules, it made a careful distinction between its general powers under its charter and its administrative powers under its Rules.

When the Association acts in the processing of a dispute in any of its Tribunals, it acts as administrator on behalf of the parties for their particular arbitration.

The powers of the administrator are governed entirely by the parties to each particular dispute. It is by their mutual agreement to arbitrate under the Rules or direction of the Association that the Association becomes their administrator. These powers, although specified in the Rules, may not be the same for all arbitrations, for any conditions or modifications agreed to by the parties in their submission, or other reference to arbitration, take precedence over similar provisions contained in the Rules. In the application of this principle, the Association, as administrator for the parties, can have no duties or functions except those conferred by mutual agreement of the parties, nor can it assume any other function without their knowledge or specific authorization.

But in order to meet the technical requirements of arbitration laws and in order to avoid writing long and comprehensive rules in submissions and clauses, and in order to provide a uniform practice in tribunals, the Association offers standard rules of procedure. Acceptance of these Rules by the parties, with such modifications as they agree upon, is necessary to constitute the Association their administrator.

These Rules define precisely the powers of the administrator. Their provisions are carefully separated into routine duties which the clerks assigned to tribunals perform in like manner for all arbitrations;[1] and exceptional powers which the administrator performs only occasionally, when so requested by the parties, or when they fail or are unable to exercise their prior rights in the manner and within the time limits specified in the Rules.

These exceptional powers, which may be occasionally exercised by the administrator, are intended only to prevent the frustration of an arbitration through failure or neglect or refusal of the parties or of a party to exercise their prior right.[2]

In the application of these Rules, the impartiality of the administrator should be no less than that required of a Panel arbitrator. The administrator is there to carry out the will and the intentions of the parties, to show favor to neither party, to perform no service for one party that is not available to the other party. A communication from one party affecting the proceeding is immediately transmitted to the other party. When, under the Rules, lists or notices are to be sent out simultaneously, it means simultaneously, with no discretion to do otherwise.

The administrator, being the channel through which parties communicate with the arbitrator when the occasion demands, finds this principle of impartiality tested in unexpected ways, for there is no way of anticipating what requests a party will make or what information he will require. Therefore, the policy of keeping each party fully advised of every such communication and request is highly important. This occurs, for example, when a party seeks to submit some additional information to the arbitrator when the hearings have been closed; or seeks to obtain from the arbitrators their reasons for making an award.

For the kind of service which the administrator is called upon to perform under its Rules, the Association created a new type of

[1] See Ch. X, p. 76, for statement of routine duties performed by clerks and rights and duties performed by parties and arbitrators.

[2] For statement of these occasional powers, see Ch. X, p. 81.

administrator and established principles of conduct not hitherto generally prevailing.

This new type of administrator is a corporate administrator of an independent character, having no connection or identification with any party and not personally interested in the award. The Association is, therefore, a wholly impartial administrator under no obligations to any party or arbitrator in any manner, and performing only the services prescribed in the Rules.

This is, in fact, a different type of administrator from one acting for a trade group which requires non-members or outside traders to arbitrate within the terms and conditions laid down by one of the parties, namely a member of the group, and is under a duty to render special service to its members. Under such circumstance, the non-member has no participation in making the Rules and no alternative but to accept them.

This new type of corporate administrator is a responsible trained administrator. Its authority is exercised through a Tribunals Department with a competent and trained Tribunals Vice President in charge. He is trained not only in processing an arbitration but in the general duties of his office. He has a labor arbitrations staff, a commercial arbitrations staff, an accident claims tribunal staff, an international arbitrations staff and a special motion picture arbitrations staff. There is also attached to this Department a legal research staff that compiles court decisions, is familiar with arbitration laws, and which furnishes general information. Its services are also available to attorneys for legal information. These respective staffs function under the Rules of the different systems and are concerned only with the processing of arbitrations. They are not concerned with the general policies or educational work of the Association. By centering this responsibility, parties are at all times assured of the speedy and economical processing of their arbitration.

The trained administrator also furnishes the arbitrator with the tools for his office. He has a right to expect a copy of the Rules and instructions for his guidance in applying them. He expects to be shown consideration in the use of his time and that he will be freed from unfamiliar detail. He is also furnished with agreeable surroundings in which to hold hearings and assumes that his award will be accepted in the spirit of arbitration.

The trained administrator is also a paid administrator. The schedule of fees which it is entitled to receive for its services is set forth in the Rules and is strictly adhered to as being the amount agreed to by the parties when they elected to arbitrate under the Rules. These fees are paid into the treasury of the Association and help to maintain the system and pay the actual cost of the proceeding.

This new type of administrator is both a neutral and a silent administrator. It holds no economic or social viewpoints that influence its administration of any particular arbitration. This is a particularly important characteristic in administering labor arbitrations where theories as to the respective rights of management and labor might seriously affect an impartial processing of cases involving such questions. In the administration of elections to determine the bargaining agency, both the arbitrator and the administrator must be free from any viewpoint that would influence the processing of the election.

Nor does the administrator hold or express opinions upon any award rendered. It issues no publicity and makes no public comment upon any matter submitted to arbitration in a tribunal. It carries out to the full the belief that a proceeding is the parties' affair and any comment or publicity is theirs to express.

This new type of administrator has no judicial functions in the determination of the controversy nor does it influence the decision of arbitrators. The principle of separating executive and judicial functions is strictly maintained. Even when the contract of the parties authorizes the Association to act as arbitrator, it will always assume the functions of an administrator and will submit to the parties names from which to choose arbitrators, or will, by authorization of the parties, appoint a member of a Panel to hear and determine the controversy.

This principle represents a sharp departure from practices in some trade organizations where the group is concerned with the kind of decision rendered, and where its officials, acting as arbitrators, not infrequently have to take into consideration the effect of the award upon their own membership or make an award that will please the trade. The tendency of international agencies to grant executives judicial powers of settling disputes is one which may eventually lead to bias or the miscarriage of justice and is strictly avoided in all administration of international trade arbitrations by the Association.

This modern administrator is a democratic and not an arbitrary one. It recognizes local pride in the selection of members of its National Panel from the different communities. It uses the facilities and services of other organizations when these are available. It functions under joint clauses which are approved by the Association and other agencies, under arrangements for the mutual use of their respective facilities. It is friendly to joint arbitration committees, representing different tribunals, to determine the locale of an arbitration when parties cannot agree thereon, particularly in international arbitrations. It reserves to parties their full rights and goes all out to help parties exercise them before assuming any powers of its own. It encourages representation of parties by counsel in its proceedings. It assumes no duties not specifically conferred by all of the parties either in the Rules or by subsequent written stipulation.

It is a function of the administrator to see that procedural parity among the parties is strictly maintained and that no one party obtains an advantage over another through failure on its part to maintain procedural parity. In labor arbitrations, this principle cannot be too meticulously followed, for in this field of human relations the slightest deviation or oversight serves to arouse suspicion and any omission or dereliction may be regarded as intentional.

This type of administrator does not encroach upon the rights of the parties in a proceeding. The temptation is always in the direction of usurping rights and powers, especially when an administrator believes it can exercise these powers more expeditiously and effectively than can the parties. The Association has resisted such temptation and has found that slight delays in which to persuade the parties to exercise their prior rights is a much better way to promote the amity of a proceeding than for the administrator peremptorily to assume these rights upon a slight pretext of delays, or inefficiency of a party.

This new type of administrator possesses a high degree of integrity. This is not only evidenced in the choice and qualifications of its clerks, but in the ethical standards that govern the administrator. Under these standards, for example, no one connected with the administration of a tribunal may accept any gratuities, gifts, or favors from parties or counsel or from any one participating in the arbitration. None of the officers of the Association may profit from a proceeding nor from any information revealed in the course of an arbitration. None of its Panel members may charge fees, except by written agreement of the parties, and all expense accounts are itemized and accounted for to the parties.

It is not within the discretion of the administrator to assume any powers or duties with respect to an arbitration that is not authorized by the parties. They may, however, by request or stipulation seek to have the administrator take on new duties. It is discretionary with the administrator to accept these new responsibilities. It is usually guided in its decision by whether it is a clerical or ministerial duty and whether it comes within the scope of the standards established for a corporate administrator.

It follows from these standards of practice for administrators, that they may not give any legal advice, nor recommend lawyers to a party. When parties are represented by counsel, all notices, exchange of documents, and other services performed in making arrangements for or administering the proceeding are sent to the counsel rather than to the parties; the delivery of the award is also made to counsel.

An administrator of this type also performs certain pre-case services. It furnishes forms for making submissions, and for demands for arbitration, and for clauses in contracts for reference of future disputes to arbitration. It furnishes its Rules and information concerning their use. It conveys information upon the cost of the arbitration and concerning the kind of arbitrators that are available for the settlement of their type of dispute. It furnishes counsel for both parties with digests of laws and court decisions when this information is essential to the reference of a matter to arbitration.

An administrator of this type also has post-tribunal and post-award responsibilities. These consist of keeping the files and returning exhibits to the parties, of furnishing *facsimile* copies of records that may be required for court action. It also will, if both parties agree, transmit to the arbitrators any requests for explanation or interpretation of the award. It also answers any protests or comments on the award or upon the arbitrators.

Even though neither the proceeding nor the award is usually made public, the administrator nevertheless has a public responsibility. If justice has been done through a fair and just determination of the issue, through hearings in which each party is satisfied that he has had an equal and full opportunity to be heard before a fair and impartial arbitrator, then arbitration gains in public estimation and good has been done to the community or trade affected by the dispute. If the contrary be true, then evil has just as surely been done. If the administrator fails to provide the safeguards that keep an arbitration free from bias, fraud, corruption, overcharging, irresponsibility in handling funds or accounting for them, then just as surely there is an unfavorable public reaction to arbitration itself. If the administrator itself is not free from self-interest, or from influence by either party and does not steer an absolutely impartial course between them, then suspicion replaces confidence and the public is the loser through non-resort to arbitration.

This public responsibility lays upon the administrator the solemn duty of maintaining in the highest possible degree integrity and impartiality in the exercise of all of its functions and of avoiding self-seeking throughout its entire operations. These are among the things which increase public confidence in arbitration and enhance its benefit to society.

Administrators of international systems of arbitration, notably those of the Western Hemisphere, have found acceptance of this new type of administrator advantageous and as the Rules of these systems are similar to those of the Association, the practice followed by administrators in these international systems is identical. The extension of the practice followed by modern administrators to international systems of arbitration on the basis of experience in the Western Hemisphere should prove of substantial advantage to arbitration.

CHAPTER XVI

The Arbitration Clause as an Instrument of Civilization

«««« »»»»

REFERENCE has been made to the importance of the legislation which gave legal validity and enforceability to the promise to arbitrate a future dispute when an arbitration clause in a contract so provided. Emphasis has also been placed upon the efficacy of a promise to arbitrate a future dispute as a means of controlling controversy and discord. It has been shown that where this promise to arbitrate obtains generally in any industrial group, or in any segment of society, its effect is to reduce the amount of discord and dispute, even to the point where the formal process of arbitration becomes unnecessary. It is certain that any instrumentality which reduces the burden of waste and cost of disputes to a nation is an activating power for the advancement of civilization. It is even more certain that the constant action which arbitration, as an ameliorating influence, wages against resort to force is an invaluable national asset.

That these conclusions may not sound chimerical but are deeply rooted in American experience, there follow three illustrations from many, where special systems have been established and the results justify these conclusions.

In the description of the Motion Picture Arbitration System,[1] the promise of the distributors to submit to arbitration, upon the demand of the exhibitor, worked such magic in a highly disputatious industry that only a small percentage of the anticipated 5,000 complaints materialized. Automatic settlements became the rule where previous to the installation of arbitration, they were the exception.

[1] Ch. XII, p. 92.

In other areas of the amusement industry, a similar situation prevails. When Actors' Equity Association first used an arbitration clause in its standard contract, references to arbitration were frequent. In recent years, such has been the cultivation of the spirit of arbitration, that submissions of disputes in tribunals is not only rare, but increasingly settlements are effected by the parties during the process of arbitration. What was once known as a most contentious industry has now become a model of good behavior in respect to the infrequency of disputes.

In 1939, the Air Transport Association set up arbitration facilities for the arbitration of disputes among their members. The machinery was incorporated in the Air Transport Rules of Arbitration to be administered by the Association. Under this plan, rules and panels, specially chosen and located at convenient air bases were established, but the Tribunals of the Association were to be used, thus avoiding duplication and cost. Under the leadership of the late Colonel Edward H. Gorrell and its counsel, Howard C. Westwood, the industry determined that it would be free from internal litigation in order that its members might work together for the greater use of air transport.

Arbitration was not imposed upon any carrier, but the use of arbitration clauses in all inter-carrier agreements was recommended as a general trade practice. The reason assigned for using the machinery of the Association was the recognition of a situation that had troubled other trade associations, namely that the assumption of judicial functions by members of an organization had often resulted in friction and the disruption of other co-operative undertakings, and that impersonal organizations not connected with the industry would afford more acceptable facilities.

Although this arrangement has been in effect for eight years, no matter has been submitted to arbitration, *the promise to arbitrate* and the prevalent spirit of goodwill engendered therein having been sufficient to effect voluntary settlements by the parties.

The fur importing industry offers a quite different illustration of the effectiveness of a promise to arbitrate a future dispute. This was a contentious industry whose method of dealing with disputes had reached such a pass that they were settled somewhat haphazardly by persons more interested in securing a verdict for the party by whom they had been appointed than in determining the merits of the controversy. The usual practice, when a dispute arose, was for each side to appoint an arbitrator, who then tried to convince the arbitrator appointed by the other side that his principal was right and an allowance should or should not be granted. When a deadlock ensued, the so-called arbitrators, really agents of the parties, commenced to bargain to secure a third person favorable to their party's point of view. As soon as the third arbitrator had been agreed upon, it was generally believed that the verdict could be foretold. If the foreign shipper's representative, the broker, had secured the appointment of the arbitrator, the allowance would be nothing or very small; but if the buyer had been able to secure the appointment of a third arbitrator from the buying group, an allowance, and frequently a generous one, would be the verdict.

Under these conditions, arbitration was not conducted by the three arbitrators alone but was in reality being held informally in the stores or on the street floors of the fur district.

In March of 1928, upon invitation from the industry, the American Arbitration Association assisted the American Fur Merchants Association to install special facilities. But first a promise was required under the by-laws of the Fur Merchants Association to the effect that a member would not sue another member without first offering to arbitrate and the defending member was required by the industry to accept the offer.

One of the interesting departures from the usual commercial arbitration practice was the method of selecting arbitrators. In an industry, which for many years had followed a system permitting each party to name an arbitrator, it was difficult, to say the least, to change that method. The representatives of brokers and shippers insisted that some method had to be devised to permit the parties to continue that right and at the same time to insure the selection of impartial arbitrators. The method was to appoint an official panel. It included sixty names, representing the different elements of the industry. These names were selected by the representatives of the brokers and merchants. The list included men familiar with every type of fur—fox, mink, Argentine lamb, Persian lamb, muskrat, leopard, dog, rabbit and every other animal whose skin was used in the fur industry, and also men who carried on the processing of such skins—dressers, dyers and fur coat and trimming manufacturers.

When a dispute arose and the matter was filed with the Fur Tribunal, the official panel was submitted to the party filing the dispute. From the panel, he selected three persons he believed competent to serve. These names were submitted to the defending party. He was requested to select one of them and also to select three names from the official panel from which the complaining party was then asked to select one. Two members of the arbitration board were thus appointed by mutual agreement of both parties.

As part of this method, a special panel of arbitrators was appointed. It contains thirty names of persons, selected by the representatives of the brokers, the merchants, and the American Arbitration Association. These thirty members were leaders in the industry and again representative of all of its sections. From this Panel, the Association was required to appoint the third arbitrator, selecting a person having the knowledge and experience necessary for the determination of the pending dispute.

This system of arbitration also provided that an appeal from the award might be taken to a special appeal board of arbitrators within a period of seven days after it was rendered. The brokers, representing as they did shippers in the far corners of the world, believed that those shippers might view with some suspicion a proceeding conducted in the country of the buyer, and would feel more confidence in a proceeding recommended by American traders and be more willing to accept the arbitration clause if a review might be had of the decision, when desired by a party.

These somewhat elaborate preparations in a highly contentious industry contemplated the disposal of a large volume of disputes. The contrary happened. Members of the Panels, being thoroughly familiar with conditions and trade practice within the industry, have discouraged members from submitting trivial or extravagant claims, and contestants have learned to adjust minor matters that had hitherto found their way into litigation or arbitration. Also, the number of appeals have been small.

What actually happened, however, was that the acceptance of a promise to arbitrate a future dispute changed the attitude of parties toward controversy. Fear of its consequences is removed; and certainty of a continuing friendship is assured. The high costs and risks of controversy are avoided. Controversy thereby assumes less importance in the routine of trade, it is taken more calmly and threats of resort to force lessen. The increasing exercise of self-restraint, self-confidence, and self-regulation are the natural outcome of these promises.

These illustrations from among many,[2] indicate how arbitration clauses have become an instrument of civilization. But in order to have them continue as such instruments, certain conditions must prevail.

The *first* is that the written promise to arbitrate a future dispute is an indispensable element, for without this none of the benefits above noted, become steadily possible.

The *second* is that arbitration becomes an instrument in civilization in the degree to which these promises to arbitrate future disputes come into general use in all kinds of human and contractual relations where conflict and dispute threaten that civilization.

The *third* is, that care must be taken to cultivate the spirit of arbitration in connection with the adoption of clauses, for they alone are not sufficient unless they embody and continually demonstrate the presence of good faith, confidence, and goodwill.

The *fourth* is, that the presence of these arbitration clauses should strengthen the belief in a system of free enterprise by emphasizing individual responsibility and competence in the control of disputes, and by applying self-restraint, self-regulation and by increasing self-confidence which promises to arbitrate embody or encourage.

The *fifth* condition is that a clause should always be directed toward the prevention rather than the cure of a dispute and to the realization that in proportion as it reduces the acuteness of controversy and induces parties to effect their own settlements, it contributes to the advancement of civilization.

The *sixth* is, that the use of a general clause is a greater instrument for civilization than a limited one, for in this age of unprecedented economic difficulties, the kinds of disputes that will arise cannot be foreseen and if one emerges that does not come within

[2] The *Year Book on Commercial Arbitration in the United States* contains many further illustrations of the decrease in disputes and in arbitration when a trade adopts a standard arbitration clause for the use of its members.

the provisions of the clause, then it becomes a trouble-maker for civilization.

A country is immensely more tranquil and secure that builds up reserves of goodwill and good faith among its people. Arbitration clauses are a means of increasing them. Their prevalence indicates a high level of these reserves. Therefore, the cultivation of the spirit of arbitration as an American way of life makes for a strong nation of happy individuals and of cooperative organizations. To this end, the arbitration clause is being used in the organization of American arbitration and in international systems projected for the benefit of all peoples.

Part III

AMERICAN CONCEPT AND ORGANIZATION OF INTERNATIONAL COMMERCIAL ARBITRATION

CHAPTER XVII

The Inter-American System

«««« »»»»

One of the first acts of the Association was to lay a foundation of knowledge for an international system of arbitration among the twenty-one American Republics. The first step was a survey, made in 1926, of arbitral practice and laws in Mexico.

The choice of the American Republics for the first experiment was a happy one, for the ground had been well cultivated by the Pan American Union in its arrangements for the settlement of political disputes. There had also been discussions from time to time of proposals for the settlement of commercial disputes.

For example, the first Pan American Financial Conference, meeting in 1915, had endorsed the principle of commercial arbitration; and the Fifth International Conference of American States, meeting in 1923, had adopted a resolution suggesting that chambers of commerce in the different Republics should reach agreements among themselves for the arbitration of commercial controversies and establish a system to allow easy and satisfactory solution of differences between merchants and manufacturers. In 1928, addressing the International Conference of American States on Conciliation and Arbitration, President Coolidge said:

"The great value of the plan for arbitration lies in the fact that it both furnishes knowledge and assurance that differences will be adjusted and adjusts them. This has a very large influence on the public temper. The desire to bring differences to mutual accord and satisfaction by negotiation rather than by conflict is more and more apparent.

"We shall greatly promote this spirit if we provide ourselves before the event with the necessary judicial machinery and promulgate rules of procedure to govern the composing of differences. Neither industries nor nations can make much progress in this direction, if, when a dispute arose, it was necessary to establish a tribunal and determine on the rules of action before anything could be done about the real controversy. To be compelled to stop to go through that process would probably result in having not one dispute, but many differences of opinion. An implement becomes manifoldly more valuable if it is already at hand when needed."

In the meantime, the Inter-American High Commission had been requested to study the principles of obligatory arbitration as a means of solving differences and to report its findings. In the meantime, in order to adjust differences following the first World War, the Chamber of Commerce of the United States had made arrangements with chambers of commerce in other American Republics for the settlement of differences and had indicated the trend which a more permanent organization might take. These early experiments, together with the report made by the Inter-American High Commission,[1] furnished the background for what eventually became the Inter-American System.

In 1931, these various experiments and resolutions took more final form, through the leadership of the American delegation to the Fourth Pan American Commercial Conference, meeting in Washington. It adopted a Resolution requesting the Pan American Union to have a thorough inquiry made as to the possibility of the commercial interests of the Republics, joining with those of other countries, in supporting an active system of arbitration for the settlement of trade disputes.

The adoption of this Resolution was notable in that it called for an inquiry leading to action in which efficiency and expediency were emphasized and it called for a report to be distributed to member states, with a view to obtaining action at the next International Conference of American States.[2]

[1] See V. Vita, *Comparative Study of American Legislation Governing Commercial Arbitration* Washington, (1928).

[2] Resolution XVII: "To request the Pan American Union to have a thorough inquiry made as to the possibilities of the commercial interests of the American Republics joining with the commercial interests of other countries in the support and active use of a system of arbitration to be utilized in disputes in trade between all countries, with a maximum of efficiency and expedition and avoidance of duplication, and to distribute its report on the results of such inquiry, together with a concrete questionnaire regarding the various aspects of the subject, to all American Republics for their consideration and suggestions for its practical development—the report to be distributed as quickly as possible to all member States with a request that the questionnaires be returned to the Pan American Union before May 31, 1932. . . ."

In accordance with the provisions of this Resolution, the Pan American Union, with the collaboration of the American Arbitration Association, made a survey of the laws and practice of arbitration in each American Republic. A comprehensive questionnaire was sent out to government officials, trade and commercial organizations, lawyers and educators, and the material received included texts of the prevailing arbitration laws and rules of procedure and practice by private commercial organizations. The findings were embodied in a report made to the Seventh International Conference of American States, meeting in Montevideo, in December, 1933.[3]

Briefly, the survey and report indicated that, while differences existed as to the arbitration laws, those of the Latin-American countries, being based upon the Spanish version of the Code Napoleon, while those in the United States were based upon the English common law, a foundation existed for the commercial interests joining together in support of an Inter-American System of Arbitration, as shown by: (1) active trade relations between members of different Republics which require some means of settling controversies, (2) existence of similar commercial groups in different Republics through which such a system could be supported, (3) activities of chambers of commerce interested in both local and inter-American trade and their willingness to enter into arrangements with chambers of commerce in other Republics, and (4) views of lawyers and businessmen and organizations in each Republic in favor of such a system.

The report recommended that the form of co-operation necessary to establish an Inter-American System of Arbitration should be developed not officially between governments but between trade and commercial organizations operating in the different Republics; and that standards should be adopted for amending the existing arbitration laws to make legal procedures more uniform and better adapted to trade conditions and for making rules of procedure more effective.

After due consideration of this Report and of the recommendation, the Seventh International Conference of American States, in

[3] *Commercial Arbitration in the American Republics—Documents for the Use of Delegates to the Seventh International Conference of American States,* No. 2, (1933).

1933, authorized the appointment of an Inter-American agency charged with the responsibility of establishing an Inter-American System of Arbitration.[4]

The adoption of this Resolution affords the only illustration in the history of commercial arbitration where a Conference, consisting of official representatives of states, has formally authorized a private international trade agency, to be operated independently of official control, but with the co-operation of the Pan American Union offering its advice and assistance in the undertaking.

This Conference was also remarkable for another achievement which made arbitration history. It approved of a series of eight legislative principles for the improvement of arbitration law and tribunal procedures. As these principles were the first to be officially approved by a group of states and have constituted a foundation for arbitration advancement, they are embodied in this record:

(a) Agreements to arbitrate, whether relating to existing or future controversies to be valid and enforceable, and where enforcement is not provided for by law, trade discipline is to be provided.

(b) Parties to have the power to designate arbitrators and to fill such vacancies or to provide a method therefor.

(c) Proceedings by *de facto* arbitrators to be more precisely defined by the parties or organization under whose auspices the arbitration is to be held.

(d) The full impartiality of the arbitrator to be provided for, with the right of challenge or removal, by the organization under whose auspices the arbitration is being conducted in a manner provided for in the rules or regulations governing the proceedings.

(e) An uneven number of arbitrators to be provided for under the rules, all of whom are to participate in the proceedings from the beginning.

(f) Awards in all instances to be unanimous or by majority vote.

(g) Waiver of the right of appeal to be provided for in the rules, which shall be binding on the parties, and which will limit the ground for appeal to procedural matters and to such questions of law as both parties agree to submit to the court.

(h) The wider use of discipline by the organization whose members participate in an arbitration and refuse to abide by the award where the law is inadequate to compel performance of the terms of the award.

[4] Resolution XLI: "That with a view to establishing closer relations among the Commercial Associations of the Americas, entirely independent of official control, an Inter-American Agency be appointed, in order to represent the commercial interests of all Republics, and to assume, as one of its most important functions, the responsibility of establishing an Inter-American system of arbitration."

These Resolutions were not allowed to remain dead letters, as had so often happened in the past, for there was real purpose and interest behind them, created largely by the survey in which all Republics had participated. The Governing Board of the Pan American Union, upon the initiative of its late Director General, Dr. L. S. Rowe, at its April meeting in 1934, requested the American Arbitration Association and the Council on Inter-American Relations jointly to establish a System.[5] Representatives of these groups met later in the same month and founded the Inter-American Commercial Arbitration Commission.[6] Under its constitution, representatives of the business interests of each Republic were appointed members of the Commission, and provision was made for the appointment of National Committees in each Republic to carry forward its work. The Commission elected as its first Chairman, Spruille Braden. Upon his appointment as Ambassador to Colombia, he became Honorary Chairman of the Commission and Thomas J. Watson was elected Chairman.

The Commission is administered from a central office located at 9 Rockefeller Plaza, New York City, and operates through the National Committees and members located in each of the American Republics. The functions and activities of the Commission and its National Committees include:

(1) The maintenance and administration of an Inter-American System of Arbitration for the adjustment of claims and controversies arising out of trade and commerce among the American Republics.

(2) The promotion of the widespread and uniform use of the Commission's arbitration clause in inter-American commercial contracts.

(3) The modernization and standardization of arbitration law and procedure in all of the American Republics in accordance with the principles adopted by the Seventh International Conference of American States.

(4) The maintenance of a close liaison with the commercial organizations and interests of the Western Hemisphere in order that

[5] The Council on Inter-American Relations having been dissolved in 1936, the American Arbitration Association continued its sponsorship of the work of the Commission and provided it with the necessary facilities.

[6] For members of the Commission, see Ch. XXV, p. 211.

they be represented and participate in the operation of the Inter-American System of Arbitration.

In furtherance of its activities, as the Seventh International Conference had intended, the Commission has had the cordial co-operation of government agencies, trade and commercial organizations in each Republic. To the friendly support of Cordell Hull, then Secretary of State, the Commission owes much of its progress, through endorsement and friendly action by American embassies and consulates in Latin-American countries. To the United States Department of Commerce, particularly through the devoted and untiring efforts of the late Guerra Everett, the Commission is indebted for improvement in its technique. Without their exercising direct control, the Commission has enjoyed from other official agencies a high degree of co-operation as, for example, from the United States Post Office Department, from members of the Governing Board of the Pan American Union and from Latin-American consulates located in the United States. Representatives of the business and professional interests have served as members of the Commission and on its law, banking, business relations and other Committees, thereby bringing to the Commission wide support from all Republics.[7]

In all of this assemblage of goodwill and co-operation, that of the late Dr. L. S. Rowe was the keystone, for due to his wise guidance and unfailing effort, the Commission went steadily forward with few blunders, and with no unpleasant incidents. This was the more remarkable considering that it was a new experiment handicapped somewhat by differences of languages and of varying trade practices.

Early in the history of the Commission, however, it was found that many of the disputes which were causing misunderstandings and ill will, particularly between North and South American traders, were not adapted to arbitration. Others were of a character requiring explanations and adjustments rather than formal hearings. Still others lent themselves best to solution through the use of the good offices of the Commission, particularly when the cost of an arbitration would have been prohibitive.

In order better to develop the adjustment services of the Commission, which form by far the greater part of its activities, the

[7] For members of Committees, see Ch. XXV, p. 214.

Commission established an Inter-American Business Relations Committee.[8] When complaints are received by the Commission, this Committee acts as an intermediary between the parties. It clears up misunderstandings and effects explanations or settlements, thus maintaining cordial relations among the traders.

Through an understanding with the former Director General of the Pan American Union during the early period of establishing the Commission, no charge had been made for adjusting services. Only when a matter was submitted to formal arbitration, requiring hearing rooms and administrative services, was the fee fixed in the Rules, charged in equal amounts to each party.

The organization of research and education by the Commission has paralleled, if not kept pace, with that of the American Arbitration Association. For example, the activities of the Commission are reported in a special section of the *Arbitration Journal*. The Commission has sponsored the annual "*Guia* Arbitration Award," presented by J. E. Sitterley and Sons, Inc. of New York City, which is given each year to a Latin-American Chamber of Commerce or commercial organization in recognition of its outstanding contribution to arbitration in foreign trade. A monthly bulletin is published, covering the Commission's activities and is distributed to members of the Commission, its committees, commercial organizations, and official agencies.

The Commission has published a treatise on international arbitration, written by a Colombian attorney, Dr. Alvaro Herran Medina, entitled *Del Arbitraje Comercial Internacional*, which was distributed to universities, commercial organizations, and official agencies throughout the Hemisphere.

Rules of Procedure and descriptive pamphlets outlining the facilities and services of the Commission, printed in English, Spanish, and Portuguese, have been distributed in all of the American Republics through trade associations, banks, chambers of commerce, consular offices, and official agencies. Of special assistance have been the resolutions adopted at conferences of inter-American agencies such as the Inter-American Development Commission, the Inter-American Bar Association, and the Inter-American Council of Commerce and Production. The meetings of local chambers of commerce

[8] For members of the Committee, see Ch. XXV, p. 212.

and trade associations have offered an opportunity for the dissemination of information concerning arbitration and have stimulated the co-operation of these organizations in the Commission's educational work.

Much of the research and educational work of the Commission has been made possible by grants from the Office of Inter-American Affairs. In 1942, the first grant enabled the Commission to send its Executive Secretary to Latin America to organize National Committees and to enlist the co-operation of commercial associations. In 1946, an additional grant was given to the Commission which made possible a new survey of facilities and services in Latin America, and the publication and distribution of literature in English, Spanish, and Portuguese among the business men and commercial agencies of the American Republics. This grant has also enabled the Commission to prepare a report for submission to the Ninth International Conference of American States to be held in Bogota, Colombia, in 1948.

As the Pan American Union had no appropriation available for the work of the Commission, the American Arbitration Association assumed the responsibility of housing the Commission and of providing its annual budget. This budget covers secretarial and clerical services, operating expenses, and educational program, including publication and distribution of Rules, reports, monthly bulletins, and other educational matter. This budget is now met in part by inter-American memberships and by special contributions.

The practice of arbitration in Inter-American Commercial Arbitration Tribunals takes place under the Rules of the Commission. These Rules are similar to those of the American Arbitration Association, and the principles, policies, and standards of the Inter-American system are similar. The Commission is the administrator of the system. It operates through a personnel of clerks in the same manner as does the American System. Through this similarity, Americans may practice arbitration in either an American Arbitration Tribunal or in an Inter-American Tribunal, with the assurance that the procedures will be identical and the administrative services will be of the same competence.[9]

[9] See *Western Hemisphere Systems of Commercial Arbitration* by Martin Domke and Frances Kellor, published in *University of Toronto Law Journal*, Vol. 6, (1946), p. 307.

In the course of its operations over a period of twelve years, the Commission has had more than a thousand claims submitted to it. It has been instrumental in adjusting many other differences through its educational work and particularly through the use of its arbitration clause which in itself induces settlements without direct intervention by the Commission.

During the periods of peace and war in which the Commission has functioned, it has been instrumental in strengthening goodwill and co-operation among the American Republics, in promoting the commercial welfare of each Republic and in increasing solidarity of interest among the Republics. The usefulness of the Commission was especially apparent during the war when it functioned smoothly and effectively as a Western Hemisphere defense and war instrument.

The Commission has demonstrated that people of widely different cultures and traditions and languages, far distant from each other, can dispose of their differences without enmity or resort to force.

CHAPTER XVIII

Canadians and Americans Complete the Western Hemisphere System

«««« »»»»

ALTHOUGH Canada and the United States had been settling their political differences by arbitration for more than a century, this policy had not been supplemented by any permanent arrangement for the settlement of commercial controversies between Canadian and American business men. This was true, notwithstanding that the boundary line between the two countries was crossed by more people, more trains, more money, more newsprint, more tourists, more automobiles and planes than any other boundary.

A system of commercial arbitration for the Western Hemisphere was, therefore, incomplete without including the twenty-second country in that Hemisphere. It was in the belief that all countries in this Hemisphere should participate in an international trade arbitration system that the American Arbitration Association opened negotiations with the Canadian Chamber of Commerce in 1938, with a view to establishing joint facilities for the settlement of trade disputes.

As some doubt existed concerning the effectiveness of provincial arbitration laws in Canada to sustain such a system, and whether they offered the necessary security for the legal enforcement of agreements and awards, it was decided to postpone action until a study had been made of these laws. This study was made possible through a scholarship fund contributed in 1939 by Thomas J. Watson. The study was completed by Brooke Claxton, now Minister of National Defense, in September, 1942.[1]

[1] Published in 1943 under the title of "*Commercial Arbitration under Canadian Law.*" *Canadian Bar Review,* Vol. 21, p. 171.

It was found that eight of the nine Canadian provinces had arbitration laws which closely followed the provisions of the English Arbitration Act of 1889 and therefore closely approximated the best of the modern arbitration statutes in the United States. Under these laws, agreements to submit existing or future disputes to arbitration are valid, enforceable, and irrevocable, and the award of an arbitrator is final and binding.

In Quebec, the ninth province, the arbitration law differed somewhat, in that the arbitrator must be named and the dispute stated in the agreement to arbitrate. Arbitration clauses referring to future disputes would therefore not, of themselves, constitute a valid agreement to arbitrate. The study pointed out, however, that the provisions of the Quebec law could be effectively supplemented by a well-drawn submission,[2] and concluded, that "the laws of the provinces of Canada, as they are today, provide a satisfactory basis for the systematic extension of the practice of settling commercial disputes along desired lines."

An Organization Committee had been appointed, following a meeting of the Directors of the Canadian Chamber of Commerce in 1939. Five members from the Canadian Chamber of Commerce and five from the American Arbitration Association were entrusted with the task of formulating a plan of organization, drafting Rules and a standard clause, and setting up panels of arbitrators in their respective territories.

The agreement, drafted by Brooke Claxton, and entered into by the Canadian Chamber of Commerce and the American Arbitration Association provided for a joint Commercial Arbitration Commission.[3] This agreement came into effect with the promulgation of joint rules and of a standard arbitration clause and with the election of officers of the Canadian-American Commercial Arbitration Commission.[4]

[2] Subsequent examination of decisions indicates a trend in the court's attitude in Quebec toward the recognition of future disputes agreements.

[3] It was signed on May 20, 1943, on behalf of the Canadian Chamber of Commerce by R. F. Jellett, President; P. A. MacFarlane, Chairman of the Executive Committee, and D. L. Morrell, Secretary; and on behalf of the Association by H. O. King, President; Frances Kellor, First Vice President, and Malcolm Muir, Secretary.

[4] For members of the Commission, see Ch. XXV, p. 215.

As the Canadian-American arrangement comprises what is believed to be the first bilateral private international arbitration agreement and may serve as a model for other bilateral agreements in which Americans become interested, the following text of the agreement is presented in full:

1. *Creation of the Commission.* To assist in promoting good trade relations between the United States of America and Canada, The Canadian Chamber of Commerce and the American Arbitration Association hereby establish The Canadian-American Commercial Arbitration Commission.

2. *Purpose.* The purpose of the Commission is to promote the use of arbitration in trading and commercial transactions between Canadians and Americans, and to provide facilities for the arbitration of controversies arising out of such transactions.

3. *Membership of Commission.* The Canadian-American Commercial Arbitration Commission is constituted by the Association and the Chamber each appointing an equal number of representatives as members. These members may appoint such officers and for such time as they deem desirable. Any vacancy shall be filled by the organization which appointed the person to be replaced.

4. *Sections, Headquarters and Facilities.* The representatives appointed by the Chamber shall be the Canadian Section of the Commission, and the representatives appointed by the Association shall be the American Section of the Commission. Each Section shall be responsible for the development and maintenance of arbitration facilities in its country. The headquarters and branches of the Commission shall be at such places in Canada as are designated by the Chamber and at such places in the United States, its territories or possessions, as the Association designates. The administrative control of the Canadian Section is vested in the Chamber, and of the American Section in the Association, but the Chamber and Association agree to consult and co-operate with each other in carrying out the purposes of the Commission and to exchange information and services to further its objects.

5. *Panels of Arbitrators.* Each Section agrees to maintain panels of arbitrators of sufficient number and quality at such places as trading and commercial transactions and the settlement of controversies may require.

6. *Rules of Procedure.* Each Section agrees to collaborate on the formulation of Rules of Procedure designed to provide for the just, amicable, and speedy settlement of commercial controversies in accordance with the arbitration law in the various jurisdictions. These Rules, when approved or amended from time to time by both Sections of the Commission, shall be known as the Rules of Procedure of the Canadian-American Commercial Arbitration Commission.

7. *Arbitration Clause in Contracts.* Each Section agrees to collaborate in the formulation of an arbitration provision which it will recommend for

insertion in all commercial contracts entered into between Canadians and Americans in their trade transactions. When approved by both Sections, this provision shall be known as the Canadian-American Commercial Arbitration Clause.[5]

8. *Arbitration Tribunals.* Tribunals established hereunder for the hearing of controversies shall be known in both countries as 'Canadian-American Commercial Arbitration Tribunals,' and shall be established at the request of the parties and made available in the manner and upon the conditions set forth in the Rules of Procedure.

9. *Education in Use of Facilities.* Each Section agrees to carry on in its country educational work in the use of its facilities or it may agree to take part in programs to be carried on jointly or in the name of the Commission in both countries.

10. *Financial Support.* Each Section shall provide the funds for carrying on the work of the Commission within its national boundaries, or may contribute to the maintenance of the general work of the Commission, or authorize the Commission to raise funds for its work in such manner and amount as the Commission by joint action of a majority of both Sections, may approve. All individual case fees shall be payable to that Section of the Commission in whose Tribunal the case is heard.

11. *Modification.* This arrangement shall continue in force subject to any modification from time to time agreed upon in writing until such time as the parties, after 120 days' notice, agree to some other arrangement or to terminate this arrangement.

After the agreement was signed, the following supplemental agreement relating to cancellation of the joint agreement was executed:

1. The parties to the Joint Agreement dated 20th May, 1943, agree that said Agreement may be cancelled by either party giving to the other 120 days' notice in writing of intention to cancel.

2. The question as to which party hereto shall have the right after such cancellation to the use of the name 'Canadian-American Commercial Arbitration Commission' shall be determined if possible by negotiation between the parties. If within 60 days of the notification of intention to cancel no agreement has been reached, the question shall be determined by arbitration to be completed seven days before the notified date of cancellation. Such arbitration shall be held by a Board of Arbitrators of which one member shall be designated by each of the parties hereto and the third, who shall act as Chairman, shall be designated by the Director General of the Pan

[5] *Arbitration Clause*: Any controversy or claim arising out of or relating to this contract or the breach thereof, shall be settled by arbitration, in accordance with the Rules of Procedure then obtaining of the Canadian-American Commercial Arbitration Commission established by the American Arbitration Association and The Canadian Chamber of Commerce, and judgment upon the award rendered may be entered in any court having jurisdiction thereof.

American Union or, if that office is vacant or the incumbent is unavailable, then by the Acting Director or Assistant Director General, whichever is then performing the duties of the Director General. The arbitration shall be held at the place selected by the Board of Arbitration. Both parties hereto agree to accept the decision of such Board of Arbitration or a majority thereof as final and binding and hereby pledge their good faith thereto.

3. If, at the time of cancellation, there are funds in the possession or under the control of the Commission as to which equitable title has not been settled by negotiation, this question shall also be decided by the Board of Arbitration. Funds under the control of the respective Sections of the Commission shall revert upon cancellation to the respective parties.

The Commission operates through two Sections: The Canadian Section has headquarters at the Canadian Chamber of Commerce, Board of Trade Building, Montreal, Quebec, and the United States Section has headquarters at the American Arbitration Association, 9 Rockefeller Plaza, New York City. Each Section has a Secretary who functions as clerk of the Arbitration Tribunals for that Section, or who appoints a clerk for this purpose.

Each Section maintains a National Panel of Arbitrators, consisting of business and professional men carefully selected from persons recommended by leading trade, commercial, and professional organizations. The members of these Panels serve without remuneration, under the Rules of the Commission. Two hundred and seventy members of Panels are now available in nineteen cities in Canada and all members of the National Panel in the United States are available for service. An Arbitration Tribunal is set up for each controversy referred to the Commission.

The Commission maintains Standard Rules of Procedure that govern a proceeding in accordance with the provisions of the applicable law, but parties arbitrating under these Rules may request the adoption of special rules to meet unusual circumstances.

The general administrator of these Arbitration Tribunals, in each country, is a standing Arbitration Committee of three members, appointed for each country by the respective Sections. The clerk of each Arbitration Tribunal performs the administrative functions prescribed in the Rules, except where the Rules specifically provide that the Arbitration Committee itself shall act.

A joint Arbitration Committee, composed of members of the two Arbitration Committees and a Chairman, acts in the special instances referred to in the Rules. The Chairman of this Committee is appointed by the Canadian-American Commercial Arbitration Commission and serves for one year. The Rules provide that he will alternately be a citizen of Canada and of the United States.

While it is contemplated that all of the hearings in any case will usually be held in the country where the proceedings were initiated, it is permissible for the parties to agree otherwise and, with the concurrence of the arbitrators, to arrange for some of the hearings to be held in one country and one or more to be held in another country.

When there is no agreement by the parties as to the location, the party desiring arbitration may initiate the proceeding by communicating with the Section of the Commission in his own country. The Secretary will endeavor to ascertain the wishes of the parties as to the place of hearing, but in the event that the parties fail to agree, the Tribunal in which the arbitration is to be held shall be designated by the Joint Arbitration Committee of the Commission.

At a meeting in February 1944 at Toronto, an agreement was reached to make the Canadian-American Rules available in disputes between Canadians and Latin-Americans, thereby making inter-American as well as American facilities available to Canadians and Canadian facilities available to Latin-Americans. To put this understanding more specifically into effect, a joint arbitration clause for the Western Hemisphere was developed, whereunder parties may agree to use any one of the three Western Hemisphere arbitration systems.[6]

The facilities of the Canadian Section are also available for the settlement of disputes arising between parties resident in Canada and for foreign trade disputes which may arise between Canadians and traders in other countries outside of the Western Hemisphere. Under these arrangements, the arbitration of disputes is not only provided for throughout the Western Hemisphere, but its twenty-two countries are equipped with facilities and services that are available for international trade in which the nationals of any of these countries engage with nationals of other countries.

[6] See Annex II, p. 231.

CHAPTER XIX

The Unification of Law and Practice Makes Progress in the Western Hemisphere

«««« »»»»

ALTHOUGH each of the Western Hemisphere Systems of Arbitration—the American, the Inter-American, and the Canadian-American—is organized separately and administered by a different organization, they present in operation a unified system of arbitration for the international trade of twenty-two countries. While they differ profoundly in their inception—that of the American System having been created by business and professional men and lawyers, that of the Inter-American being quasi-official in that a political conference authorized it, and that of the Canadian-American being initiated by joint agreement of the Association and the Canadian Chamber of Commerce—the pattern followed in all of them admits of their unification while retaining to each System its full independence of operation.

As the unification of arbitration law and practice constitutes one of the major problems in the development of international commercial arbitration systems, the methods followed in the Western Hemisphere to advance such unification may be of interest in a further discussion of the broader subject.[1]

By the unification of arbitration law and practice, Western Hemisphere arbitration organizations have had in mind the adoption of legislative standards which would provide for a uniform and systematic development of arbitration law in essential particulars in

[1] See Ch. XXII, p. 161, for reference to studies now under way for the unification of arbitration law.

all twenty-two countries. The adoption of legislative standards for the American Republics by the Seventh International Conference of American States in 1933, the promulgation of a Draft Act by the Association in 1927, and the survey of provincial laws in Canada, indicating that the main principles of the British arbitration law had been adopted, set the pattern for the Western Hemisphere.[2] Toward this goal of similarity in arbitration laws, the American Arbitration Association, the Inter-American and the Canadian-American Commercial Arbitration Commissions are steadily progressing.

In the meantime, as legislative processes are necessarily slow, the Western Hemisphere organizations have attained a high degree of similarity in procedures, by adopting for each system rules of procedure that, in effect, are sufficiently alike to assure parties in dispute of similar standards, and methods in the processing of an arbitration. The Rules of the American Arbitration Association have set the pattern, followed by the adoption of similar Rules by the Inter-American and Canadian-American Commissions.

The practical effect of this unification is that parties need learn only one kind of procedure, and only one form of administration. They have available in each one of the twenty-two countries identical facilities and services and a trained administrative personnel. While each system is administered separately and retains its full powers of self-regulation, co-ordination has taken place through the adoption of similar rules and through acceptance of similar principles, standards, and viewpoints in their adoption.

Having similar rules of procedure, it then became practical to advance unification a further step by the approval of a joint arbitration clause under which parties could hold their arbitration in any one of the countries, under the Rules of their own choice.[3] This clause provides that any controversy or claim arising out of or relating to the contract shall be settled under the Rules of the American Arbitration Association. If, however, one or more of the parties are domiciled in one of the Republics of Latin America, then the Rules of the Inter-American Commercial Arbitration Commission shall apply. The arbitration will then be held in the locale

[2] See Ch. XVII, p. 128, for Declaration of Legislative Principles.
[3] See Annex II for text of clause, p. 231.

agreed upon by the parties, or upon their failure to agree, it will be determined by the Commission under its Rules.

A second provision in this clause specifies that if one or more of the parties to this agreement is domiciled in Canada, the Rules of the Canadian-American Commission shall apply, except where the other party is domiciled in a Latin-American Republic, in which case the parties may agree to arbitrate under the Rules of the Inter-American Commission or the Canadian-American Commission, as they may prefer. If any questions arise as to which Rules are applicable, a joint arbitration committee of three members appointed one each by the three organizations has authority to determine the question.

Under this joint clause, parties are given wide latitude to exercise their right to determine in what country and under what Rules they will arbitrate, but the arbitration will not be frustrated through their failure to agree.

A third method in this process of unification, *first*, through acceptance of legislative principles, *second*, through similarity in rules of procedure, and *third*, through recommendation of a joint clause making all systems available, has been the use of conferences. A general conference of all Western Hemisphere organizations was held in 1943. This has been supplemented by meetings held in Latin-American Republics and in Canada. The purpose of these conferences and meetings is to keep in harmony the thinking and planning of commercial arbitration in the Western Hemisphere, to improve techniques, to exchange ideas and views, and to plan educational activities. These conferences also serve to bring into accord the administrators of the three systems, in matters of common policy.

A *fourth* method of co-ordination has been through the exchange and distribution of publications, by which the experiments, experiences, and explorations of one organization are placed at the disposal of the others. For example, *The Arbitration Journal* serves the interests of all organizations, reports upon the activities of each, and is distributed in the 22 countries of the Western Hemisphere to commercial and educational organizations.

More recently, the three organizations have united in participating in the educational activities of the International Commercial Arbitration Committee, having assumed joint responsibility for preparing the reports for two Working Committees, one on Arbitration Education and the other on Co-ordination of Arbitration Systems. This joint participation indicates the close co-ordination in which these organizations act.[4]

These Western Hemisphere organizations are again co-ordinating their interests and efforts in calling a Conference for late 1948 to include representatives of organizations or systems in other countries with which the American Arbitration Association and the Inter-American Commercial Arbitration Commission are associated in the mutual use of their respective facilities.

These methods of co-ordinating the commercial arbitration interests and systems of the Western Hemisphere would, however, tend to become mechanical devices unless separately in each country and jointly, the spirit of arbitration was not constantly cultivated. There preceded the establishment of the Inter-American System nearly half a century of the cultivation of a spirit of goodwill and co-operation among the Republics through the Pan American Union. This continued through many basic agreements which were restated in bilateral or multilateral conventions. A long period of the cultivation of good relations also preceded the establishment of the Canadian-American Commission.

Permeating this entire Western Hemisphere structure of commercial peace is the cultivation of the spirit of arbitration through the education of the peoples of each country in the knowledge and use of arbitration, through the establishment of panels of arbitrators and through general education. This personal, friendly contact accomplishes more than the mere unification of laws and procedures —it takes the ameliorating influence of arbitration through all of the channels of trade and advances good understanding; it bridges the differences created by diverse languages, customs, and tradition; and puts into active practice on the individual level, the aspirations and purposes set forth in treaties and conventions on the political level.

[4] For account of organization of the Committees, see Ch. XXII, p. 161.

CHAPTER XX

The Problem of Education in International Arbitration

«««« »»»»

THE problem of education in international arbitration looms ominously on the horizon. So dense is the ignorance concerning international commercial arbitration, that to suggest systematic education is to arouse such incredulity as to question its necessity or worthwhileness. In fact, in many quarters there is downright opposition to the idea of such education.

Those interested in planning such education are equally in the dark as to where to begin and in what order. The chief problem is the initial one of lack of funds with which to make the necessary studies, assemble the workers, and chart the course. Although extensive funds are available for the advancement of peace and security, none seems to have been directed to the practical necessity of acquainting people with the mechanics of peace that are involved in the settlement of economic disputes.

This is true, notwithstanding the fact that the Western Hemisphere Systems, both political and commercial, have endured because large sums of money have been spent in making basic studies and in creating permanent machinery that is concerned primarily with the settlement of disputes. Similar funds have not been made available for activities devoted to these same ends in other countries.

The task is stupendous. To begin with foundations: What are the laws and practice of arbitration in different countries? Are the people interested and do they participate in the practice? Are the prevailing principles and standards such as to permit of the national laws and practice affording a stable foundation for an international structure? It is significant that the studies begun by the International Chamber of Commerce and the American Arbitration Association in 1927 still remain the outstanding handbooks on commercial arbitration in Belgium, France, Germany, Great Britain, Italy, The Netherlands, Sweden, and Switzerland.

In view of the momentous political and economic changes taking place since the war, it would seem that the first essential in any educational program would be a survey of existing national laws and practice, similar to that made in the Americas in 1933, that would give an over-all picture and serve as a chart of the areas where improvements are needed, or where new facilities are required, or where other action should be taken. To construct international systems of arbitration without sound national support is, in the end, to court disaster. The absence of such information explains in part the American plan of organizing international arbitration from the Western Hemisphere basis by means of bilateral arrangements with agencies in countries that possess sufficiently stable foundations to support international arbitration.

The main problem in education in international commercial arbitration, however, is to bring its knowledge and use to the understanding of the people who engage in international trade or who depend upon that trade for their well-being. In the United States and the other Republics, this education is intensive. It is carried on through trade and commercial organizations and their publications, and by means of business institutions, in the foreground of which are banks, insurance companies, and other financial institutions. In 1947, the Association began the publication of an International Arbitration Bulletin which now has a wide circulation in many countries. One of the features of this Bulletin is a supplement on American arbitration techniques which are being interpreted to readers in other countries. Unfortunately, outside of the Western Hemisphere such publications cannot be put into the language of the people of different countries and cannot, therefore, become a real stimulus to their thinking and interest.

Disputes in international commerce are of two kinds: they may be procedural disputes; that is, differences over how to settle an issue; or they may be substantive disputes over things of ascertainable value. Not infrequently, disputes are so violent over how to settle them that the real matter in issue is never reached. Therefore, there seem to be two main lines of education: first, in the techniques so that those who are willing to arbitrate may know arbitration and how to use it effectively; and, second, in the general education of those unfamiliar with the subject and whose interest must first be aroused. Under general education, it is certainly necessary that more people know about the nature of controversy, its means of growth, and its cost and waste in human relations. How much this is needed was made evident when there was published in 1944 a study on Arbitration in International Controversy.[1] Although that study outlined both procedural and substantive controversies and indicated the volume of disputes that was likely to come, so optimistic was the public mood, at that time, that it failed to heed the warning which has subsequently been so fully justified.

In a previous chapter, the adventures in education and research in the Western Hemisphere were outlined.[2] Nothing comparable to this planned study and training is taking place elsewhere, although it is now generally admitted that international structures of commercial peace cannot be constructed without them. What may prove to be an opening wedge into this wide area of unawareness of arbitration was the action taken at the Conference in Paris in 1946, when a Committee on Education was appointed and assigned to the Western Hemisphere organizations for a report.[3] When completed, it will doubtless be the first report of its kind on the subject. It is within the province of this report not only to assemble knowledge from all countries but to formulate a program of education on international commercial arbitration.

None of the educational experiments have undertaken any systematic education of governments in the application of arbitration. In democratic countries, this may have to be preceded by public interest impressing itself upon the governments. In other countries, like the Soviet Union, which has a complete domestic and foreign system of arbitration, and where the reference of disputes is compulsory through state facilities provided by the government, education of the people may not be so feasible. Instruction in institutions

[1] Frances Kellor and Martin Domke, *Arbitration in International Controversy*, published by the Commission to Study the Organization of Peace and the American Arbitration Association, (1944).

[2] See Ch. VII, p. 44.

[3] For account of the Conference, see Ch. XXII, p. 160.

of learning, and the teaching of arbitration generally are so rudimentary in the various international courses as to be scarcely worth mentioning.[4] Complete courses are practically unknown.

The indifference of international agencies to this subject may be seen in the educational program of UNESCO where no reference appears and in the first Charter of the International Trade Organization, where it seems to be taken for granted that any references to arbitration will be applied automatically—a tradition thoroughly disproved by the Permanent Court of Arbitration at The Hague and by the Council of the League of Nations.

Mention has been made of the trend toward organizing a science of arbitration. It is abundantly clear that organizing the existing knowledge on arbitration and expanding education through such knowledge are essential elements in the creation of such a science.

This education is now being undertaken through a Research Institute for the Advancement of the Science of Arbitration projected by the American Arbitration Association. Its membership will comprise educational and research experts from different countries.

These fragmentary approaches to the subject, together with the glimpses of the vast areas uninhabited by any educational action, serve to highlight the problem of education and to indicate the need of a systematic approach and carefully organized program. A tentative approach to such a program is made possible through the Committee on Education of the International Commercial Arbitration Committee, now engaged in preparing its report. But, even with a well-formulated program, the projection of its recommendations or program into action among the many peoples of the world remains the single greatest problem in making international arbitration an effective instrument against war.

[4] A textbook on arbitration is the first study being made under the R. Emerson Swart Memorial Research Fund, established under the auspices of the American Arbitration Association in 1947.

CHAPTER XXI

American Action in International Commercial Arbitration

«««« »»»»

From its experience in constructing international commercial arbitration institutions and systems in the Western Hemisphere, and from its experiments in co-ordinating these systems, the American Arbitration Association learned some of the problems involved, and encountered some of the barriers to be scaled. Out of these undertakings has grown the pattern which the Association is following in its undertaking to advance the organization of international commercial arbitration systems outside of the Western Hemisphere.

From this pattern has emerged the vision and program which the Association is putting into operation as rapidly as funds and economic conditions in other countries will permit. It is a long-range program looking toward the eventual establishment of a universal system, in which existing organizations and facilities will take their place in performing their share and in developing the larger program. Perhaps the most concrete way of unfolding this pattern is to present some of the arrangements already entered into by the Association, as tending toward the establishment of a universal system of commercial arbitration.

The first type of arrangement utilizes a joint arbitration clause and the mutual use of respective facilities and services of co-operating organizations in an undertaking to provide both American and foreign parties to contracts with machinery of a somewhat uniform type, thus assuring them of competence, integrity, and efficiency in arbitrations.

The first of these arrangements was entered into by the Association with the Manchester (England) Chamber of Commerce in 1939.

This arrangement, suspended during the war, has been recently revised (1946) and now provides for the use of a joint clause whereunder arbitrations are held in the United States under the Rules of the Association or of the Chamber of Commerce of the State of New York or of the General Arbitration Council of the Textile Industry. If the arbitration is to be held in Manchester, then the procedure is under the Rules of that Chamber. When the parties have not agreed upon the alternatives to the Association's Rules in the United States then the latter prevail. As this arrangement is primarily concerned with textile disputes, it seemed advisable to include a wider range of rules so as to provide for all contingencies.

Application for arbitration under this arrangement may be made either to the Manchester Chamber of Commerce or to the American Arbitration Association, and arrangements will be made for the arbitration by the organization under whose Rules it is to be held and at the place designated by the parties. Failing their agreement, they, or either of them, may request the President or acting President of the International Chamber of Commerce to determine the place of arbitration and his decision shall be final.

In 1939, the Association entered into an arrangement with the International Chamber of Commerce. This first arrangement provided that the two co-operating organizations would recommend the use of a joint clause in contracts to which an American was a party and when the arbitration was held in the United States, it should be conducted under the Rules of the Association and when held elsewhere, under the Rules of the Chamber. In the event that the parties could not agree upon the locale, an Arbitration Committee, consisting of one person named by the Association and one by the Chamber, and a third person, not a member of either organization, would decide the locale. Owing to the war, this arrangement did not come into active use.

It was revised and approved by the Congress of the Chamber, in June, 1947. Under the present arrangement, the use of a joint clause is continued whereby arbitrations are to be held in the United States under American Arbitration Association Rules, unless by written agreement they adopt the Rules of the International Chamber of Commerce. Conversely, arbitrations to be held outside of the United States are to be held under the Rules of the Chamber, unless by written agreement the parties adopt the Rules of the Association.[1]

An alternate clause makes provision whereby the parties designate the place and the Rules at the time of entering into the contract.

For the better administration of arbitrations that may be provided for under either of these clauses, the Chamber and the Association have agreed upon an administrative procedure, as follows:

A joint Arbitration Committee of three members—one appointed by the Chamber and one by the Association and the third to act as chairman—is to be chosen by these two. He is not to be a member of either of the co-operating organizations. The sole function of this Committee is to determine the locale when the parties are unable to agree upon it. The locale determines the Rules to be used and the decision by the Committee is binding. The Committee is authorized to adopt its own procedure for resolving this issue.

The Chamber and the Association have also agreed to undertake other activities which they believe will expedite arbitrations and encourage the use of their joint clause.

One is the establishment of such international panels of arbitrators as may be necessary to carry out the provisions of the agreement and to advise each other of the personnel of the panels. These panels may be published, in the discretion of either co-operating organization.

Each co-operating organization also agrees to administer each other's rules in any territory where they may be applicable and where the organization has facilities. For example, an arbitration called for in the United States under Chamber Rules would be administered by the Association in its Commercial Arbitration Tribunals and with their facilities and services. An arbitration called for in Brussels or some other locality, under the Rules of the Chamber or those of the Association, would be administered by the Chamber through its facilities. This arrangement will establish a mutual use of facilities and services not hitherto achieved under other arrangements.

The new agreement also clarifies a doubt that existed under the first agreement. It states explicitly that the arrangement between

[1] For text of Arbitration Clauses, see Annex II, p. 232.

the Chamber and the Association does not exclude or interfere with such other arrangements as either organization may wish to make with other persons or organizations in foreign countries for the advancement of the use of arbitration or for clauses to be used in connection with such other arrangements.

The new agreement also provides for general co-operation between the two organizations in advancing international arbitration through the increased use of their respective organizations and in the exchange of information.

Also, for the first time in history, two organizations pledge their combined efforts to advance a science of international arbitration through research, education, and such joint publications as they may agree upon.[2]

In 1947, the Association concluded an arrangement with The London Court of Arbitration for the use of a joint clause. It provides that any controversy or claim arising out of or relating to the contract of which it is a part, shall be settled by arbitration. If held in England, it shall be conducted under the Rules of The London Court of Arbitration and the construction, validity, or performance of the contract shall be governed by the Law of England. If the arbitration is held in the United States, it shall be conducted under the Rules of the American Arbitration Association. In the event that the parties have not designated the locale or are unable to agree thereon, either party may apply to the International Law Association in London to decide the locale and its decision shall be final.[3]

A new feature of this arrangement is the implementation of the clause whereby delays in determining the locale will be obviated

[2] See Ch. XX, p. 146.

[3] Any controversy or claim arising out of or relating to this contract or breach thereof shall be settled by arbitration. If the arbitration is held in England, it shall be conducted under the Rules of The London Court of Arbitration and the construction, validity or performance of the contract shall be governed by the law of England. If the arbitration is held in the United States, it shall be conducted under the Rules of the American Arbitration Association. Judgment upon the award rendered may be entered in any court having jurisdiction thereof. In the event that the parties have not designated the locale of the arbitration and are unable to agree thereon, either party may apply to the International Law Association in London to decide the locale and its decision shall be accepted by the parties thereto.

and the use of the clause will be enhanced. Both the clause and its implementation are being brought to the attention of British and American business interests.

The extension of a similar arrangement between the American Arbitration Association and other British Chambers of Commerce is now under consideration as a means of offering wider protection from disputes in British-American trade.

A second type of arrangement follows the Canadian-American plan of establishing a bilateral commission, having sections operating in each country but providing a central organization for administrative purposes, maintenance of joint rules, and the development of educational work. The plan was first proposed in 1939 in the form of a Philippine-American Trade Arbitration Commission. Its development was retarded by the war and has since been restored by an arrangement between the American Arbitration Association and the Chamber of Commerce of the Philippines.[4] As soon as the economic reconstruction of the Philippines permits, it is expected that the arbitration law will be amended to conform in principle with American modern statutory laws. In the meantime, a temporary clause has been approved, pending the completion of arrangements, under which arbitrations are being held under the Rules of the Association.[5]

This type of co-operative arrangement has also been proposed for Chinese-American trade. Early in 1945, the Association, at the request of the Department of State, submitted a memorandum recommending that there be established a Joint Trade Arbitration Commission for the settlement of any disputes or differences arising out of business and trade relations between Chinese and Americans. This memorandum was submitted through American official channels to the Chinese Government, which approved the proposal and appointed a Delegation comprising leading Chinese businessmen and bankers to confer with a committee of American business men and bankers.[6]

Meeting in joint session, this group of American and Chinese business men approved a proposal under which the American Arbi-

[4] For members of the Commission, see Ch. XXV, p. 215.

[5] For text of clause, see Annex II, p. 233.

[6] For members of the Chinese-American Trade Arbitration Conference, see Ch. XXV, p. 215.

tration Association and an agency approved in China would establish joint facilities for the settlement of Chinese-American trade disputes. Pending the establishment of a co-operating organization in China, which has been delayed by internal conditions, the Chinese-American Trade Arbitration Conference authorized the use of a temporary arbitration clause providing that until such time as the proposed Commission approves of a clause, arbitrations should be held under the Rules of the American Arbitration Association which could apply them in the locality designated by the parties.[7]

This arrangement has not yet been concluded as the Chinese Government has first undertaken to establish a Chinese Arbitration Association as the co-operating organization with the American Arbitration Association in creating the Commission, and to act as the Chinese Section of the Commission. Also, it has been necessary to clear the proposal with different government agencies in order that the proposal may proceed without opposition when it goes into execution.

Negotiations for the establishment of a similar Commission are now pending with the Soviet Union through the Foreign Trade Arbitration Commission of the All Union Chamber of Commerce. A similar proposal is now before the Turkish Ministry of Economics, with a view to using Turkish Chambers of Commerce for the advancement of Turkish-American trade arbitration.

A third type of arrangement is under discussion between the Association and The Netherlands Chamber of Commerce in New York. While the proposal is for the use of a joint clause, the availability of mutual facilities in The Netherlands will require study and formulation, owing to changing conditions and other effects of the war throughout the Dutch Empire. As finally concluded, it will make available the facilities of other trade associations in the United States that represent the buyers and sellers of commodities from the Netherlands and may require an expansion of the activities of the Netherlands Chambers of Commerce, in addition to those now organized in New York and at the Hague.[8]

Under all types of arrangements, the Association carries on educational work through trade and commercial organizations and

[7] For text of clause, see Annex II, p. 234.

[8] See Anton D. Bestebreutje, "Netherlands-American Trade Arbitration," *Arbitration Journal*, (New Series) Vol. II, (1947), p. 311.

their publications and through other economic agencies in much the same way as for the Western Hemisphere Systems.

The servicing of these combined systems presents a problem; as does also the tendency of Americans to use an arbitration clause in a foreign trade contract without inquiring whether any facilities exist in the country where they are trading.[9] This situation resolves itself into the primary problem of providing impartial and competent arbitrators in such localities, together with Rules of Procedure and administrators of those Rules.

Supplementing the undertaking of the International Chamber of Commerce to establish Panels of arbitrators in different localities (as provided for in the revised agreement of 1947), the International Business Relations Council of the American Arbitration Association[10] has undertaken through American business enterprises which have agencies or organizations abroad to obtain nominations for advisors and correspondents to keep the Association advised, in the leading trade centers of the world, of conditions that create trade misunderstandings or controversies and that require settlement. The Council will also sponsor conferences for the advancement of arbitration and promote other activities for the improvement of international trade relations that might otherwise give rise to controversy.

The further problem of setting up standards of qualifications for members of these Panels and for their training in law and techniques, as well as in the fundamental principles of arbitration, is also involved in an American pattern of international commercial arbitration. This subject, as well as courses of instruction in institutions of learning, will receive the careful consideration of the Research Institute for the Advancement of a Science of Arbitration, when its organization is completed.

For areas where no facilities exist or where the existing agencies are not in a position to function effectively, and where Americans desire to put arbitration clauses into effect, the Association has approved an emergency clause which provides that if the arbitration is not held in the United States, the Association is authorized to make arrangements for the arbitration to be held under its Rules,

[9] See *International Trade Bulletin* for June 1947, containing a Warning on the indiscriminate use of clauses in foreign trade contracts.

[10] For members, see Ch. XXV, p. 215.

or under such Rules as it may designate, in any locality or territory agreed upon by the parties or, failing their agreement, on the locality designated by the Association. Under this clause, the Association undertakes to find administrators for its Rules in other countries, or to use Rules of other organizations for such emergencies.[11]

The administration of its Rules in other countries requires a short and concise manual of instructions for the administrator who has not had the opportunity of being trained at the headquarters of the Association.

At the Conference being called in the fall of 1948, the pattern for a universal commercial arbitration system will be examined in the light of these types of arrangements and with a view to considering measures of co-ordination, some of which are set forth as the American Vision of a Universal System of Commercial Arbitration.[12]

The fourth element in the American pattern of international commercial arbitration is the policy followed by the United States Government. An outstanding illustration is afforded by the action taken at the Chicago Conference on International Civil Aviation in 1944. The Convention, which came into force on April 4, 1947, provides for arbitration by executive decisions of the International Civil Aviation Organization in Montreal. It will maintain Panels of arbitrators and administer proceedings pursuant to modern principles of settlement of disputes. Rules governing such settlement have been issued by the Council of this Organization. At the Chicago Conference, the American Arbitration Association was instrumental in submitting proposals and later in formulating the procedure.

The new China-United States Treaty of Friendship, Commerce, and Navigation, of November 2, 1946, now pending in the Senate, contains what is perhaps the furthest advance of support by a government of private commercial arbitration, contained in the following paragraph:

> In the case of any controversy susceptible of settlement by arbitration, which involves nationals, corporations or associations of both High Contracting Parties and is covered by a written agreement for arbitration, such

[11] For text of clause, see Annex II, p. 231.

[12] See Ch. XXII, p. 157.

agreement shall be accorded full faith and credit by the courts within the territories of each High Contracting Party, and the award or decision of the arbitrators shall be accorded full faith and credit by the courts within the territories of the High Contracting Party in which it was rendered, provided the arbitration proceedings were conducted in good faith and in conformity with the agreement for arbitration.

The support given by the United States Government through the State Department in advancing bilateral arbitration commissions and joint clauses is a part of this pattern; as has also been a series of round-table conferences, held at Brookings Institution, in which, members of the State and Commerce Departments participated. It may also be noted that in the processing of commercial attachés for foreign service in embassies and consulates abroad, information about and instruction in arbitration procedure is included. These illustrations are indicative of the interest and co-operation which extends in many directions.

The most recent international agreement on a multilateral basis in which the United States plays a leading part, namely the International Trade Organization, provides for a mechanism to settle disputes between the states which may arise out of the operation of that Organization. The American Arbitration Association availed itself of the opportunity of hearings of the Executive Committee on Economic Foreign Policy, of the Department of State, to present its views for an improvement of the Draft Charter.

As these different elements of bilateral commissions, arrangements for use of joint clauses, and introduction of arbitration in international agreements and conventions are integrated, they indicate the broad outlines of American policy on international commercial arbitration.

CHAPTER XXII

American Vision of Universal Commercial Arbitration

«««« »»»»

THE American Arbitration Association knows that a way to international peace and security lies through world trade by the organization of international systems of arbitration. The successful organization of a Western Hemisphere system for its 22 countries carries assurance of this knowledge. The success of the tentative international arrangements, entered into between the Association, commercial organizations, and agencies in other countries since the close of the second World War, carries further conviction that a universal system of commercial arbitration may become a reality.

For itself as the chief engineer of this planning, the Association has adopted a Declaration of Principles, as follows, to guide its participation in the building of national and international systems of commercial arbitration:

1. Conflict is a fundamental law of human nature. It is universal and ineradicable. Out of conflict grow grievances and disputes. Commerce must, therefore, be concerned with their amelioration, control, and direction as well as their elimination.

2. Economic conflict, wherein things of ascertainable value are at stake, presents the most disastrous controversies of far-reaching power. As they most vitally affect the welfare, happiness, and progress of peoples all over the world, the control of economic conflict and disputes should be a first concern.

3. Since neither law nor government can deal successfully with individual conflict and controversy in their initial stages, the voluntary effort of international traders, acting through self-discipline,

restraint, and self-regulations, must be scientifically utilized in this direction.

4. Voluntary arbitration, fully and freely exercised by individuals, offers an expeditious alternative to force and thereby contributes to the safety, happiness, and tranquillity of all people. It is a part of the process by which people govern themselves, through free enterprise and freedom of contract.

5. Arbitration, being an instrumentality for the administration of justice, as well as for the advancement of understanding, its methods of strengthening confidence and co-operation among nations and among their peoples, should be impartial, non-profit-making, and non-partisan.

6. As the welfare of the United States is inseparable from that of other nations, the advancement of international peace and security, through arbitration as a part of economic relations, and through its use by international organizations or in contracts, conventions, treaties and other instrumentalities or arrangements, is a major responsibility of Americans.

7. As the general purpose of arbitration is to advance goodwill, good faith, confidence and co-operation through the establishment of a belief in and a practice of arbitration as a counterbalance to the organized forces of destruction let loose through conflict and war, the scientific organization of arbitration is indispensable if it is to have adequate power to combat organized force.

In order to put these principles into action and to make world peace through world trade more than a slogan and more than a dream, the Association has laid out a program for building a universal system of commercial arbitration.

First, as the second World War has so changed the political alignment of states and has so disrupted the internal economic conditions in many states, and as new types of governments and laws are coming into force, and as state trading and other forms of government trading are emerging, the status and trend of arbitration in many countries are unknown. Therefore, a survey of the interest in arbitration developments, proposals, practice, laws, and of the relation of arbitration to postwar conditions would be advisable as a first step in planning any comprehensive systems of international commercial arbitration, particularly in countries where new forms of freedom or of government are under consideration or in process. This survey should proceed country by country and be uniform as to the data to be obtained.[1]

Second. It would appear from experiments in the Western Hemisphere, that national associations of all of those interested in improving human relations through the development of a knowledge and practice of arbitration among the people of a country, and also as a foundation for an international system, would be desirable. For unless the people of a country acquire the habit of using arbitration in their immediate relationships, they cannot be expected to support their governments or exert their influence behind international systems. Furthermore, experience has shown that arbitration developed solely through commercial organizations whose other economic activities or policies subordinate the practice of arbitration, are not likely to advance universal systems of arbitration. For they lack the freedom to co-operate on a broad plan. All of the Western Hemisphere organizations and systems enjoy the freedom of action which independent national organizations afford.

Third. Without waiting for complete surveys or the organization of national arbitration associations, and because the world is in such a turmoil of disputes, immediate steps should be taken to strengthen existing facilities and services or, where none exist, to establish new ones. This can be begun by the improvement of national arbitration laws, by improving techniques, by establishing qualified panels of arbitrators and by instituting educational work among the people of the different countries. Some will need these activities more than others; for in countries that are backward in arbitration experience or that need reconstruction, the task will be greater than in countries where arbitration facilities and services have not been upset. For these reasons, the planning of such measures becomes an important element in establishing a universal system. The ideal situation is that eventually every area of trade should have arbitration machinery, competent administrators, and adequate rules of procedure

[1] A forthcoming publication of the International Chamber of Commerce, entitled *Commercial Arbitration and the Law throughout the World,* will contain a survey of statutory law provisions concerning arbitration agreements, procedures, and enforcement of awards as a practice manual, but does not cover the survey above suggested.

in order that trade disputes may be disposed of rapidly, fairly, and competently.

Fourth. Arbitration laws in the different countries, to be well applied by international arbitration systems, should attain a higher degree of uniformity, according to mutually acceptable standards, such as, for example, were approved at the Seventh International Conference of American States in 1933, or those prepared by the International Institute at Rome for the Unification of Private Law. Such standards would tend to establish uniform procedures in the different countries and would eventually lead to the adoption of an international procedure that could be used generally by arbitrators in different countries.

Fifth. Methods of referring international trade disputes to arbitration differ so widely in various countries that the suggestion for a universal arbitration clause for international trade contracts is under consideration. Progress has been made in the Western Hemisphere where traders in 22 countries may use one clause which assures them of facilities or services, at their election, of any one of the three systems. This experiment demonstrates that the idea is practical. Further steps were taken by the American Arbitration Association when it became associated with other organizations in the use of joint clauses under which the facilities and rules of either participating organization may be used. The arrangements made by the Association with the International Chamber of Commerce, and with the London Court of Arbitration, offer illustrations. A very considerable extension of these arrangements will doubtless be necessary before a universal clause is approved under which all systems of arbitration become available.

Sixth. In a publication entitled *Arbitration in International Controversy*, the Association proposed as an essential part of a program the holding of international arbitration conferences.[2] The first conference of this kind was the Western Hemisphere Conference on Arbitration and Foreign Trade held in 1943. It was highly serviceable in bringing about closer unity among the Western Hemisphere systems. Following the suggestion for international conferences, the International Chamber of Commerce in 1946 called a Conference at which eight organizations were represented. An International Commercial Arbitration Committee was created and under it four

[2] See *Arbitration in International Controversy* (1944), p. 98.

Working Committees are examining important aspects of international commercial arbitration.[3]

Seventh. The training of international arbitration personnel is an essential part of the maintenance of arbitration systems. This personnel includes the arbitrators before whom parties in dispute appear, the parties to contracts who use arbitration and the administrators of the systems. By reason of the importance and wide range of the issues that international commercial arbitration involves, the casual person selected by agreement of the parties, just because they can agree upon him and irrespective of judicial and personal qualifications, no longer satisfies the demand for just and fair and competent arbitrators' decisions. The impromptu administrator of rules, or administrators preoccupied with trade or other economic duties, can no longer give the expert, disinterested, and competent administrative service which organized arbitration requires.

Eighth. The active co-operation of governments and their official agencies is essential to the building of international systems of arbitration. National associations can be built in many countries only with government approval or with their participation. Expansion of international facilities in new areas generally require government approval and often their direct participation. Negotiations between the Association and agencies in foreign countries must often proceed through the State Department, or at least with its knowledge. Incorporation of provisions in treaties, conventions, and other governmental instrumentalities are of necessity advanced only with governmental approval. The Liaison Committee of the Chinese-American Trade Arbitration Conference offers a case in point as does

[3] The following are member organizations of this Committee: The International Chamber of Commerce, The London Court of Arbitration, The International Institute for the Unification of Private Law, The International Law Association, The Foreign Trade Arbitration Commission and Maritime Arbitration Commission, All-Union Chamber of Commerce, The American Arbitration Association, The Inter-American Commercial Arbitration Commission, and the Canadian-American Commercial Arbitration Commission.

The four Working Committees were assigned as follows: (1) Committee for the Unification of the Law on Arbitration and the Enforcement of Arbitral Awards, assigned to the London Court of Arbitration; (2) Committee for the Co-ordination of Arbitration Systems, assigned to the Western Hemisphere organizations; (3) Committee on Arbitration between Governments and Individuals, assigned to the International Institute for the Unification of Private Law; (4) Committee on Arbitration Education, also assigned to the Western Hemisphere organizations.

also the China-United States Treaty of Friendship, Commerce, and Navigation, recently concluded but not yet approved by the United States Senate.[4] The arbitration provisions in the Convention on International Civil Aviation also offer a case in point as to the steps to be taken in the introduction of arbitration in international agreements.[5]

Ninth. The cultivation of good business relations as a sound basis for the building of international arbitration systems is a necessary part of any program for extending international systems. The American Arbitration Association has recently created an International Business Relations Council which it hopes will serve as a model for advancing good international business relations as an element in strengthening international systems of arbitration.[6]

Tenth. Publications on arbitration should be both expanded and integrated in a manner to provide, in all languages and in all appropriate publications, the information, news, and other data that is required to make systems of arbitration effective and that will effect exchange of views, opinions, points of view, and data as a means of public education.

Eleventh. Judging by the indifference to, or ignorance of, the importance of arbitration to international official agencies, and by the unscientific way in which arbitration, when adopted, is introduced in international charters, conventions, treaties, or other agreements, it would seem that a major undertaking would be the education of the makers of such instrumentalities so that provisions would be more generally adopted, be more carefully drawn, and would express the intent of the parties to them to control such disputes as would arise out of the conditions which these agreements seek to regulate. Such agencies as the United Nations, Unesco, International Trade Organization, and many others offer the opportunity for such education.[7]

Twelfth. Direction of the attention of national and international

[4] For text of arbitration provision, see Ch. XXI, p. 155.

[5] Martin Domke, "International Civil Aviation Sets New Pattern," *International Arbitration Journal,* (1945), p. 20.

[6] For members of Council, see Ch. XXV, p. 215.

[7] Martin Domke, "The International Trade Organization. Settlement of Disputes-Provisions of the Draft-Charter," *Arbitration Journal,* (New Series) Vol. II, (1947), p. 222.

thought and discussion to the possibility of controlling future disputes, as well as their systematic settlement, through a science of arbitration designed to avoid the mounting menace of conflict, is a part of the realization of a vision of universal arbitration. The American Arbitration Association has taken the first concrete action in this direction, not only in the development of its national and international systems of arbitration but through the authorization of a Research Institute for the Advancement of a Science of Arbitration. It will devote its efforts to studies and discussions that will advance the scientific organization of arbitration.

A vision of universal arbitration implies, therefore, for its realization: (1) That postwar information be brought up to date, by national surveys; (2) that consideration be given to organizing national associations for the advancement of arbitration; (3) that existing systems of international arbitration be strengthened, and that new ones be created; (4) that attempts be made to unify arbitration laws; (5) that consideration be given to the adoption of a universal clause; (6) that periodic international conferences be held; (7) that training of arbitration personnel, including arbitrators and administrators, be undertaken; (8) that co-operation of governments be sought, particularly in their capacity as state traders; (9) that good business relations be cultivated as necessary to systems of arbitration; (10) that publications on arbitration be expanded; (11) that education of international official agencies be undertaken; and (12) that attention be directed to the importance of organizing arbitration as a science.

Part IV

MEN AND EVENTS

CHAPTER XXIII

Twenty Years of Progress

«««« »»»»

Arbitration has long been an international policy of the United States. Beginning with the Jay Treaty of 1794, between the United States and Great Britain, the policy has been expressed through a long series of conventions, treaties and other arrangements to which the United States has been a party.[1]

The record with respect to commercial and labor arbitration is more recent and less defined. The people, in their voluntary use of arbitration, have not consistently kept pace with the international policy. In the past twenty years, the advance has been more marked than in any other period of American history.

Some of the significant policies now obtaining in commercial and industrial arbitration are for the first time here briefly recorded:

1. The long-established American policy with respect to governments is now being applied in international trade relations of Americans. Commercial treaties contain specific applications, notably in the China-United States Treaty of Friendship, Commerce, and Navigation.[2] Government policy in this direction also appears in the Convention on International Civil Aviation, in the Draft Charter of the International Trade Organization and in the support given to bilateral trade arbitration commissions and other forms of organized international commercial arbitration sponsored by private organizations and nationals of different countries.

[1] See "*Arbitration and the United States*"—a Summary of the Development of Pacific Settlement of International Disputes with Special Reference to American Policy. World Peace Foundation Pamphlets, Vol. IX, Nos. 6-7, (1926).

[2] See Ch. XXII, p. 155.

2. A very considerable body of Americans have subscribed to and are advancing a definite policy of commercial arbitration which has been set forth in a Declaration of Principles. As adopted by the American Arbitration Association, this may be said to define in a preliminary way a policy in this field of conflict.[3]

3. The voluntary nature of arbitration as an American policy has been steadily maintained. During two World Wars, and particularly during the last World War, numerous efforts have been made to introduce compulsory features by law or by directive,[4] but without any fundamental change in this policy. When the issue has been presented, the courts have been alert to sustain the policy of voluntary arbitration.[5] The American Arbitration Association has steadfastly maintained this policy throughout its history.

4. Commercial and industrial arbitration originated in the United States as part of its system of free enterprise. That policy has been carried steadily forward, with a view further to developing the initiative, responsibility and self-regulation that form so large a part of the spirit of free enterprise and which are also characteristic of the voluntary exercise of arbitration by a free people. Government interference with the exercise of this right within the framework of business enterprise has been limited. The activities noted in the preceding chapters have continued this policy.

5. American policy is not to restrict the right of individuals to use their own resources in the settlement of disputes. The application of this policy has opened new areas of conflict to arbitration by choice of the people. In civil affairs, illustrations are afforded by the use of arbitration in the settlement of accident claims and domestic relations disputes. In commercial relations, any matter that can be made the subject of a contract is arbitrable. In labor relations, the questions range over a wide variety of subjects—wages, seniority, dismissals, and interpretation of agreements both as to their terms and application. The modern arbitration laws which make agreements to arbitrate future disputes legally valid and

[3] For Declaration of Principles, see Ch. XXII, p. 157.

[4] The nearest approach to compulsory arbitration occurred by directive of the War Labor Board as a measure of war production.

[5] *Matter of Feuer Transportation, Inc.* 295 N. Y. 87, (1946), on p. 91: "A quarter of a century of its operation has demonstrated its usefulness and general acceptability."

enforceable have greatly widened the areas of conflict that are now submissible to arbitration. The wide use of collective bargaining agreements has increased the usefulness of arbitration in avoiding work stoppages.

6. Public interest in commercial and labor arbitrations has created what is in effect a new policy. Public indifference to the high cost and immense waste of commercial and labor disputes has changed to one of public concern. Such disputes are no longer regarded as the private affair of the contesting parties, hence the public clamor for arbitration when a strike is threatened, or the demand from trade groups that its members settle their differences speedily and amicably. Public interest is now concerned with such matters as the settlement of accident claims and with trade practices in a great industry like that of the motion picture. This change from indifference to awareness indicates an increasing public concern over private disputes. The awakening of public interest is one of the outstanding results of public education, along the lines outlined in a previous chapter.[6]

7. During the last twenty years a new philosophy has arisen to direct future policy on arbitration. This is the philosophy of foresight, of prevention, and of faith and belief that disputes can be controlled and be used to advantage. The doctrine of inevitability is tempered by the certainty of prevention. The old concept that only parties in dispute held a stake in its settlement has given way to consciousness of the cost to the public, even in seemingly trivial disputes. The old concept that the country can afford a high rate of cost and waste is disappearing as there comes to light data on the enormity of this waste. It was a Bulletin of the U. S. Department of Commerce which said that next to war, commercial litigation is the largest single item of preventable waste in civilization.[7] This concern over costs is even more prevalent in labor disputes, for costs greatly exceed the consequences of commercial disputes in their extension to those not directly concerned in the dispute and in their cost to the public.

It is, however, in the practice of arbitration that progress is most outstanding. In 1926, when the national organization of American

[6] See Ch. XX, p. 144.
[7] See *Commerce Reports*, June 30, 1924.

arbitration began, there was one headquarters; now there are 31 offices; there was one local panel of 400 men; now there are national panels with a membership of more than 12,000; there were facilities and services in one city; now they embrace 1,537 communities in the United States; there was one system of tribunals; now there are four in the United States, three in the Western Hemisphere, and two international systems; the administrative personnel consisted of seven people; now it is well over one hundred; there was no American literature to direct the work of Tribunals; now there are several technical publications. The Board of Directors of the Association numbered seven members in 1926; now business or the professions are represented by 115 members of the Board; there were five modern state arbitration laws; now there are fifteen and a Federal law. From an expenditure of a few thousand dollars annually, now more than half a million dollars a year are spent upon organized national arbitration in the United States.

If matters submitted to arbitration are reckoned as indicators of progress, then over the period of twenty years, approximately 30,000 disputes have been referred to the Association. If the use of clauses is reckoned as a test of progress, the few hundred that reported use of such clauses in 1926 now have increased to thousands.

It is, however, the increasing prevalence of these clauses and the failure of disputes to emerge in any great number under them that tells the real story of progress, for they indicate that the voluntary control of disputes is becoming effective and that the promise to arbitrate a future dispute is actually reducing the volume of disputes. A high rate of clause users with diminished arbitrations, therefore, furnishes the greatest single item of gain.[8] As previously indicated, the number of settlements effected during an arbitration proceeding itself, gains steadily, indicating the high degree of accord that is developing during the process of arbitrations.

If progress is indicated by the expanding knowledge of arbitration, then such progress is little less than phenomenal. Where once the word arbitration was practically unknown, it is now featured in daily headlines; it is presented and discussed in a wide range of American periodicals; labor arbitration awards are reported and

[8] See Ch. XVI, p. 117, on The Arbitration Clause as an Instrument of Civilization.

courses of instruction are given; court decisions are assembled and published; conferences are held and public interest is aroused over the radio and in the press. This advance is primarily the result of twenty years of research and education.[9]

It is also in the development of a general practice of arbitration, in which parties are now represented in 77 per cent of their arbitrations by legal counsel, that the most outstanding progress has been made. That the practice increases annually, along with the establishment of machinery and the accompanying education in its use is indicated by the Association's record, in which it appears that, in 1947, more than 2,000 matters were referred to arbitration in its different Tribunals.

Certain outstanding improvements have occurred during the progress of the practice of arbitration as, for example, in the type of administrator and its competence, in the selection and training of arbitrators, in the increased acceptance of rules, in the separation of bargaining processes from judicial proceedings and in the stabilizing of costs and in methods of accounting to parties for deposits made for expenses.

The chronology, which follows, reveals in a more methodical manner, not only progress, but some of the events that have made possible that progress.

[9] See Ch. VII, p. 44, on Adventures in Research and Education.

CHAPTER XXIV

Chronology of Events

«««« »»»»

THIS chronology of the organization of American Arbitration indicates the diversity of the activities undertaken and the events held under the initiative of the Association, toward the creation of a science of arbitration and in the advancement of the organization of the knowledge and practice of arbitration as a part of that science. It presents an over-all picture of the manner in which these activities have been integrated, not only in the organization of the American system of arbitration but of the Western Hemisphere and international systems. It is believed to be the first chronology of such activities and events and of systematic progress and may prove helpful in the organization of institutions or systems of arbitration in other countries.

AMERICAN CHRONOLOGY

1920 Enactment of first modern Arbitration Law—New York State

1922 Organization of the Arbitration Society of America

1923 Enactment of New Jersey Arbitration Law

Organization of arbitration system for the motion picture industry by the Film Boards of Trade

First conference of the bench, bar, and business leaders to consider arbitration

1924 "Arbitration Week." First co-operative effort of 60 leading trade and commercial organizations to promote arbitration

1925 Enactment of United States Arbitration Law

Organization of the Arbitration Foundation, Inc.

Enactment of Massachusetts and Oregon Arbitration Laws

Enactment of Territory of Hawaii Arbitration Law

Calling of an "Arbitration Conference" of representatives of trade, commercial and professional organizations, and of the Judges of all of the New York courts

First agreement for the administration of arbitrations for an industry made with Actors' Equity Association

1926 Organization of the American Arbitration Association

First case filed with the Association the day after its organization was a labor case under the standard form contract of Actors' Equity Association, A.F. of L.

Appointment of the National Panel of Arbitrators

Formulation of Draft State Arbitration Act as a model for modern statutory arbitration laws

1927 Publication of the first *Year Book on Commercial Arbitration in the United States*

Enactment of California Arbitration Law

Adoption of the Association's standard arbitration clause by the New York furniture moving and warehousing industry through the New York Furniture Warehousemen's Association—the second industry so to act

First Code of Ethics published by the Association, entitled "Suggestions for the Guidance of Arbitrators"

1928 Association begins Surveys of State Arbitration Laws under fellowships presented to leading universities

First general Arbitration Conference held at the University of Virginia

Publication of *Suggestions for Practice of Commercial Arbitration in the United States*

Enactment of Louisiana and Pennsylvania Arbitration Laws

Agreement for the administration of arbitration for an industry made with the American Fur Merchants Association and the Fur Brokers Association

1929 Enactment of Arizona, Connecticut, New Hampshire, and Rhode Island Arbitration Laws

1930 Publication of *A Treatise on Commercial Arbitrations and Awards* by Professor Wesley A. Sturges of the Yale Law School

Adoption of standard arbitration clause and agreement for arbitration under AAA Rules for the cloth and garment trades by the Wool Institute (now the National Association of Wool Manufacturers), Industrial Council of the Cloak, Suit and Skirt Manufacturers, Merchants Ladies Garment Association, New York Clothing Manufacturers Exchange, Textile Shrinkers Association, and Textile Adjusters Association

1931 Publication of first *Code of Arbitration Practice and Procedure*
Enactment of Wisconsin and Ohio Arbitration Laws

1932 Establishment of National Council on Trade Relations to study applicability of arbitration in correction of unfair inter-trade practice, particularly in the retail field

1933 Accident Claims Tribunal established

Arbitration under the Association's rules included in many Codes of Fair Competition under the National Industrial Recovery Act

1934 City Court of the City of New York has general calendar call and urges arbitration be used to settle cases that cannot be tried for two and a half years

Special Panel of Arbitrators appointed in co-operation with the Bar Association of the City of New York to relieve congested court calendars

1935 The dental professional and trade organizations agree to submit all disputes to arbitration under AAA Rules

Joseph P. Kennedy, Chairman of The Security and Exchange Commission, announces at an AAA luncheon an eleven-point program for changes in Stock Exchange procedure, including recommendation of impartial arbitration of disputes between customers and brokers

Council on Trade Agreements submits plan for voluntary self-regulation of industry with use of arbitration as judicial part of some regulations

Committee on Arbitration appointed by the Bar Association of the City of New York

Organization of Insurance Arbitration Council

1936 Public observance of Tenth Anniversary of the Association

American Bankers Association approves modern arbitration law in its recommended program for state legislation

1937 American Institute of Architects adopts new arbitration procedure for Standard Building Contracts and provides for administration by the AAA

First publication of the *Arbitration Journal*

Establishment of Voluntary Labor Arbitration System by the Association, together with Rules for labor arbitrations

1938 First course in Arbitration Law given at the New York University Law School

First nation-wide union representation determination held under the voluntary labor arbitration machinery of the American Arbitration Association (National Broadcasting Company, Columbia Broadcasting System, and the American Federation of Radio Artists)

1939 Adoption of arbitration by the Air Transport Industry, using the Association's facilities

Participation in World Trade Center at New York World's Fair

1940 Consent Decree established facilities for Motion Picture Arbitration System in 31 cities in the United States

Educational Conference of insurance executives called by the State Superintendent of Insurance of New York State

Summary of questions submitted during three years' operation of Labor Tribunal, issued by the Association

1941 Survey of Canadian Arbitration Laws

Use of 31 Motion Picture Tribunals for Labor and Commercial Arbitration in advancing war production

Symposium on Arbitration conducted by the Association of the Bar of the City of New York

Enactment of Michigan Arbitration Law

Publication of *Arbitration in Action*

Conference of Impartial Chairmen to discuss procedures and standards and formulation of rules

Association publishes "The American Arbitrator and His Office"—a Code for behavior in office

1942 Arbitration machinery expanded for wartime use in the Americas

AAA Labor Advisory Council of 100 labor leaders organized

WLB established and urged inclusion of voluntary labor arbitration clauses in all collective bargaining agreements, thereby accelerating services of the Association's tribunals

1943 Monthly illustrated magazine on arbitration published

Enactment of Arbitration Law in Washington

Labor union officials added to Board of Directors of American Arbitration Association

First comprehensive survey of state labor arbitration laws made by U.S. Department of Labor in consultation with the Association

First nation-wide union representation determination, by mail ballot, held under the voluntary labor arbitration machinery of the American Arbitration Association (Prudential Insurance Company of America and the United Office & Professional Workers of America, C.I.O.)

1944 Membership of National Panel of Arbitrators reaches 10,000

1945 In-Service Course for New York City Teachers held at Association headquarters

Conference of 11 New York State Teachers College Presidents and Faculties to outline courses of study for teaching arbitration

Course in Industrial Arbitration given at the Graduate School of Business Administration, New York University, by AAA executive

AAA made country-wide poll of attitude toward compulsory arbitration. Revealed overwhelming majority opinion of both management and labor against compulsion—refuting Gallup poll—based on "sampling" of few hundred

AAA administers its first labor arbitration in Canada, signalizing entry into this field at the International level

Joint labor arbitration seminar held by University of Minnesota and American Arbitration Association

First *Blue Book* published, listing 500 firms in 60 major industries and the international unions which have adopted American Arbitration Association arbitration clauses

1946 AAA arbitration clauses in collective bargaining agreements in the textile industry exceed 400

Resumption of publication of the *Arbitration Journal* (New Series)

Publication of *Code of Ethics for Arbitrators*

Course in Arbitration Law given at Yale Law School

Publication of *Labor-Management Arbitration Letter* inaugurated by American Arbitration Association

1947 Labor Relations Institutes, with instruction in voluntary arbitration, organized in country's leading universities by United Steelworkers of America, C.I.O.

The United States Arbitration Act of 1925 enacted into positive law by the Congress, Public Law 282, approved July 30, 1947

Arbitration Committees of the Bar Association of the City of New York and the New York County Lawyers Association present practice arbitration in co-operation with the American Arbitration Association

Connecticut State Bar Association devotes one session of its annual convention in New Haven to arbitration in co-operation with the Assembly of Judges of the State of Connecticut and the American Arbitration Association

National Association of Hosiery Manufacturers recommends Association's arbitration clause for all sales contracts

Largest commercial award for royalties on patent licensing agreement, amounting to approximately $1,800,000 paid within three weeks of its rendition

INTER-AMERICAN CHRONOLOGY

1927 Preliminary study of commercial arbitration in Central and South American countries undertaken by Guerra Everett, then on the staff of American Arbitration Association (later, Chief, Division of Commercial Laws, Bureau of Foreign and Domestic Commerce, U. S. Department of Commerce)

1928-9 Study continued; Inter-American Commercial Arbitration Council of American Arbitration Association organized; special panel of arbitrators appointed in the United States

Sixth International Conference of American States, meeting at Havana, recommends that the Inter-American High Commission study the "principle of obligatory arbitration as a means of solving the differences between merchants residing in different countries"

1928 Inter-American High Commission publishes report by V. Vita, "Comparative Study of American Legislation Governing Commercial Arbitration"

1931 Fourth Pan American Commercial Conference, meeting in Washington, D.C., requests Pan American Union to have an inquiry made as to commercial interests of the American Republics joining with commercial interests of other Republics in the support and active use of a system of arbitration (Resolution XVII)

1932 Pan American Union requests the American Arbitration Association to co-operate in such inquiry. Pan American Union sends out questionnaires; replies are returned to American Arbitration Association

1933 American Arbitration Association files report with Pan American Union; published as Document #2 for use of Delegates to Seventh International Conference of American States at Montevideo, Uruguay

Seventh International Conference of American States in Resolution XLI authorizes the creation of an Inter-American Commercial Agency, one of whose functions is to be the establishment of an Inter-American System of Commercial Arbitration

1934 Governing Board of Pan American Union by resolution requests the Inter-American Commercial Arbitration Council of the American Arbitration Association and the Committee on Inter-American Commerce of the Council on Inter-American Relations to undertake the organization of such a body

Inter-American Commercial Arbitration Commission organized Spruille Braden appointed Chairman

1935 Constitution, By-Laws, Standard Rules, and Clause of Commission completed and organization of National Committees begun

1938 Commission Reports to Eighth International Conference of American States

Eight National Committees reported organized

Colombia adopts modern arbitration law (Law No. 2 of 1938), making agreements to arbitrate future disputes valid and enforceable

Inter-American Section of *Arbitration Journal* published

1939 Spruille Braden becomes Honorary Chairman of Commission; Thomas J. Watson takes Chairmanship

1940 Business Relations Committee of Commission organized

Commission participates in New York World's Fair—International House

1942 Executive Secretary of Commission visits Mexico, Colombia, Ecuador, Peru, and Cuba

1943 Handbook *Del Arbitraje Comercial Internacional,* published in Colombia under auspices of Commission and Colombian National Committee

Commission participates with American Arbitration Association in First Western Hemisphere Conference on Foreign Trade and Arbitration

1944 Commercial Associations Committee of Commission is established

Commission resolves to make facilities available to residents of Puerto Rico and of British, Dutch, and French possessions in the West Indies and Central and South America

1945 Standard Arbitration Rules of Commission revised

Commission and Canadian-American Commercial Arbitration Commission develop joint arbitration clause with American Arbitration Association to cover Western Hemisphere

1946 Executive Secretary of Commission visits Argentina, Brazil, Chile, Ecuador, Mexico, Peru, Uruguay, and Venezuela

Commission represented at first International Arbitration Conference organized by International Chamber of Commerce in Paris

1947 Commission files report with Pan American Union for Ninth International Conference of American States

Reports 1,031 matters submitted for arbitration or adjustment

Eighteen National Committees organized

INTERNATIONAL CHRONOLOGY

1928 Publication of Handbooks on arbitration laws and practice in foreign countries, in co-operation with the International Chamber of Commerce

Publication of *International Year Book on Civil and Commercial Arbitration*

1934 Establishment of a London-New York Arbitration Service under a joint clause by American Chamber of Commerce in London and the American Arbitration Association

1939 Arrangement between the International Chamber of Commerce and the American Arbitration Association for use of joint clause and facilities

Arrangement with Manchester (England) Chamber of Commerce and the American Arbitration Association for use of joint clause and facilities

Arrangement between Permanent Court of Arbitration and the American Arbitration Association for recommendation of use of arbitration facilities

1941 Use of American Arbitration Association in War Purchasing Contracts by British, Canadian, Australian, French, Dutch, and other Purchasing Missions

1942 Canadian Law survey completed as basis for Canadian-American agreement

1943 Canadian-American Commercial Arbitration Commission organized

First Western Hemisphere Conference held in New York on Foreign Trade and Arbitration

1944 Publication of *Arbitration in International Controversy* as foundation for expanding international arbitration

Negotiations opened by the American Arbitration Association through the State Department with the Chinese Government for the establishment of a Chinese-American Trade Arbitration Commission and Liaison Committee of Chinese and Americans appointed

Co-operation with American Delegation of International Civil Aviation Conference (Chicago) in promoting modern arbitration standards in international convention and agreements

1945 Liaison Committee submits draft proposals for the organization of the Chinese-American Trade Arbitration Commission

Publication of *International Arbitration Journal* with special supplement on arbitration in international civil aviation

Round-table Conferences on actual problems of international arbitration (United Nations' proceedings; trade agreements) with officials of U. S. Departments of State and Commerce, members of universities, of bench and bar held in Washington, D. C., Boston, Mass., and New Haven, Conn.

1946 International Commercial Arbitration Day held during International Week in New Orleans

Participation in Conference on International Commercial Arbitration held in Paris under the auspices of the International Chamber of Commerce

Soviet-American Trade Arbitration Commission proposed by the Association to the All-Union Chamber of Commerce in Moscow

1947 Publication of first *International Trade Arbitration Bulletin*

Joint agreement between International Chamber of Commerce and American Arbitration Association revised and expanded

Agreement between American Arbitration Association and London Court of Arbitration for use of joint clause and mutual use of services, concluded

Participation in work of Committee on Commercial Arbitration, International Law Association in London

International Business Relations Council appointed by the Association, with H. L. Derby as Chairman. Meeting held on November 19 and program approved

Research Institute for the Advancement of a Science of Arbitration authorized by the American Arbitration Association

Netherlands-American arbitration service projected through co-operation of the Netherlands Chamber of Commerce in New York and the American Arbitration Association

Japanese-American trade arbitration proposal submitted to military authorities in Tokyo

Turkish-American Trade Arbitration Service in co-operation with Turkish Chambers of Commerce, proposed to Turkish Ministry of Commerce

International Trade Arbitration Practice presented at Yale Law School

Chinese Government advises that a national association of arbitration is being organized in China as a basis for co-operation in establishing a Chinese-American Trade Arbitration Commission

CHAPTER XXV

Builders of American Arbitration

«««« »»»»

AMERICAN arbitration, as described in the foregoing chapters, in both policy and practice, has been built in the true American way—by the participation of many individuals and organizations. There seems to be no better way to describe the progress of its organization than to indicate to some degree the personality of those who have built it.

In this story of organization, there have been three missionaries—men who have felt the call of the spirit of arbitration to an almost fanatical degree and to whom they gave very real devotion. These three men were Moses H. Grossman, founder of The Arbitration Society of America; Charles L. Bernheimer, organizer of the Arbitration Foundation and Chairman of the Arbitration Committee of the Chamber of Commerce of the State of New York, and R. Emerson Swart, late President of the American Arbitration Association.

For not quite two years, Mr. Swart carried forward both the spirit and fact of arbitration as a leader in a campaign to make it a greater instrumentality for peace and security for Americans and peoples in many lands. He might have been a Quaker, so gentle and persuasive was his approach to the problems that surround controversy and so profound was his faith in the good in his fellowmen. He was certainly a philosopher in his understanding of mankind and of its needs and in his planning for the general welfare. Disregarding warnings that his span of life might be cut short unless he curbed his zealous spirit in its ceaseless urge to serve, he drove himself relentlessly forward to the very end.

There were two other men whose belief and faith in arbitration and constant support made them founders of the Association. These two men were Lucius R. Eastman who, as chairman of the consolidating committee and later as President and Chairman of the Board of the Association, made the present organization possible; and Felix M. Warburg, who, as Chairman of the Board, gave the Association much of its wide understanding of human relations and the financial assistance to carry on its work.

At the time of his death in 1943, *Arbitration in Action* published the following appreciation of Mr. Eastman's services to the Association:

January the twenty-sixth was the seventeenth anniversary of the founding of the American Arbitration Association. For all of these years and during the turbulent year that preceded its founding, one man has stood steadfastly at the helm, piloting the first attempt anywhere in the world to organize arbitration on a national plan and looking forward to the day when, as a science, it would heal more infallibly the wounds and scars left by controversy. His last act for arbitration was to sponsor *Arbitration in Action*, the first publication of its kind to chart a new course for permanent peace in the economic affairs of men and nations.

In future days there may be other claimants for the foundership of modern, organized arbitration in the United States, but there are men who will remember that it was born out of bitter controversy and that the man chosen to bring about peace and to build the new structure with the aid of all reconciled factions was Lucius R. Eastman; and that to his perseverance and tolerance and patient negotiation and the collaboration of Felix M. Warburg, in the early dark days, the Association owes its life and progress.

He lived to see arbitration spread from a tiny acorn planted in one small room with a staff of three into an organization of a hundred, with close to ten thousand men serving as volunteer arbitrators over the nation on his invitation; and to see an organization expand from the single commercial tribunal into the fields of labor, accidents and many special trade tribunals, including that of the motion picture industry under a Consent Decree. To him it meant faith justified in a high degree and a realization of the forthright and upright dealing of men with each other, which was the ideal he bequeathed to the new organization to follow in all its ways.

In his vision of peace through arbitration during his long term of service, he did not waver; in his patience and tact and wisdom in dealing with shortcomings and misunderstandings of men in controversy, he did not falter. From the integrity and principles that were wrought into the foundation of arbitration, no departures were permitted. To him there was never but one right way and that was always the hardest for us. His conscience was a hard taskmaster for the infant organization. Lethargy was to him the unforgivable sin and new ideas, fervent ideals and first adventures in the realm of commercial peace were a challenge which he spurred his associates on to meet. His genius for friendship, and the warmth of his own, brought to arbitration many steadfast friends and expanded its outlook.

He was never too proud to change his mind or too obstinate to learn by experience or too timid to try a new experiment. To every conference table he brought the results of this attitude of mind, to help shape new policies and to find new exits from problems.

We here in the Association have no sense that he has left the plans for the future in lesser hands, or that there will depart from the day's work any of the fine traditions and standards that he brought to it. On the contrary, these are so woven into the fabric of this young but intrepid champion of peace, that he goes marching along with it into new fields to conquer. As arbitration finds its way into world peace, as it fulfills its mission on the western hemisphere (an achievement which never failed to cheer him in the dark days of war and under the strain of its adjustments), more will be known of the inspirational power of this founder and friend of modern organized arbitration and of this exponent of goodwill and friendship and cooperation and his impact upon the lives of this generation and those to come.

It was to Mr. Warburg's wisdom, generosity, fine sense of public service, aversion to war and genius for persuasion that the American Arbitration Association owes its weathering of the first years of its turbulent existence and the flowering of its ideas and plans into constructive action.

These five men were able to gather about them, in the development of American arbitration, representative Americans and organizations who became the actual builders of American Arbitration as it exists today. These builders reveal so wide a range of interest, and exemplify so fully the American way of building a democratic institution that their personnel and the setting in which they functioned is presented. It disposes of any implication that organized American arbitration has been the achievement of any one person, group or organization, or that it has at any time been dominated by any one interest or viewpoint.

Outstanding in the service of all of these individuals and groups has been disinterest in personal credit and refusal personally to profit by any share that they may have as builders and a sense of public service that has subordinated private interests. It is unnecessary to add that at no time in the history of the Association have the personal interests of these builders swayed any arbitrator in any tribunal, or charted a course of development that was not dictated by the ideals and purposes revealed in the previous chapters.

Consolidation Committee, 1925-26

Lucius R. Eastman, Chairman; Anson W. Burchard, John F. Fowler and James H. Post for the Arbitration Foundation; Henry Ives Cobb, Frank H. Sommer and Felix M. Warburg for the Arbitration Society of America.

First Board of Elected Directors, 1926

Andrew Adie, Helen Astor, Jules S. Bache, W. J. L. Banham, Charles L. Bernheimer, Willis H. Booth, Archibald Bowman, Frederick Brown, James Brown, Anson W. Burchard, Henry Ives Cobb, C. Frank Crawford, Lincoln Cromwell, Richard C. Curtis, Elizabeth Cutting, J. Winter Davis, Kenneth Dayton, William L. DeBost, Gano Dunn, Lucius R. Eastman, Frederick H. Ecker, Charles G. Edwards, Harold E. Emmons, Ben Erdman, John H. Fahey, A. Lincoln Filene, John F. Fowler, Michael Friedsam, James W. Gerard, Julian Goldman, Moses H. Grossman, Charles L. Guy, Charles T. Gwynne, Will H. Hays, August Heckscher, Charles E. Heitman, Charles Evans Hughes, Edward N. Hurley, Hermann Irion, Huger W. Jervey, William B. Joyce, Frances Kellor, Frederic Kernochan, William E. Knox, Alvin W. Krech, Henry Goddard Leach, Samuel McRoberts, E. J. Mehren, John L. Merrill, Arthur S. Meyer, Robert H. Montgomery, W. W. Nichols, John B. Niven, James A. O'Gorman, Homer S. Pace, Thomas B. Paton, Ramsay Peugnet, H. Hobart Porter, James H. Post, Roscoe Pound, David H. McAlpin Pyle, Samuel Rea, William C. Redfield, Robert Goodwyn Rhett, Charles T. Root, Julius Rosenwald, John E. Rousmaniere, David A. Schulte, Charles M. Schwab, Charles B. Seger, Finley J. Shepard, Franklin Simon, Frank H. Sommer, William Sproule, Alfred P. Thom, Arthur S. Tompkins, J. H. Tregoe, Felix M. Warburg, Paul M. Warburg, William R. Willcox, Benjamin Winter, B. N. Wunder and Owen D. Young.

Members of Successive Boards of Directors

James S. Alexander, George Backer, David G. Baird, J. Stewart Baker, William D. Baldwin, Julius Barnes, Herman B. Baruch, A. A. Berle, Jr., Paul Block, Walter E. Bonwit, George P. Brett, Jr., Herman G. Brock, Irving T. Bush, Rear Adm. Richard E. Byrd, W. Gibson Carey, Jr., Edwin H. Cassels, Irwin S. Chanin, Charles Cheney, Horace B. Cheney, Harley L. Clarke, Henry Ives Cobb, Jr., Russell Colgate, Charles A. Coolidge, Maxwell Copelof, Harvey Wiley Corbett, P. E. Crowley, Clarke G. Dailey, S. H. Dalrymple, Donald K. David, William C. Dickerman, Victor J. Dowling, Michael Francis Doyle, Russell Duane, Homer A. Dunn, Francis I. du Pont, Mrs. E. Marshall Field, Haley Fiske, Jr., Henry C. Flower, Jr., L. F. Gieg, Jerome D. Greene, Harry F. Guggenheim, Lew Hahn, P. M. Haight, Edward K. Hall, Natalie Hays Hammond, William M. Holmes, Frank R. Hope, Louis J. Horowitz, Nathan Isaacs, Cornelius F. Kelley, Robert P. Lamont, Monte M. Lemann, P. W. Litchfield, L. F. Loree, Clarence H. Low, Thomas H. McInnerney, John D. McKee, George V.

McLaughlin, Donald R. McLennan, Mrs. Eleanor Nash MacWilliam, James R. MacColl, John Markle, L. L. Marshall, Stephen I. Miller, James J. Minot, Jr., C. Stanley Mitchell, William S. Moore, William Fellowes Morgan, Jr., Dave Hennen Morris, Charles Nagel, George W. Naumburg, Floyd B. Odlum, John E. Otterson, Eugenius H. Outerbridge, William Barclay Parsons, Col. Richard C. Patterson, Jr., F. W. Pershing, Ellis L. Phillips, Gen. Palmer E. Pierce, Chester D. Pugsley, Edgar Richard, Kermit Roosevelt, Samuel N. Rosenman, Mrs. C. C. Rumsey, R. B. Scandrett, Jr., J. E. Sitterley, Peter M. Speer, W. A. Starrett, R. Emerson Swart, H. R. Swartz, Alfred H. Swayne, Robert E. Tally, Frank A. Tichenor, William H. Vanderbilt, George S. Van Schaick, Robert J. Watt, Harry A. Wheeler, C. V. Whitney, Daniel Willard, Langbourne M. Williams, Jr., Benjamin L. Winchell, Evans Woollen, Quincy Wright, Evan E. Young.

1947 Board of Directors

Robert E. Allen, James R. Angell, Robert W. Atkins, William W. Bodine, Willis H. Booth, J. Noble Braden, Spruille Braden, Edward J. Brown, Owsley Brown, George A. Brownell, John S. Burke, H. Donald Campbell, Henry Munroe Campbell, Paul Carrington, James S. Carson, George W. Carter, Ward Cheney, Leo M. Cherne, J. Luther Cleveland, Julius Henry Cohen, Ralph F. Colin, S. Sloan Colt, L. K. Comstock, William H. Coverdale, Morton R. Cross, George C. Cutler, Archie O. Dawson, Kenneth Dayton, Thomas M. Debevoise, H. L. Derby, Chester R. Dewey, Marshall Dill, Georges F. Doriot, Robert W. Dowling, Paul Dullzell, George L. Eastman, Lee J. Eastman, Mrs. Lucius R. Eastman, Ferdinand Eberstadt, John H. Fahey, Lincoln Filene, Paul Fitzpatrick, Robert I. Gannon, Lloyd K. Garrison, Harvey D. Gibson, Sylvan Gotshal, William J. Graham, Basil Harris, Frederick E. Hasler, A. Hatvany, R. S. Hecht, Charles E. Heitman, Lewis A. Hird, Garrett S. Hoag, Charles R. Hook, Jr., Walter Hoving, James F. Hughes, Mrs. Lytle Hull, William P. Hunt, Hermann Irion, Henry Ittleson, Floyd W. Jefferson, Thomas Roy Jones, Joseph P. Kasper, Frances Kellor, Fred I. Kent, H. O. King, Mrs. H. O. King, Arthur S. Kleeman, O. A. Knight, S. Whitney Landon, Richard W. Lawrence, Robert Lehman, Samuel D. Leidesdorf, Sam A. Lewisohn, B. A. McDonald, David J. McDonald, John T. McGovern, Edward F. McGrady, James H. McGraw, Jr., Walter H. Mann, George Meany, Sidney A. Mitchell, Gilbert H. Montague, Thomas A. Morgan, Malcolm Muir, B. H. Namm, Lawrence Ottinger, Franklin E. Parker, Jr., Maurice E. Peloubet, Gordon W. Reed, Arthur M. Reis, Gordon S. Rentschler, Emil Rieve, Morris S. Rosenthal, William Rosenwald, Raymond Rubicam, J. W. Schwab, George H. Sibley, Eugene F. Sitterley, Reginald Heber Smith, Kenneth M. Spence, Mrs. Roger W. Straus, Wesley A. Sturges, Arthur Hays Sulzberger, Mrs. R. Emerson Swart, Eugene P. Thomas, R. J. Thomas, Arthur T. Vanderbilt, Frederick M. Warburg, Paul Felix Warburg, Thomas J. Watson, Sidney J. Weinberg, George Whitney, Charles E. Wilson, Matthew Woll.

Honorary Presidents and Regional Vice Presidents, 1926

Honorary Presidents: Newton D. Baker, Charles L. Bernheimer, Moses H. Grossman, Herbert Hoover, Charles Evans Hughes.

Regional Vice Presidents: Horace B. Cheney, Connecticut; Monte M. Lemann, Louisiana; James R. MacColl, Rhode Island; Charles Nagel, Missouri; John H. Puelicher, Wisconsin; Robert Goodwyn Rhett, South Carolina; Julius Rosenwald, Illinois; Franklin Simon, New York; Robert E. Tally, Arizona; E. G. Van Hoesen, Idaho; Evans Woollen, Indiana.

Board of Trade Vice Chairmen, 1927

DIVISION I

1. *Groceries, General.* H. W. Charles, President, Charles & Co., N. Y. C.; P. C. Staib, Francis H. Leggett & Co., N. Y. C.; T. H. Roulston, Roulston, T. H., Brooklyn.

2. *Grocers' Food Specialties.* Ralph B. Annis, American Association Importers of Spanish Green Olives; G. Lowenstein, Fred Fear & Co., Brooklyn; Wm. Archibald, Pres. and Treas., Archibald & Lewis Co., N. Y. C.; C. V. Armstrong, Pres., Charles E. Armstrong, Inc., N. Y. C.; Alfred Klopfer, Bakers' Weekly, N. Y. C.; R. U. Delapenha, Pres., R. U. Delapenha & Co., Inc., N. Y. C.; John Magee, Pres., John Magee & Co., Inc., N. Y. C.; J. S. Neuman, Pres., Neuman & Schwiers Co., Inc., N. Y. C.; H. Steinhardter, Steinhardter & Nordlinger, N. Y. C.; Henry von Bremen, Von Bremen, Asche & Co., N. Y. C.; H. L. Sills, Singlo-Sills Co., N. Y. C.; E. C. Rogers, Mgr., N. Y. office, Standard Rice Co., N. Y. C.; Harry D. Tipton, Southern Baking Co., N. Y. C.; Andre L. Causse, N. Y. C.

4. *Coffee and Tea Importers and Dealers.* Harry L. Jones, Jones Bros. Tea Co., Brooklyn; William Bayne, Jr., N. Y. Coffee & Sugar Clearing Assn.; Samuel Zechnowitz, Pres., Consolidated Tea Co., Inc., N. Y. C.; Benjamin B. Peabody, T. Barbour Brown & Co., N. Y. C.; Adolph C. Israel, A. C. Israel & Co., N. Y. C.

5. *Sugar, Syrup, etc.* H. A. S. Van Dalen, Orvis Bros., N. Y. C.; Lewis C. Henry, Lewis B. Henry's Sons, N. Y. C.; D. S. Wadsworth, Trukane Products Co., Inc., N. Y. C.; Keen Tameling, N. Y. C.; John Farr, Vice Pres., Central Aquirre Sugar Co., N. Y. C.; Carlos Garcia, Pres., Garcia Sugars Corp., N. Y. C.

6. *Confectionery, Bakers, Confectioners and Soda Fountain Supplies.* Joseph S. Auerbach, D. Auerbach & Sons, N. Y. C.; Herman R. Habicht, Habicht, Braun & Co., N. Y. C.; Frederick K. Nieschlag, Pres., Nieschlag, Scheerer & Co., Inc., N. Y. C.; William N. Evans, Pres. and Treas., Rockwood & Co., Brooklyn; Horace C. Moses, Sec., Wood & Selick, Inc., N. Y. C.; Herman W. Hoops, Hawley & Hoops, N. Y. C.

7. *Flour and Grain.* Thomas R. Van Boskerk, George W. Van Boskerk & Son, N. Y. C.

8. *Meat and Poultry.* B. B. Butts, Butts & Miller, N. Y. C.

9. *Sea Food.* William H. Cornell, Pres., Wallace, Keeney, Lynch Corp., N. Y. C.

10. *Country Produce and Fruits.* Ralph Horton, Sheffield Farms Co., N. Y. C.; N. J. Eschenbrenner, Pres., Lewis, Mears Co., N. Y. C.; L. J. Lippmann, J. & G. Lippmann, N. Y. C.; P. H. Keifer, N. Y. C.; Walter L. Long, Gen. Manager, United Fruit Co., N. Y. C.

12. *Ice: Cold Storage.* William Fellowes Morgan, Pres., Brooklyn Bridge Freezing & Cold Storage Co., Brooklyn; C. C. Small, Pres., Knickerbocker Ice Co., N. Y. C.; Frank A. Horne, Pres., Merchants' Refrigerating Co., N. Y. C.

DIVISION II

1. *General Merchandise, Wholesale, including Resident Buyers.* Alfred Fantl, N. Y. C.; John Block, Treas., Kirby, Block & Fischer, Inc., N. Y. C.; Milton J. Greenbaum, Felix Lillienthal & Co., N. Y. C.

2. *Department, Retail Dry Goods and Women's Wear Specialty Stores.* Jacob A. Livingston, Pres., J. A. Livingston, Inc., N. Y. C.; Louis E. Salomon, Pres., "Worth," Inc., N. Y. C.

DIVISION III

1. *Dry Goods Commission Merchants, Manufacturers, etc.* Charles L. Bernheimer, N. Y. C.; Isaac D. Bachmann, Pres., Bachmann, Emmerich & Co., Inc., N. Y. C.; Fred S. Bennett, Pres., Fred S. Bennett, Inc., N. Y. C.; Carl Cavalsky, Treas., Debenhams (U.S.A.), Ltd., N. Y. C.; Benedict Erstein, Pres., L. Erstein & Brother, Inc., N. Y. C.; Lincoln Cromwell, William Iselin & Co., N. Y. C.; Isaac Kommel, I. Kommel Company, N. Y. C.; Arthur Kreeger, Kreeger Brothers, N. Y. C.; David Langenzen, Pres., Langdon Textile Co., Inc., N. Y. C.; Francis R. Masters, Lawrence & Company, N. Y. C.; Henry W. Howe, N. Y. C.; James R. Leask, N. Y. C.; Samuel McConnell, Edward McConnell & Co., N. Y. C.; Samuel Pearsall, Pres., Pearsall & Co., Inc., N. Y. C.; Max J. Shapiro, Treas., Shapiro Brothers Factors Corp., N. Y. C.; James D. Hopkins, Vice Pres., Textile Banking Co., Inc., N. Y. C.; E. M. Townsend, E. M. Townsend & Co., N. Y. C.; Edmund Wright, Pres., Edmund Wright-Ginsberg Co., Inc., N. Y. C.; Alfred L. Helwitz, N. Y. C.; Harry T. Rounds, Sussex Print Works, N. Y. C.; George J. Swift, Northern Textile Co., N. Y. C.; Gustav Veit, Pres., York Manufacturing Co., Inc., N. Y. C.; Gerrish H. Milliken, Deering Milliken Co., N. Y. C.

3. *Woolens and Worsteds, Trimmings, Linings, etc.* Frank C. Kay, Hager, Clark & Co., N. Y. C.; Morton H. Meinhard, Morton Meinhard & Co., N. Y. C.; William Alsberg, W. Alsberg & Co., N. Y. C.; Morris Garfunkel, N. Y. C.

4. *Silk Goods and Allied Lines, Dyeing and Cleaning.* I. Israel, V. P., Champlain Silk Mills, N. Y. C.; Charles Cheney, Cheney Brothers, N. Y. C.; B. Edmund David, B. Edmund David, Inc., N. Y. C.; Lester D. Livingston, Louis Livingston & Son, N. Y. C.; M. L. Roessel, Pres., Louis Roessel &

Co., Inc., N. Y. C.; Julius Bernstein, Majestic Silk Mills, N. Y. C.; Henry Zollinger, Pres., Zollinger & Schroth, Inc., N. Y. C.; J. R. Howlett, Howlett & Hochmeyer Co., N. Y. C.; A. D. Walker, A. D. Walker Co., N. Y. C.; Lionel F. Straus, N. Y. C.; Wm. Greenbaum, Vivanti Bros., N. Y. C.; H. R. Mallinson, Pres., H. R. Mallinson & Co., N. Y. C.; Samuel Eiseman, N. Y. C.

5. *Upholstery Goods.* Royal W. France, Salt's Textile Co., Inc., N. Y. C.

6. *Laces, Embroideries and Curtains.* Nat. N. Samuely, Pres., Pall Mall Embroidery Works, Inc., N. Y. C.; Julius Gottschalk, Pres., Reform Initial Co., Inc., N. Y. C.

9. *Hosiery, Underwear, Knit Goods.* A. Egerer, S. Augstein & Co. Elmhurst, L. I.; Sidney Worms, Pres., Franklin Knitting Mills of N. Y., N. Y. C.; Jacob Gold, J. Gold & Co., N. Y. C.; Nathan A. Kommel, A. Kommel & Sons, N. Y. C.; John H. Lang, Lang Knitting Mills, Inc., N. Y. C.; Moses Garbarsky, Ray-Mend Hosiery & Underwear Co., N. Y. C.; Samuel Siff, N. Y. C.; E. I. Bloomingdale, N. Y. C.; Max Liebhold, J. H. Semel & Co., N. Y. C.

10. *Carpets, Rugs, Matting, Oil Cloth, Linoleum, etc.* Charles J. Mentrup, Pres., C. J. Mentrup Co., Inc., N. Y. C.; Vassos Vayanos, Pres., Vayanos Brothers, Inc., N. Y. C.; J. T. Broadhurst, Pres., Standard Textile Products Co., N. Y. C.

11. *Felts, Bags, Burlaps, Clippings, Wastes, etc.* Samuel T. Bell, Bell Bag Co., N. Y. C.; E. W. Spark, Percy Kent Bag Co., N. Y. C.

DIVISION IV

1. *Fancy Goods, Novelties, Notions, Dry Goods, Sundries and Small Wares.* James A. Smith, Calhoun, Robbins & Co., N. Y. C.; Louis Reibstein, N. Y. C.; Sol Mutterperl, Pres., Sol. Mutterperl, Inc., N. Y. C.; Henry F. Samstag, Pres., Samstag & Hilder Bros., N. Y. C.; Henry L. Schwanda, B. Schwanda & Sons, N. Y. C.; Leo H. Hirsch, Leo H. Hirsch & Co., N. Y. C.

2. *Corsets.* C. N. Merritt, V. P., Crown Corset Co., N. Y. C.

3. *Gloves.* Wallace E. Meyers, Sec. and Treas., Louis Meyers & Son, Inc., N. Y. C.

4. *Leather Specialties.* Max Berkowitz, Pres., Unique Leather Goods Co., Richmond Hill, L. I.; Louis Merzbach, Levy & Merzbach, Inc., N. Y. C.; Maurice Lifton, The Lifton Manufacturing Co., N. Y. C.

6. *Toys, Dolls, Games, Children's Vehicles, etc.* Theo. Baettenhausen, Pres., F. A. O. Schwarz, N. Y. C.

DIVISION V

1. *Cloaks, Suits, Skirts, etc.* P. J. Barash, N. Y. C.; Maxwell Copelof, Copelof-Stillman & Co., Inc., N. Y. C.; William Rosenbaum, Sec., National Cloak & Suit Co., N. Y. C.; Wm. Hecht, N. Y. C.; Joseph A. Engel, N. Y. C.; Wm. Fischman, N. Y. C.; Max Lachman, N. Y. C.; Robert W. Foster, Sam Finkelstein & Co., N. Y. C.

2. *Costumes, Dresses, Waists, Petticoats, House Dresses, Kimonos, Sleeping Garments, Bathing Suits, etc.* Fred E. Frank, Sec. and Gen. Mgr., Henry

A. Dix & Sons Corp., N. Y. C.; Morry Schulman, Pres. and Treas., Schulman, Morry & Dessau, Inc., N. Y. C.; M. D. Mossessohn, Ex. Ch., United Women's Wear League of America, N. Y. C.; David N. Mossessohn, Ex. Ch., Associated Dress Industries of America, N. Y. C.; S. M. Goldberg, S. M. Goldberg Enterprises, Inc., N. Y. C.

3. *Ladies' Muslin and Silk Underwear.* A. Gussow, A. Gussow & Co., N. Y. C.

5. *Furs and Fur Goods.* J. H. Bleistein, J. H. Bleistein, Inc., N. Y. C.; Leo D. Greenfield, Leo D. Greenfield & Co., Inc., N. Y. C.; Fred Kaufman, Pres., Kaufman & Oberleder, Inc., N. Y. C.; Abraham Schiff, Fur Dressers & Fur Dyers' Assn., N. Y. C.; Chas. S. Porter, Chas. S. Porter, Inc., N. Y. C.; Joseph Kruskal, N. Y. C.; E. S. Ullman, N. Y. C.; Louis H. Solomon, Counsel for Fur Trade, N. Y. C.; Adolph Engel, Treas., A. & J. Engel, N. Y. C.

DIVISION VI

1. *Men's and Boys' Clothing.* Sol Bashwitz, Pres., Bashwitz Bros. & Co., Inc., N. Y. C.; Samuel Brill, Brill Bros., N. Y. C.; Edward Friedman, Friedman Bros. & Co., N. Y. C.; Harry Schwartz, Julius Schwartz & Sons, Inc., N. Y. C.; Klee Oppenheimer, Treas., Washington Manufacturing Co., The, Brooklyn.

2. *Men's Furnishing and Specialties, Shirts, Collars, Cuffs, Underwear, Night Shirts, Robes and Pajamas, Neckwear, Cravats, Suspenders, Belts, Garters, etc.* Louis Newman, Broom & Newman, N. Y. C.; Max Phillips, Pres., Phillips-Jones Corp., N. Y. C.; F. A. Sarg, National Shirt Shops, N. Y. C.; David Meyer, Berliner, Strauss & Meyer, Inc., N. Y. C.

3. *Hats and Caps, Hatters' Materials, etc.* Aaron Naumburg, Pres., Jonas & Naumburg Corp., N. Y. C., Milton W. Stein, Treas., Wormser Hat Stores, Inc., N. Y. C.

4. *Merchant Tailors.* George H. Tappen, Tappen & Pierson, N. Y. C.

DIVISION VII

Millinery Goods and Kindred Lines. Leon Goodman, Pres., Goodman-Nicholson Co., N. Y. C.; M. W. Amberg, Amberg, Schwab & Co., N. Y. C.

DIVISION VIII

2. *Jewelry and Precious Stones, Jewelers' Supplies and Tools.* William N. Behrens, N. Y. C.; Lazare Kaplan, S. Kaplan & Co., N. Y. C.; Arthur Lorsch, Pres., Albert Lorsch & Co., Inc., N. Y. C.; H. Ollendorff, Pres., I. Ollendorff Co., Inc., N. Y. C.; Jacob Hollander, Castle Co., N. Y. C.; David Belais, N. Y. C.

3. *Watches, Clocks, Bronzes.* J. Fahys Cook, Treas., Jos. Fahys & Co., N. Y. C.; Ralph H. Matthiessen, Pres., Western Clock Co., La Salle, Ill.

DIVISION IX

1. *Crockery, China, Glassware, etc.* Charles K. Ovington, N. Y. C.; Marcy L. Jacobs, Gotham Glass Co., N. Y. C.

DIVISION X

1. *Automobiles, Aeroplanes, Bicycles, Supplies and Accessories.* B. M. Asch, Pres., Asch & Co., Inc., N. Y. C.; Frank B. Nostrand, Dist. Mgr., Inc. Autocar Sales & Service Co., The, N. Y. C.; N. W. Durnin, Sec., Houpert Machine Co., L. I. City; A. G. Southworth, Mgr., Buick Motor Car Co., N. Y. C.; John B. Hulett, Pres., Auto Sales Corp. N. Y. C.; A. J. Brosseau, Pres., Mack Trucks, Inc., N. Y. C.; E. P. Chalfant (N. S. P. A.), Detroit, Mich., John Raskob, General Motors Corp., N. Y. C.

DIVISION XI

1. *Hides, Leather, Belting, etc.* Sylvan M. Barnet, Pres., Barnet Leather Co., Inc., N. Y. C.; Volmer H. Houlberg, Pres., Volmer H. Houlberg, Inc., N. Y. C.; Max Eisman, N. Y. C.

2. *Boots, Shoes and Footwear.* Raymond Morse, Cantilever Corp., Brooklyn; E. H. Krom, Pres., G. R. Kinney Co., Inc.; Frank Grossman, Julius Grossman, Inc., Brooklyn.

3. *Shoemakers, Findings and Supplies.* Anthony L. Aste, Pres. and Treas., Griffin Manufacturing Co., Inc., N. Y. C.

DIVISION XII

1. *Drugs, Chemicals, Manufacturing Pharmacists, Proprietary Medicines, Essential Oils, Medicinal Oils.* S. M. Hermann, Pres., Apex Chemical Co., Inc., N. Y. C.; G. V. Sheffield, Innis, Speidon & Co., Inc., N. Y. C.; Louis J. Ellinger, Kay & Ellinger, Inc., N. Y. C.; E. M. Allen, Pres., Mathieson, Alkali Works, Inc., N. Y. C.; William Jay Schieffelin, Ch. of Bd., Schieffelin & Co., N. Y. C.; J. Edward Young, Jr., Thurston & Braidich, N. Y. C.; H. J. Peffer, Treas., American Solvents & Chemical Co., N. Y. C.; Irving Hochstadter, Stillman & Van Sicklen Co., N. Y. C.; Franklin H. Kalbfleish, Pres., Kalbfleish Corp., N. Y. C.; George B. Hulme, Pres., Brooklyn Osage Oil Co., N. Y. C.

2. *Druggists' Sundries.* J. F. Jelenko, J. F. Jelenko & Co., N. Y. C.; I. Silverberg, Bonnie B. Co., N. Y. C.

3. *Colors, Dyestuffs, etc.* Herman A. Metz, Pres., H. A. Metz & Co., Inc., N. Y. C.; Ernest Gossweiler, Treas. and Gen. Mgr., Sandoz Chemical Works, Inc., N. Y. C.; Arthur L. Somers, Lavanberg Co., N. Y. C.

4. *Miscellaneous Chemical Products.* W. F. Carey, N. Y. C.; Jos. E. Roan, Binney & Smith Co., N. Y. C.; E. K. Speiden, Speiden-Whitfield Co., Inc., N. Y. C.; I. A. Hays, Union Oil Co. of California, San Francisco, California; Avery D. Andrews, Rep. of Royal Dutch-Shell Companies, N. Y. C.; Herbert J. Carr, Pres., Carr Brothers, Inc., N. Y. C.; Daniel G. Adams, Pres., Shere Lubricator Co., N. Y. C.; William B. Hill, Hoagland Laboratory, N. Y. C.

6. *Paints, Varnishes, Painters' Supplies, etc.* Henry L. Calman, Emil Calman & Co., Inc., N. Y. C.; W. E. Miller, Mgr., Coignet Chemical Products Co., Inc., N. Y. C.; F. W. Davis, Jr., Pres., Detroit Graphite Co., N. Y C.;

Fred W. Herz, Pres., National Varnish Co., L. I. C.; J. W. Robson, Pres., Standard Varnish Works, N. Y. C.; H. E. Hendrickson, S. Winterborne & Co., N. Y. C.; Geo. V. Horgan, Gen. Mgr., National Paint, Oil & Varnish Assn. N. Y. C.

DIVISION XIII

2. *Typewriters, Mimeograph, Multigraph, Computing, Recording, Registering, Sealing, Check Protection and Writing Machines and Supplies, etc.* B. L. Winchell, Ch. and Pres., Remington Typewriter Co., N. Y. C.

4. *General Stationery.* H. W. Rogers, Wilbur & Hastings, N. Y. C.; Aaron Gottlieb, Pres., L. Gottlieb & Sons, Inc., N. Y. C.

5. *Stationers' Supplies and Specialties.* Benjamin Rosenthal, Pres., Russel Playing Card Co., N. Y. C.

DIVISION XIV

1. *Book and News Paper, Cardboard, Cigarette Paper, Gummed Paper, Pasteboard, etc.* Samuel Samuels, Sec., American Corrugated Paper Products Corp., N. Y. C.; J. A. McKelvey, Atterbury & McKelvey, N. Y. C.; Wm. B. Ebbets, Sec. & Gen. Mgr., Coy, Disbrow & Co., Inc., N. Y. C.; Alvah Miller, H. C. Craig & Co., Inc., N. Y. C.; A. L. Kennelly, Pres., Kennelly Paper Co., Inc., N. Y. C.; Edgar Richard, Pres., Pejepscott Paper Co., N. Y. C.; Edward A. Westfall, V. P., H. A. Craig & Co., N. Y. C.; Joseph H. McCormick, Herman Scott, Chalfant, Inc., N. Y. C.

2. *Writing Paper, Envelopes, etc.* Spencer Lathrop, Lasher & Lathrop, Inc., N. Y. C.; W. D. Ramsburg, Gen. Mgr., Standard Envelope Co., Inc., N. Y. C.; G. Alfred Knoche, N. Y. C.; B. A. Franklin, Strathmore Paper Co., Mittenague, Mass.

3. *Wrapping Paper, Paper Bags, Twine, etc.* Max Weill, Treas., The Mutual Paper Co., Inc., N. Y. C.; Wm. V. Hawkins, Columbian Rope Co., N. Y. C.; George W. T. Skinner, Pres., Skinner & Co., N. Y. C.

5. *Waste Material.* Charles M. Haskins, Natl. Assn. Waste Material Dealers, N. Y. C.

DIVISION XV

1. *Printing and Binding Machinery, Printers' Supplies, etc.* H. R. Swartz, Pres., R. Hoe & Co., N. Y. C.

2. *Printing and Binding.* Joseph E. Hindle, Pres., J. E. Hindle Co., Inc., N. Y. C.; Raymond E. Baylis, Pres., Eugene C. Lewis Co., N. Y. C.; Erich E. Lehsten, New York Rep., Maryland Color Printing Co., N. Y. C.; Nathan Eibschutz, Pres., The Night & Day Press, Inc., N. Y. C.; John C. Powers, Pres., The John C. Powers Co., Inc., N. Y. C.; Robert H. Wessman, Treas., J. F. Tapley Co., L. I. C.; Charles Francis, Pres., Chas. Francis Press, N. Y. C.

3. *Engraving, Lithographing, Embossing, Stamping, Designing, etc.* Philip Sheinkman, Lutz & Sheinkman, Inc., N. Y. C.; R. J. Shoemaker, American Lithographic Co., N. Y. C.; C. S. Hammond, C. S. Hammond & Co., N. Y. C.

DIVISION XVII

1. *Leaf Tobacco.* Ery Kehaya, Pres., The Standard Commercial Tobacco Co., N. Y. C.; Fred Singer, Pres., Singer & Mayer, Inc., N. Y. C.; Ernest Ellinger, Pres., Ernest Ellinger & Co., N. Y. C.

2. *Cigars, Cigarettes, Tobacco and Cigarette Boxes.* E. A. Kline, E. A. Kline & Co., N. Y. C.

3. *Tobacconists' Sundries.* Leopold Demuth, Pres., Wm. Demuth & Co., N. Y. C.

DIVISION XVIII

1. *Architects.* Thomas Hastings, Carrere & Hastings, N. Y. C.

2. *Contracting Engineers, Building Construction, Building and General Contractors, etc.* Otto M. Eidlitz, Marc Eidlitz & Son, N. Y. C.; Harry Alexander, Harry Alexander, Inc., N. Y. C.; George J. Atwell, George J. Atwell Co., Inc., N. Y. C.; Walter B. Faddis, Cauldwell-Wingate Co., N. Y. C.; Edward Parsons Corning, Pres., Edward Corning Co., N. Y. C.; Benjamin Leavin, Pres., Eastern Construction Co., Inc., N. Y. C.; John C. Hatzel, Pres., Hatzel & Buehler, Inc., N. Y. C.; Gustave Lobo, Pres., Kelvin Engineering Co., Inc., N. Y. C.; Fred T. Ley, Pres., Fred T. Ley & Co., Inc., N. Y. C.; T. C. Desmond, N. Y. C.; Max Baumann, N. Y. C.; W. Boardman Reed, The Engineers' Club, N. Y. C.; John A. Mulligan, Pres., John A. Mulligan, Inc., N. Y. C.; James O. Oliver, James O. Oliver & Co., N. Y. C.; Andrew J. Post, Sec., Post & McCord, Inc., N. Y. C.; A. Milton Napier, Pres., Tide-Water Building Co., N. Y. C.; John L. Flagg, Pres., Watson-Flagg Engineering Co., N. Y. C.; L. J. Horowitz, Thompson Starrett Co., N. Y. C.; Henry G. Turner, Turner Construction, N. Y. C.; Wm. Kennedy, Pres., Wm. Kennedy Construction Co., N. Y. C.; P. J. Carlin, Pres., P. J. Carlin Construction Co., N. Y. C.; J. R. Kilpatrick, V. P., George A. Fuller Co., N. Y. C.; Peter Grimm, Building Managers & Owners' Assn., N. Y. C.; Charles A. Stone, Stone & Webster, N. Y. C.

3. *Masonry Materials, Plasterers' Materials.* M. W. Haney, W. Schuette Co., N. Y. C.; Albert Moyer, Asst. Pres., Vulcanite Portland Cement Co., N. Y. C.; Charles Aubrey Nichles, V. P., Empire Construction Co., N. Y. C.; Franklin Brook, Gen. Counsel, Standard Soapstone, N. Y. C.

4. *Lumber and Timber.* W. W. Schupner, Sec. Man. Dir., Natl. Amer. Wholesale Lumber Assn., N. Y. C.; E. L. Barnard, Bronx, N. Y.

5. *Sash, Doors, Trim, Skylights, Floors, etc.* Alexander Konta, V. P., Perfect Window Regulator Co., Inc., N. Y. C.

6. *Mantels, Grates, Tiles, etc.* William W. Jackson, Pres., Edwin A. Jackson & Bro., Inc., N. Y. C.; Benjamin D. Traitel, Pres., The Traitel Marble Co., Long Island City.

7. *Plumbing, Ventilation, Gas and Steamfitting and Supplies, Asbestos and Magnesia Products.* J. B. Owens, Pres., Empire Floor & Wall Tile Co., N. Y. C.; E. F. Keating, Pres., E. F. Keating Co., N. Y. C.

9. *Gas and Electric Fixtures.* Edwin R. Welles, Pres., The Fink Co., Inc., N. Y. C.

10. *Elevators, Elevator Appliances, Repairs, etc.* Marcellus Staley, Pres., Staley Electric Elevator & Machine Co., N. Y. C.

11. *Hoisting Machinery, Derricks, Cranes.* Percy M. Brotherhood, N. Y. C.

13. *Building Supplies, Miscellaneous.* B. A. Schutz, V. P., Central Foundry Co., N. Y. C.; Eugene Pitou, Pres. and Sec., Patent Scaffolding Co., N. Y. C.; H. D. Lounsbury, N. Y. C.; W. S. Quigley, Pres., Bradley Fireproof Products Co., N. Y. C.

DIVISION XIX

1. *Cabinet Woods and Veneers.* M. Hill, Hawes (Willard) Co., Inc., N. Y. C.

2. *Furniture, Interior Decorations, Works of Art and Decoration.* Andrew J. Connell, College Point, L. I.; Max Guggenheim, N. Y. C.; P. D. Wright, N. Y. Sample Furniture Co., N. Y. C.

3. *Wall Paper.* Henry Burn, Pres., Robert Graves Co., The, N. Y. C.

DIVISION XX

Bank, Office, Store Fittings, Display Frames and Furniture. W. H. Mount, Mount & Robertson, Inc.; Richard A. Jonas, Oxford Filing Supply Co., Bklyn., C. W. Knox, Minneapolis School Supply Co., Minneapolis, Minn.; R. T. Clayton, Educational Exchange Co., Birmingham, Ala.

DIVISION XXI

1. *Iron, Steel, Various Metals.* W. H. Pouch, Pres., Concrete Steel Co., N. Y. C.; Berthold Hochschild, Amer. Metal Co., N. Y. C.; P. L. Guiterman, Vice President, Guiterman & Co., N. Y. C.; Charles M. Smith, Pres., Colonial Iron Co., N. Y. C.; Max Bauman, Pres., Geo. S. Holme Co., N. Y. C.; Philip J. Goodheart, Cast Iron Pipe Foundry, N. Y. C.; Milton L. Lissberger, Pres., Marks, Lissberger & Son, L. I. C.

2. *Railway Supplies.* Warren J. Lynch, V. P., American Steel Foundries, N. Y. C.; C. F. Quincy, Pres., Q. & C., Co. N. Y. C.; B. B. Greer, Pres., N. Y. Air Brake Co., N. Y. C.; R. W. Marshall, Pres., Transit Equipment Co., N. Y. C.

4. *Machinery, Machinists' Tools, Supplies, etc.* Medad E. Stone, Pres., Tucker Co., Inc., N. Y. C.; C. Philip Coleman, Pres., Worthington Pump & Machinery Co., N. Y. C.; Grant N. Spear, N. Y. C.

DIVISION XXII

1. *Builders' and Cabinet Hardware, Tools, Cutlery, etc.* Clement M. Biddle, Pres., Biddle Purchasing Co., N. Y. C.; Frank J. Oliver, Pres.-Treas., Oliver Brothers, Inc., N. Y. C.; John H. Towne, Yale & Towne Mfg. Co., N. Y. C.

2. *House Furnishing Goods.* F. L. Goetz, Long Island City; W. J. Berry, C. H. and E. S. Goldberg, N. Y. C.

4. *Brass Goods, Metal Goods, Metal Ceilings, Sheet Metals, Sheet Metal Products, Tin-Foil, etc.* Fred J. Treiber, Stieglitz-Treiber Co., N. Y. C.

DIVISION XXIII

1. *Electrical Apparatus and Supplies—Radio Sets and Accessories.* J. J. Raftery, Pres., J. H. Bunnell & Co., Inc., N. Y. C.; Wm. Dubilier, Pres., Dubilier Condenser & Radio, N. Y. C.; Alex Eisemann, Pres., Freed Eisemann Corp., Bklyn.; Wm. R. Goodman, Treas., Sperry Gyroscope Co., Bklyn.; H. B. Gilmore, Sec., Western Electric Co., Inc., N. Y. C.; Chas. E. Stephens, Mgr., Westinghouse Electric & Mfg. Co., N. Y. C.; R. W. Smith, Natl. Assn. of Light Equipment Dealers, N. Y. C.; E. W. Rice, Jr., Hon. Ch. B. of D., General Electric Co., N. Y. C.

2. *Electrical Contractors.* L. K. Comstock, Ch. of Bd., L. K. Comstock & Co., N. Y. C.; Charles L. Eidlitz, Chas. L. Eidlitz Co., N. Y. C.

DIVISION XXIV

1. *Light, Heat and Power Service.* Cornell S. Howley, Consolidated Car Heating Co., N. Y. C.; Arthur Williams, V. P. Commercial Relations, New York Edison Co., N. Y. C.; Frank W. Smith, V. P., United Electric Light & Power Co., N. Y. C.; John W. Lieb, Pres. Electrical Testing Laboratories.

DIVISION XXVI

1. *Railroads.* Gerhard M. Dahl, Bklyn.-Manhattan Transit Corp., N. Y. C.; Juliens L. Eysmans, V. P., Penn. R. R. Co., Phila.; B. F. Yoakum, N. Y. C.

2. *Express, Delivery Service, Domestic and Foreign Forwarding, Freight Agents, Ship Brokers.* Fred O. Nelson, Jr., Pres., Fred O. Nelson Co., Inc., N. Y. C.

3. *Steamship Companies and Agents, Ship Brokers, Marine Engineering, Drydocks, Towing, Lightering, etc.* Chas. M. Barnett, Clinchfield Navigation Co., Inc., N. Y. C.; Fred B. Dalzell, V. P., Dalzell Towing Co., Inc., N. Y. C.; J. J. Glatzmeyer, Asst. Sec., Merritt-Chapman Scott Corp., N. Y. C.; E. P. Morse, V. P. and Gen. Mgr., Morse Dry Dock & Repair Co., N. Y. C.; Chas. H. Potter, Pres., Potter SS Co. Inc., N. Y. C.; Frank C. Munson, Munson SS Line, N. Y. C.; Howard E. Jones, Jas. W. Elwell & Co., Inc., N. Y. C.

5. *Cartage.* J. A. Hoffman, V. P., Motor Haulage Co., Inc., Bklyn.

6. *Warehousing Wharfage, Household Storage, Moving, Packing, and Safe Deposit.* Mason F. Grymes, N. Y. C.

DIVISION XXVII

1. *Hotels, Restaurants and Caterers, Equipment and Supplies.* Arthur L. Lee, Mgr. Dir., Hotel McAlpin, N. Y. C.; David H. Knott, Pres., Knott Hotels Corp., N. Y. C.; Wm. Childs, Jr., V. P., Childs Co., N. Y. C.

DIVISION XXVIII

1. *Amusement Interests, Industrial Expositions, etc.* Nathan Hirsch, Aywon Film Co., N. Y. C.; C. B. Paine, University Picture Co., N. Y. C.;

Winthrop Ames, N. Y. C.; Frank W. Darling, L. A. Thompson Scenic R. R. Co., N. Y. C.; R. F. Woodhull, Dover, N. J.; Sol Raives, N. Y. C.

DIVISION XXIX

1. *Photographers, Art, Photographic and Kindred Lines.* J. L. Long, Practical Drawing Co., Dallas, Texas.

DIVISION XXX

1. *Music Trades.* Chas. H. Votey, Aeolian Company, N. Y. C.; W. Rodman Fay, Pres., G. Schirmer, Inc., N. Y. C.; Mark P. Campbell, Pres., Brambach Piano Co., N. Y. C.

DIVISION XXXI

1. *Newspapers, Publishers, Booksellers and Kindred Lines.* Charles Scribner, Jr., Chas. Scribner's Sons, N. Y. C.; J. A. Holden, Sec., R. R. Bowker Co., N. Y. C.; Charles W. Gerstenberg, Prentice Hall Inc., N. Y. C.; Bernon T. Woodle, Pres., International Trade Developer Corp., N. Y. C.; J. Malcolm Muir, V. P., McGraw Hill Co., Inc., N. Y. C.; A. H. Nelson, V. P., The Macmillan Co., N. Y. C.; Wm. A. Johnston, Pres., Motion Picture News, Inc., N. Y. C.; C. C. Lane, Bus. Mgr., New York Eve. Post, Inc., N. Y. C. Wm. W. McIntosh, V. P., Oxford University Press—American Branch, N. Y. C.; Frederick A. Stokes, Frederick A. Stokes Co., N. Y. C.; Wm. A. Friedman, Carey Craft Press, N. Y. C.; Fritz Frank, Iron Age Publishing Co., N. Y. C.; Harry P. Burt, A. L. Burt Co., N. Y. C.; Wm. S. Johnston, Ch. of Bd. of Dir., F. M. Lupton Publishers, Inc., N. Y. C.; Edwin S. Friendly, New York Sun, N. Y. C.; Arnold Sanchez, New York Times, N. Y. C.; Louis Wiley, New York Times, N. Y. C.; Roy W. Howard, Ch. of Bd. of Dir., Scripps-Howard Newspapers, Inc., N. Y. C.; A. Knopf, Pres., A. Knopf, Inc., N. Y. C.; Lee W. Maxwell, Pres., Crowell Pub. Co., N. Y. C.; Franklin W. Lee, F. W. Lee, Pub. Co., N. Y. C.; Truman S. Morgan, F. W. Dodge Corp., N. Y. C.; Charles G. Phillips, N. Y. C.; Edward H. Davis, U. S. Tobacco Journal, N. Y. C.; Chas. W. Price, Ch. of Bd., International Trade Press, Inc., N. Y. C.; A. C. Pearson, United Publishers' Corp., N. Y. C.

2. *Dramatists.* Channing Pollock, N. Y. C.; Arthur Richman, Pres., American Dramatists, N. Y. C.

DIVISION XXXII

1. *Banks and Trust Companies.* Saul Singer, Bank of United States, N. Y. C.; Wm. S. Irish, V. P., First National Bank of Brooklyn, Bklyn.; A. P. Smith, Pres., Franklin National Bank in New York, N. Y. C.; R. W. Poor, Garfield National Bank, N. Y. C.; Willard V. King, N. Y. C.; James S. Jonas, Pres., Manufacturers' Trust Co., N. Y. C.; Louis G. Kaufman, Pres., Chatham Phoenix Natl. Bk., N. Y. C.; Victor A. Lersner, Pres., Bowery Savings Bank, N. Y. C.; Robert S. Adamson, Ch. B., Natl. Amer. Bank, N. Y. C.; Arthur J. Morris, Pres., Industrial Acceptance Corp., N. Y. C.; Geo. E. Roberts, Natl. City Bank of N. Y.

2. *Bankers and Brokers.* Edward Allen Pierce, N. Y. C.; Fredk. A. Far-

rar, N. Y. C.; M. W. Harrison, National Association Owners Railroad Securities, N. Y. C.; C. B. Hibbard, N. Y. C.; Richard W. Lawrence, Pres., Bankers' Coml. Security Company, N. Y. C.; Clarence Y. Palitz, N. Y. C.; Credit Alliance Corp., N. Y. C.; Sam A. Lewisohn, Adolph Lewisohn & sons, N. Y. C.; Arthur D. Mendes, Times Sq. Trust Co., N. Y. C.; Edmund C. Lynch, Merrill, Lynch & Co., N. Y. C.; Alfred H. Newburger, Newburger, Henderson & Loeb, N. Y. C.; Acosta Nichols, Spencer Trask & Co., N. Y. C.; Matthew C. Brush, Pres., Amer. Internatl. Corp., N. Y. C.; W. C. Langley, Pres., Anderson Cotton Mills, N. Y. C.; Henry R. Ickelheimer, Heidelbach, Ickelheimer & Co., N. Y. C.; James A. Stillman, Dir. American Internatl. Corp., N. Y. C.; Lionel Sutro, N. Y. C.; Arthur Lehman, Lehman Bros., N. Y. C.; R. E. Dowling, City Investing Co., N. Y. C.; Samuel Sachs, Goldman Sachs & Co.

DIVISION XXXIII

1. *Fire Insurance Companies, Managers, General Agents, etc.* Hamilton Fish, Jr., John C. Paige & Co., Inc., N. Y. C.; Wm. Y. Wemple, Sec., Meinel & Wemple, Inc., N. Y. C.; Joseph John Keon, Pres., Amer. Insurance Assn., N. Y. C.

2. *Life Insurance Companies, Managers, General Agents, etc.* James G. Basinger, Con. Eng. & Econ., Home Life Ins. Co., N. Y. C.; Wm. A. Marshall, Chairman, Home Life Insurance Co., N. Y. C.

3. *Marine Insurance.* Philip Thiel, T. F. Wilmot & Co., N. Y. C.; Douglas P. Cox, Appleton & Cox, Inc., N. Y. C.

4. *Fidelity, Casualty, Title and Foreign Credit Insurance.* R. R. Brown, American Surety Co. of N. Y., N. Y. C.; Henry J. Davenport, Pres., Home Title Insurance Co., Bklyn.; Charles H. Holland, Pres., Independence Companies, Phila.; Joseph D. Bookstaver, Gen. Agt., Travelers Ins. Co., N. Y. C.

5. *Insurance Brokers, Adjusters, etc.* Wm. C. De Lancy, De Lancy, Kipp & Swan, N. Y. C.

DIVISION XXXIV

1. *Real Estate Dealers, Agents, Brokers, Investors, etc.* Clarke G. Dailey, Alliance Realty Co., N. Y. C.; Lawrence B. Elliman, Pease & Elliman, N. Y. C.; Wm. H. Cary, Cary, Harmon & Co., Bklyn.; Logan Billingsley, Billingsley Realty Co., N. Y. C.; Max Goldsmith, Pres., Alger Realty Co., N. Y. C.; Alfred R. Kirkus, N. Y. C.; Stuart Hirschman, Pres., Bayside-Flushing Co., N. Y. C.; Joseph P. Day, N. Y. C.; Frank Bailey, Ch. B., Benson Nurst Co., N. Y. C.; J. Wilson Dayton, Bayside, L. I.

DIVISION XXXV

1. *Export and Import Merchants.* Wm. Harris Douglas, Arkell & Douglas, Inc., N. Y. C.; Charles Hardy, Pres., Associated Metals & Minerals Corp., N. Y. C.; I. B. Catz, Pres., Catz American Co., Inc., N. Y. C.; A. S. Cookman, N. Y. C.; H. T. Seymour, V. P., Dodge & Seymour, Ltd., N. Y. C.; Geo. C. Fernandez, R. Fabien & Co., N. Y. C.; A. C. Fox, A. C. Fox & Co., N. Y. C.; Waldemar H. Grassi, L. Gandolfi & Co., N. Y. C.; Max Gold-

smith, V. P., Goldsmith & Co., Inc., N. Y. C.; Fred H. Conklin, Conklin & Harrington, N. Y. C.; H. E. Bulling, N. Y. C.; Ralph B. Annis, Bklyn.; Frank E. Irsch, N. Y. C.; K. M. Johns, Treas., Los Fabricantes Unidos, Inc., N. Y. C.; Louis Watjen, V. P., Nash, Watjen & Banks, Ltd., N. Y. C.; Geo. F. Taylor, Geo. F. Taylor Co., N. Y. C.; K. C. Li, K. C. Li, N. Y. C.; Wm. E. Leuchtenberg, Alpha-Lux Co., N. Y. C.; Wm. Hosken, N. Y. C.; G. A. Paul, N. Y. C.; Wm. H. Lake, Graham, Hinkley & Co., N. Y. C.; Adolph Wimpfheimer, Adolph Wimpfheimer & Co., N. Y. C.; James R. Lewis, N. Y. C.; E. Stanley Glines, N. Y. C.; P. L. Guiterman, Guiterman Co., Inc., N. Y. C.; Waldemar Muller, V. P., Daarnhaumer & Co., Inc., N. Y. C.

2. *Ores, Mine Products, Smelting and Refining.* Philip W. Henry, Pres., Achotla Mines Co., N. Y. C.; A. P. Cobb, V. P., New Jersey Zinc Co., N. Y. C.; Olin J. Stephens, N. Y. C.

DIVISION XXXVIII

1. *Accountants and Auditors.* James Frederick White, N. Y. C.; Wm. Henry Dennis, N. Y. C.; James A. Councillor, Pres., American Society of C. P. A., Washington, D. C.; C. W. Finney, Pres., American Institute of Accountants, N. Y. C.

3. *Consulting Engineers.* John J. Cone, Pres., Robert W. Hunt Co., N. Y. C.; Homer L. Bartlett, Brooklyn.

5. *Lawyers and Doctors.* Drury W. Cooper, Cooper, Kerr & Dunham, N. Y. C.; Geo. H. Engelhard, Engelhard, Pollak, Pitcher & Stern, N. Y. C.; Holland S. Duell, Klauder-Weldon Dyeing Machine Co., N. Y. C.; James M. Gifford, Merrill, Rogers, Gifford & Woody, N. Y. C.; Geo. F. Allison, N. Y. C.; Henry B. Twombly, N. Y. C.; Herman E. S. Chayes, D.D.S., N. Y. C.; Paul R. Stillman, M.D., N. Y. C.; Walter H. Crittenden, N. Y. C.; Thaddeus P. Hyatt, Metropolitan Life Insurance Co., N. Y. C.; Louis O. Bergh, Marvin & Bergh, N. Y. C.

DIVISION XXXIX

2. *Advertising.* Geo. E. Harris, Pres., Dauchy Co., N. Y. C.; Edward Kramer, Kramer Direct Advertising, N. Y. C.; E. D. Hill, Treas., McCann, H. K. Co., N. Y. C.; M. Robert Herman, V. P., Albert Frank & Co., N. Y. C.; Gilbert Kinney, V. P., J. Walter Thompson Co., N. Y. C.

DIVISION XL

Sporting Goods and Allied Lines, Firearms, Ammunitions and Explosives. Abram Davega, Davega-Lurie, N. Y. C.; T. A. Dwyer, The Brunswick-Balke Collender Co., N. Y. C.; H. Boardman Spalding, V. P., Spalding, A. G., & Bros., N. Y. C.

DIVISION XLIII

Rubber, Rubber Goods and Kindred Lines. Robert Badenhop, N. Y. C.; Francis R. Henderson, Pres., Henderson, Helm & Co., Inc., N. Y. C.;

Chas. T. Wilson, Pres., Charles T. Wilson Co., Inc., N. Y. C.; J. Maguire, Pres., Maguire Rubber Co., N. Y. C.; Max Loewenthal, N. Y. C.

DIVISION XLIV

Brooms, Bristles, Brushes, etc. Wm. F. Howard, Howard Brush Co., N. Y. C.; L. W. Wolff, Huesmann & Co., N. Y. C.; A. McEwen, Pres., Ox Fibre Brush Co., N. Y. C.

DIVISION XLVII

2. *Nursery Stock, Seeds, Bulbs, Plants, etc.* Frederick W. Kelsey, Pres., F. W. Kelsey Nursery Co., N. Y. C.

3. *Fertilizer and Insecticides.* Myron S. Hazen, American Ag. Chemical Co., N. Y. C.

DIVISION XLVIII

Cooperage, Wooden Boxes and Kindred Lines. Lowell Green, 1st. V. P., Green Co., Inc., N. Y. C.; J. H. Dunning, Pres., J. H. Dunning, Corp., N. Y. C.

DIVISION XLIX

Miscellaneous, Including Public Officials. Percy Mendelson, Pres., Laundry Board of Trade, N. Y. C.; Edwin Lane, Pres., Carolyn Laundry, N. Y. C.; John H. Love, N. Y. C.; John Duval Gluck, Capital & Labor Bureau Economic Research, N. Y. C.; Arthur M. Foran, Comptroller of Customs, New York City; James N. Jarvie, N. Y. C.; Benj. Dennison, N. Y. C.; Milton W. Harrison, Pres., Natl. Assn. Owners of R. R. Securities, N. Y. C.

Unassigned. E. N. Spelden, N. Y. C.; Otto B. Shulhof, N. Y. C.; J. S. Betts, N. Y. C.; Walter F. Ripperger, N. Y. C.

AFFILIATED TRADE ASSOCIATIONS, 1929

American Bottlers of Carbonated Beverages; American Association of Felt and Straw Goods Importers; American Association of Wholesale Opticians; American Fur Merchants Association; American Wholesale Coal Association; American Zinc Institute; Association of Electragists, International; Association of Stock Exchange Firms of New York City; Authors League of America; Automobile Merchants Association of New York; Builders Exchange of Los Angeles; Dramatists Guild of the Authors League of America; Fur Brokers Association of New York; Indianapolis Building Congress; Industrial Alcohol Institute; Institute of Scrap Iron and Steel; Jute and Gunnies Importers Association; Laundry Board of Trade; Managers Protective Association; Master Sign Makers Association; National Association of Amusement Parks; National Association of Purchasing Agents; National Association of Importers of Hides and Skins; National Coal Association; National Council of American Importers & Traders; National Retail Dry Goods Association; National Standard Parts Association; New York Building Congress; New York Carpet Cleaners Association; New York Furniture Warehousemens' Association; Philadelphia Building Congress; Photo Engravers Board of Trade of New York; Shoe Manufacturers

Board of Trade of New York; Society of American Florists and Ornamental Horticulturists; Steel Founders Society of America; Tanners Council of America; Textile Adjusters Association; Wool Institute.

ORGANIZATIONS PARTICIPATING IN EDUCATIONAL WORK (1929)

American Association of Engineers, (Chicago); American Bankers Association, (New York); American Bleached Shellac Manufacturers Association, (New York); American Boiler Manufacturers Association, (New York); American Brush Manufacturers Association, (Philadelphia); American Cider Vinegar Manufacturers Association, (Rochester); American Construction Council, (Washington); American Cotton Waste and Linter Exchange, (Boston); American Drug Manufacturers Association, (Washington); American Exporters and Importers Association, (New York); American Face Brick Association, (Chicago); American Fruit and Vegetable Shippers Association, (Chicago); American Gas Association, (New York); American Gum Importers Association, (New York); American Institute of Accountants, (New York); American Institute of Architects, (Washington); American Institute of The City of New York; American Institute of Consulting Engineers, (New York); American Institute of Electrical Engineers, (New York); American Institute of Marine Underwriters, (New York); American Institute of Mining and Metallurgical Engineers, (New York); American Institute of Refrigeration, (New York and Chicago); American Manufacturers Export Association, (New York); American Oil Burner Association, (New York); American Paper and Pulp Association, (New York); American Photo Engravers Association, (Chicago); American Society for Testing Materials, (Philadelphia); American Society of Certified Public Accountants, (Washington); American Society of Civil Engineers, (New York); American Society of Landscape Architects, (Boston); American Society of Mechanical Engineers, (New York); American Specification Institute, (Chicago); American Spice Trade Association, (New York); American Veneer Package Association, (Washington); American Walnut Manufacturers Association, (Chicago); American Warehousemens Association, (Chicago); Anthracite Institute, (New York); Artistic Lighting Equipment Association, (New York); Asbestos Brake Lining Association, (New York); Asbestos Paper and Millboard Association, (Philadelphia); Associated Dress Industries of America, (New York); Associated General Contractors of America, (Washington); Associated Industries of Florida, (Jacksonville); Associated Industries of The Inland Empire, (Spokane); Associated Industries of New York State, (Buffalo); Associated Industries of Rhode Island, (Providence); Associated Industries of Seattle, (Washington); Associated Leather Goods Manufacturers of the U. S. A., Inc., (New York); Associated Millinery Men, (New York); Associated Pennsylvania Constructors, (Harrisburg, Pa.); Associated Tile Manufacturers of New York City; Association of American Importers of Spanish Green Olives, (New York); Association of American Wood Pulp Importers, (New York); Association of Manufacturers of Woodworking Machinery, (Chicago); Atlanta Foreign Trade Club, (Georgia); Baltimore Drug Exchange Bureau; Baltimore Export Managers Club; Bankers Association for Foreign Trade, (Chicago); Better Bedding Alliance of America, (Chicago); Binders Board Manufacturers Association, (New York); Biscuit and Cracker Manufacturers Association, (New York); Brooklyn Motor Vehicle Dealers Association, (New York); Building Trades Employers Association of New York; Building Trades Employers Association, (Springfield, Mass.); Bureau of Envelope Manufacturers, (New York); California Manufacturers Association, (San Francisco); California State Society of Certified Public Accountants, (Los Angeles); California White and Sugar Pine Manufacturers Association, (San Francisco); Cardboard Manufacturers Association, (New York); Cincinnati Association of Credit Men, (Cincinnati); Clock Manufacturers Association of America, (Philadelphia); Cocoa Merchants Association, (New York); Colorado Bottlers of Carbonated Beverages, (Denver); Colorado Confectioners Association, (Denver); Colorado Manufacturers & Merchants Association, (Denver); Commercial Service Association, (Butte); Common Brick Manufacturers Association, (Cleveland); Compressed Air Socicty, (New York); Connecticut Association of Real Estate Boards, (Hartford); Connecticut Manufacturers Association, (Hartford); Connecticut Manufacturers of Carbonated Beverages, (Waterbury); Connecticut State Society of Certified Public Accountants, (Hartford); Converters Association, (New York); Cotton Yarn Merchants Association, (Philadelphia); Crockery Board of Trade, (New York); Dairy and Ice Cream Machinery Supplies Association, (New York); Dallas Cotton Exchange, (Texas); Dallas Purchasing Agents Association, (Texas); Eastern Millinery Association, (New York); Eastern Soda Water Bottlers Association, (Boston); Eastern Supply Association, (New York); Electrical Contractors Association, (New York); Employing Bookbinders of America, (New York); Employing Bookbinders of New York; Farm Seed Association of North America, (Chicago); Federated Fruit and Vegetable Growers, (New York); Federated Industries of Washington, (Seattle); First District Dental Society of State of New York, (New York); Florida Lumber & Millwork Association, (Orlando); Florists Telegraph Delivery Association, (Detroit); Foreign Exchange Club of New York; Foreign Trade Club of New Haven; Forging Manufacturers Association, (New York); Foundry Equipment Manufacturers Association, (Cleveland); Franklin Typothetae of Cincinnati; Fruit and Produce Dealers Club, (Kansas City, Mo.); Fruit and Produce Trade Association of New York; Fur Brokers Association of New York; General Contractors Association of Louisville, (Louisville, Ky); General Contractors Association of Newark, N. J. and Vicinity; Georgia Association, (Atlanta); Georgia Manufacturers Association, (Atlanta); Glass Container Association of America, (New York); Grain Dealers National Association, (Toledo); Green Coffee Association of New York City; Greeting Card Association, (New York); Hat Institute, (New York); Illinois Manufacturers Association, (Chicago); Independent Oil Men of America, (Chicago); Indiana Bankers Association,

(Indianapolis); Indiana Manufacturers Association, (Indianapolis); Industrial Congress of Arizona, (Phoenix); Industrial Council of the Cloak and Suit Industry, (New York); Institute of Carpet Manufacturers of America, (Washington); International Apple Shippers Association, (Rochester); International Association of Inventors, (Seattle); Interstate Cottonseed Crushers Association, (Dallas); Iowa Manufacturers Association, (Des Moines); Iowa Warehousemen's Association, (Sioux City); Kalamein Door Manufacturers Association, (New York); Kansas Bankers Association, (Topeka); Kansas City Association of Credit Men, (Missouri); Kansas Grain Dealers Association, (Topeka); Label Manufacturers National Association, (New York); Lace and Embroidery Association of America, (New York); Lead Industries Association, (New York); Linen Supply Association, (New York); Long Island Real Estate Board, (New York); Louisiana Manufacturers Association, (New Orleans); Maine Canners Association, (Portland); Manufacturers Association of Bridgeport, (Connecticut); Manufacturers Association of York, (Pennsylvania); Manufacturers and Employers Association of South Dakota, (Sioux Falls); Manufacturing Chemists Association of U. S. A., (Washington); Maryland Association of Certified Public Accountants, (Baltimore); Maryland Bankers Association, (Baltimore); Master Builders Association of Allegheny County, (Pittsburgh); Merchants Ladies Garment Association, (New York); Michigan Association of Certified Public Accountants, (Detroit); Michigan Grain Feed & Hay Dealers Association, (Lansing); Michigan Manufacturers Association, (Detroit); Michigan Wholesale Grocers Association, (Saginaw); Middle Atlantic Fisheries Association, (New York); Minnesota Loggers Association, (Minneapolis); Minnesota Petroleum Association, (Minneapolis); Missouri Bankers Association, (Sedalia); Missouri Grain Dealers Association, (St. Louis); Missouri Society of Certified Public Accountants, (Kansas City); Montana Bankers Association, (Helena); Motor and Equipment Association, (New York); Music Industries Chamber of Commerce, (New York); National American Wholesale Lumber Association, (New York); National Association of Band Instrument Manufacturers, (New York); National Association of Builders Exchanges, (Washington); National Association of Building Owners and Managers, (Chicago); National Association of Building Trades Employers, (Chicago); National Association of Cost Accountants, (New York); National Association of Credit Men, (New York); National Association of Dyers & Cleaners, (Silver Spring, Maryland); National Association of Finishers of Cotton Fabrics, (New York); National Association of Furniture Manufacturers, (Chicago); National Association of Manufacturers of U. S. A., (New York); National Association of Master Plumbers of the United States, (St. Louis); National Association of Men's Apparel Clubs, (Milwaukee); National Association of Merchant Tailors, (New York); National Association of Paint Distributors, (Cincinnati); National Association of Retail Druggists, (Chicago); National Association of Retail Meat Dealers, (Chicago); National Association of Steel Furniture Manufacturers, (Cleveland); National Association of Waste Material Dealers, (New York);

National Association of Wooden Box Manufacturers, (Chicago); National Association of Wool Manufacturers, (Boston); National Automatic Sprinkler Association, (New York); National Battery Manufacturers Association, (New York); National Beauty and Barbers Supply Dealers Association, (New York); National Board of Steam Navigation, (New York); National Boot and Shoe Manufacturers Association, (New York); National Builders Supply Association, (Cleveland); National Clay Products Industries Association, (Chicago); National Coffee Roasters Association, (New York); National Confectioners Association, (Chicago); National Council of American Importers and Traders, (New York); National Food Brokers Association, (Indianapolis); National Furniture Warehousemens Association, (Chicago); National Glass Distributors Association, (Chicago); National Hair and Jute Felt Manufacturers Association, (New York); National Hardwood Lumber Association, (Chicago); National Hay Association, (Winchester, Ind.); National Jewelers Board of Trade, (New York); National Knitted Outerwear Association, (New York); National League of Commission Merchants, (Washington); National Lumber Manufacturers Association, (Washington); National Macaroni Manufacturers Association, (Braidwood, Ill.); National Machine Tool Builders Association, (Cincinnati); National Paint, Oil & Varnish Association, (New York); National Peanut Butter Manufacturers Association, (Chicago); National Peanut Cleaners and Shellers Association, (Suffolk, Virginia); National Pecan Growers Exchange, (Albany, Georgia); National Pickle Packers Association, (Chicago); National Publishers Association, (New York); National Raw Silk Exchange, (New York); National Retail Furniture Association, (Chicago); National Shoe Retailers Association, (Chicago); National Slate Association, (Philadelphia); National Upholstery Textile Association, (New York); National Wholesale Druggists Association, (New York); National Wholesale Grocers Association, (New York); National Wholesale Men's Furnishing Association, (New York); Nebraska Society of Certified Public Accountants, (Lincoln); Neckwear Research Association, (New York); New England Paper Merchants Association, (Boston); New Jersey State Society of Certified Public Accountants, (Newark); New Mexico Bankers Association, (Albuquerque); New York Produce Exchange; New York State Association of Real Estate Boards, (Jamaica); New York State Hay and Grain Dealers Association, (Weedsport); New York State Society of Certified Public Accountants; New York Wholesale Grocers Association, (New York); North Carolina Association of Certified Public Accountants, (Wilmington); North Dakota Bankers Association, (Fargo); Northeastern Retail Lumbermens Association, (Rochester); North Pacific Millers Association, (Tacoma); Ohio Association of Ice Industries, (Toledo); Oklahoma, Associated Industries of, (Oklahoma City); Oklahoma Cotton Seed Crushers Association, (Oklahoma City); Oklahoma Society of Certified Public Accountants, (Tulsa); Oregon Manufacturers Association, (Portland); Oregon Society of Certified Public Accountants, (Portland); Pacific Coast Paper Box Manufacturers Association, (San Francisco); Paper Board Industries Association, (Chicago);

Pennsylvania and Atlantic Seaboard Hardware Association, (Philadelphia); Pennsylvania Institute of Certified Public Accountants, (Pttsburgh and Philadelphia); Philadelphia Board of Trade; Philadelphia Textile Manufacturers Association; Plywood Manufacturers Association, (Chicago); Printing Press Manufacturers Association, (New York); Public Utilities Advertising Association, (Chicago); Purchasing Agents Association of Kansas City; Purchasing Agents Association of New York; Quality Bakers of America, (New York); Refrigerating Machinery Association, (Philadelphia); Retail Dry Goods Association, (New York); Rhode Island Bankers Association, (Pawtucket); Rhode Island Society of Certified Public Accountants, (Providence); Rochester Association of Credit Men; Rubber Manufacturers Association, (New York); Rubber Trade Association of New York; Rug Cleaners Institute of New York, (New York); St Louis Merchants Exchange; Second District Dental Society of State of New York, (New York); Shirting Fabrics Association, (New York); Silk Association of America, (New York); Society of Industrial Engineers, (Chicago); Society of Louisiana Certified Public Accountants, (New Orleans); Society of Terminal Engineers, (New York); Southern Furniture Manufacturers Association, (High Point, N. C.); Southern Pine Association, (New Orleans); Southern Supply and Machinery Dealers Association, (Richmond, Va.); Stationers and Publishers Board of Trade, (New York); Steel Barrel Manufacturers Institute, (Cleveland); Texas Cotton Association, (Waco); Texas Society of Certified Public Accountants, (Dallas); Toy Manufacturers of the United States, (New York); United Roofing Contractors Association of North America, (Chicago); United States Fisheries Association, (New York); United States Good Roads Association, (Birmingham, Ala.); United States Shellac Importers Association, (New York); United States Trade Mark Association, (New York); United Womens Wear League, (New York); Vermont, Associated Industries of, (Montpelier); Virginia Manufacturers Association, (Richmond); Virginia Society of Certified Public Accountants, (Richmond); Washington Bankers Association, (Tacoma); Washington, Federated Industries of, (Seattle); Washington, Manufacturers Association of, (Seattle); Washington Society of Certified Public Accountants, (Seattle); Water Works Manufacturers Association, (New York); Webbing Exchange, (New York); Western Society of Engineers, (Chicago); Wholesale Dry Goods Institute, (New York); Wilmington, Manufacturers Association of, (Delaware); Wisconsin Canners Association, (Madison); Wisconsin Manufacturers Association, (Madison); Wisconsin Petroleum Association, (Milwaukee); Writing Paper Manufacturers Association, (Springfield, Mass.); Wyoming Bankers Association, (Cheyenne); York Manufacturers Association, (Pennsylvania); Youngstown Association of Credit Men, (Ohio).

ARBITRATION COMMITTEE, 1926

Charles L. Guy, Chairman; James Brown, Julius Henry Cohen, J. Winter Davis, Frances Kellor, Robert H. Montgomery, William C. Redfield, J. Noble Braden, Secretary.

Arbitration Committee, 1947

Franklin E. Parker, Jr., Chairman; James S. Carson, Ralph F. Colin, S. Whitney Landon, John T. McGovern, Wesley A. Sturges, and Frances Kellor, *ex officio* and J. Noble Braden, Secretary.

Arbitration Law Committee, 1926

Edwin L. Garvin, Edwin M. Borchard, Philip Marshall Brown, Charles C. Burlingham, Joseph P. Chamberlain, Kenneth Dayton, Charles Evans Hughes, Jr., Kenneth O'Brien, Wesley A. Sturges.

Arbitration Law Committee, 1947

Wesley A. Sturges, Chairman; William H. Ransom, Vice Chairman; John R. Abersold, Arthur A. Ballantine, Edwin M. Borchard, Robert R. Bruce, Julius Henry Cohen, Walter J. Derenberg, Phanor J. Eder, Osmond K. Fraenkel, Lloyd K. Garrison, Herman A. Gray, David E. Grant, Arthur K. Kuhn, Milton P. Kupfer, Meyer Kurz, S. Whitney Landon, Joseph Mayper, H. H. Nordlinger, Lionel S. Popkin, Frank H. Sommer, John K. Watson, Quincy Wright, Burton A. Zorn and Martin Domke, Secretary.

Research Council, 1927

Robert Adamson, Chairman, National American Bank, New York City; Albert B. Ashforth, Pres., Albert B. Ashforth, Inc., New York City; Sylvan M. Barnet, Pres., Barnet Leather Co., New York City; Clement M. Biddle, Treas., Biddle Purchasing Co., New York City; Robert Biddle, Pres., Biddle-Gaumer Co., Phila., Pa.; Leo S. Bing, Bing & Bing, New York City; John McE. Bowman, Pres., Bates-Bowman Corp., New York City; Ancel J. Brower, Pres., Blanchard Press, Inc., New York City; R. R. Brown, Pres., American Surety Co., New York City; C. W. Chabot, Chairman, Committee on Dist. Paper Industry, Erie, Pa.; L. K. Comstock, Pres., L. K. Comstock & Co., Inc., New York City; Douglas F. Cox, Pres., Appleton & Co., Inc., New York City; W. Clive Crosby, Pres., Lawrence Son & Gerrish, Inc., New York City; W. R. Cummings, Vice Pres., Monroe Calculating Machine Co., Orange, N. J.; P. C. Davis, Haskins & Sells, Seattle, Wash.; Leopold Demuth, Pres., William Demuth & Co., New York City; James H. Dunning, Pres., J. H. Dunning Corp., New York City; B. W. Dyer, Vice Pres. and Sec., Lamborn & Co., Inc., New York City; Lee J. Eastman, Pres., Packard Motor Car Co. of N. Y., New York City; William E. Ebbets, Sec. and Gen. Mgr., Coy, Disbrow & Co., New York City; S. A. Everitt, Treas., Doubleday, Page & Co., Garden City, N. Y.; A. C. Fetterolf, Vice. Pres., International Merc. Marine Co., New York City; B. A. Franklin, Vice Pres., Strathmore Paper Co., Mitteneague, Mass.; James S. Gilbert, Pres., Dexter Folder Co., New York City; Lowell Green, 1st Vice Pres., The Green Co., Inc., New York City; B. B. Greer, Pres., New York Air Brake Co., New York City; M. L. Griswold, Vice Pres., Rogers & Co., New York City; P. L. Guiterman, Vice Pres., Guiterman Co., Inc., New York City; Howard S. Hadden, Pres.,

Dorland Agency, New York City; H. A. Halligan, Vice Pres., Western Electric Co., New York City; Herbert Harley, Sec., American Judicature Society, Chicago, Ill.; Francis H. Henderson, Pres., Henderson, Helm & Co., Inc., New York City; Allerton D. Hitch, American Trading Co., New York City; A. R. Holcombe, Herald-Tribune, New York City; Frank A. Horne, Pres., Merchants' Refrigerating Co., New York City; L. J. Horowitz, Pres., Thompson-Starrett Co., New York City; Thaddeus P. Hyatt, Metropolitan Life Ins. Co., New York City; William H. Johns, Pres., George Batten Co., New York City; Henry P. Kendall, Pres., Kendall Mills, Inc., Boston, Mass.; Messmore Kendall, N. Y. C.; P. H. Kieffer, Pres., Gude Bros. Kieffer Co., New York City; Jesse L. Lasky, Vice Pres., Famous-Players-Lasky Corp., New York City; Spencer Lathrop, Pres., Lasher & Lathrop, Inc., New York City; Edmund V. Lewis, Treas., Lewis & Conger, New York City; B. U. Livingston, Jr., Vice Pres. and Mgr., Keasbey & Mattison Co., New York City; J. G. Livingston, Vice Pres., J. Livingston & Co., New York City; William Loeb, Jr., Vice Pres., American Smelting & Refining Co., New York City; Arthur Lorsch, Pres., Albert Lorsch & Co., Inc., New York City; Edson S. Lott, Pres., United States Casualty Co., New York City; James McHutchinson, McHutchinson & Co., New York City; Dr. Severo Mallet-Provost, Curtis, Mallet-Provost & Colt, New York City; John Markle, Chairman, Industrial Finance Corp., New York City; Morton H. Meinhard, Morton H. Meinhard Co., New York City; Henry F. Mendes, Touche, Niven & Co., New York City; Herman A. Metz, Pres., H. A. Metz & Co., Inc., New York City; Wallace E. Meyers, Louis Meyers & Son, Inc., New York City; Carl E. Milliken, Sec., Motion Picture Distributors and Producers of America, New York City; Stewart L. Mimms, J. Walter Thompson Co.; New York City; Jay Randolph Monroe, Pres., Monroe Calculating Machine Co., Orange, N. J.; Fletcher H. Montgomery, Pres., Knox Hat Co., Inc., Brooklyn, N. Y.; Robert H. Montgomery, Lybrand, Ross Bros. & Montgomery, New York City; William Fellowes Morgan, Pres., Brooklyn Bridge Freezing & Cold Stor., New York City; J. B. Morrell, New York City; Charles S. Morris, Pres., Metropolitan Fireproof Warehouse Corp., New York City; E. P. Morse, Sec.-Treas. and Gen. Mgr., Morse Dry Dock & Repair Co., Brooklyn, N. Y.; Frederick A. Muschenheim, Pres., Hotel Astor, New York City; Frank C. Munson, Pres., Munson Steamship Line, New York City; Kenneth O'Brien, Smythe, Haggerty, King & Corcoran, New York City; Wesley M. Oler, Pres., American Ice Co., Jersey City, N. J.; Frank J. Oliver, Treas., Oliver Brothers, Inc., New York City; Charles K. Ovington, Pres., Ovington Bros. Co., New York City; W. Douglas Owens, Vice Pres., Owens & Phillips, Inc., New York City; Homer S. Pace, Pace & Pace, New York City; George L. Patterson, Pres., Stanley & Patterson, Inc., New York City; A. C. Pearson, Vice Pres., United Publishers Corp., New York City; Andrew J. Post, Pres., Post & McCord, Inc., New York City; William H. Pouch, Pres., Concrete Steel Co., New York City; J. A. Rappaport, Sec.-Treas., Reliance Fireproof Door Co., Brooklyn, N. Y.; I. H. Reynolds, Allis-Chalmers Mfg. Co., Milwaukee, Wis.; C. A. Richards, Pres., C. A. Richards, Inc., New York City; Victor Ridder, Sec., Staats Herold Corp., New York City; Louis J. Robertson, New York City; Henry F. Samstag, Pres., Samstag & Hilder Bros., New York City; William Jay Schieffelin, Chairman of Board, Schieffelin & Co., New York City; Charles P. Schmid, Pres., Trautmann, Bailey & Blampey, New York City; Campbell Scott, Pres., Technical Advisory Corp., New York City; Robert E. Simon, Director, City Housing Corp., New York City; Reginald Heber Smith, Hale & Dorr, Boston, Mass.; Paul Starrett, Pres., Starrett Bros., Inc., New York City; Joseph H. Steinhardt, Steinhardt & Kelly, New York City; Fred M. Stewart, Pres., Fred M. Stewart Co., New York City; H. R. Swartz, Pres., R. Hoe & Co., New York City; J. H. Towne, Sec., The Yale & Towne Mfg. Co., New York City; Benjamin D. Traitel, Pres., Traitel Marble Co., Long Island City, N. Y.; Henry C. Turner, Pres., Turner Construction Co., New York City; George F. Trowbridge, George F. Trowbridge, Inc., New York City; Ludwig Vogelstein, Chairman of Board, The American Metal Co., New York City; Alex. Walker, Pres., Strong-Hewat & Co., Inc., New York City; Thomas J. Watson, Pres., Int. Business Machines Corp., New York City; Arthur Williams, Vice Pres., Commercial Relations, New York Edison Co., New York City; Thomas Williams, I. T. Williams & Sons, New York City; B. L. Winchell, Chairman & Pres., Remington Typewriter Co., New York City; and Marians L. Mora, Pres. Cuban Chamber of Commerce in U. S., New York City.

Educational Council, 1927

Prof. Spurgeon Bell, Bureau of Business Research, Ohio State University, Columbus, O.; Prof. Robert Brookings, President, Institute of Economics, Washington, D. C.; Charles K. Burdick, Dean, Cornell University Law School, Ithaca, N. Y.; Prof. Clarence N. Callender, Wharton School of Finance and Commerce, University of Pennsylvania, Philadelphia, Pa.; Dr. Frederick Cleveland, Boston University; Prof. E. J. Corwin, Princeton University; Prof. Georges F. Doriot, Assistant Dean, Graduate School of Business Administration, Harvard University, Cambridge, Mass.; James C. Egbert, Director, School of Business, Columbia University, New York City; Wm. G. Hale, Dean, Law School of the University of Oregon, Eugene, Ore.; Thomas H. Healy, Assistant Dean, School of Foreign Service, Georgetown University, Washington, D. C.; Prof. Nathan Isaacs, Graduate School of Business Administration, Harvard University; Huger W. Jervey, Dean, Columbia University Law School, New York City; Dr. Samuel McCune Lindsay, President of The Academy of Political Science in the City of New York; Everett W. Lord, Dean, College of Business Administration, Boston University; John T. Madden, Dean, New York University, School of Commerce, Accounts and Finance; C. R. Mann, Director, American Council on Education, Washington, D. C.; Stephen I. Miller, Educational Director, American Institute of Banking, New York City; Roscoe Pound, Dean, Harvard University Law School; Prof. Max Radin, School of Jurisprudence, University of California, Berkeley, California; W. A. Scott, Director, School of Commerce, University of Wisconsin, Madison, Wis.; Frank H. Sommer, Dean, New York University Law School; W. H. Spencer, Dean, University of Chicago School of Commerce and Administration; Assistant Prof. Wesley A. Sturges, Yale University Law School, New Haven, Conn.; A. Wellington Taylor, Dean, New York University Graduate School of Business Administration; John H. Wigmore, Dean, Northwestern University Law School, Evanston, Ill.; and Prof. James T. Young, Wharton School of Finance and Commerce, University of Pennsylvania.

Special Committee of Lawyers, 1933

Kenneth M. Spence, Chairman; Charles C. Burlingham, John Kirkland Clark, Alfred A. Cook, John W. Davis, Kenneth Dayton, Stanleigh P. Friedman, Chauncey B. Garver, Edward S. Greenbaum, John G. Jackson, George W. Martin, George Z. Medalie, John Reynolds, Ralph S. Rounds.

Insurance Companies that Have Submitted Cases to the Accident Claims Tribunal

Aetna Casualty & Surety Co., American Lumbermens Mutual Casualty Co., American Motorists Insurance Co., American Mutual Liability Insurance Co., American Policyholders Insurance Co., American Surety Co., Auto Mutual Indemnity Co., Butchers Mutual Indemnity Co., Century Indemnity Co., Commercial Casualty Insurance Co., Continental Casualty Co., Eagle Indemnity Co., Employers Liability Assurance Corp., Employers Mutual Liability Insurance Co., Fidelity & Casualty Co., Firemans Fund Indemnity Co., General Accident, Fire and Life Assurance Corp., General Exchange Insurance Co., Glens Falls Indemnity Co., Globe Indemnity Co., Great American Indemnity Co., Hardware Mutual Casualty Co., Hartford Accident & Indemnity Co. (New York and Chicago), Home Indemnity Co. (New York and Philadelphia), Interboro Mutual Indemnity Insurance Co., Liberty Mutual Insurance Co. (New York, Brooklyn and Chicago), London Guarantee & Accident Co., London & Lancashire Indemnity Co., Lumber Mutual Casualty Insurance Co., Manhattan Mutual Auto Casualty Co., Maryland Casualty Co. (New York and New Jersey), Massachusetts Bonding & Insurance Co., Metropolitan Casualty Insurance Co., New Amsterdam Casualty Co. (New York and New Jersey), New York Casualty Co., Norwich Union Indemnity Co., Phoenix Indemnity Co., Preferred Accident & Insurance Co., Royal Indemnity Co., Standard Accident & Insurance Co., Sun Indemnity Co., Travelers Insurance Co. (New York and Brooklyn), U. S. Casualty Co. (New York and New Jersey), U. S. Fidelity & Guarantee Co., U. S. Guarantee Co., Zurich General Accident & Liability Insurance Co.

Editorial Council, 1927

Dr. John H. Finley, The New York Times; Donald Bean, Chicago University Press; Henry S. Canby, The Saturday Review; Elizabeth Cutting, North American Review; Edward H. Dodd, Dodd, Mead & Co.; Ferris

Greenslet, Houghton, Mifflin & Co.; Will Howe, Charles Scribners' Sons; W. W. McIntosh, Oxford University Press; Edwin Mims, Vanderbilt University, Nashville, Tenn.; Wesley C. Mitchell, National Bureau of Economics Research; Dana C. Munro, American Historical Association; Thomas B. Wells, Harper's Magazine; and James S. Wilson, The Virginia Quarterly.

Arbitration Journal, Editorial Board, 1937

Honorary Editor: John Bassett Moore; Editorial Board: Lucius R. Eastman, Chairman; Irene L. Blunt, Isaiah Bowman, J. Noble Braden, Roscoe C. E. Brown, Clarence N. Callender, John B. Chevalier, Walter J. Derenberg, Lee J. Eastman, James A. Farrell, Henry C. Flower, Jr., Moses H. Grossman, Antonia Hatvany, Frances Kellor, John T. Madden, Roswell C. McCrea, Malcolm Muir, Willard L. Thorp, Frederick M. Warburg, Thomas J. Watson.

Arbitration Journal, Law Review Committee, 1937

Wesley A. Sturges, Chairman; Arthur A. Ballantine, Edwin H. Cassels, Julius Henry Cohen, Guy Richards Crump, William J. Donovan, Osmond K. Fraenkel, Lloyd K. Garrison, Chauncey B. Garver, Edwin L. Garvin, Nathan Isaacs, Milton P. Kupfer, H. H. Nordlinger, Arthur Nussbaum, Morgan J. O'Brien, Philip G. Phillips, Frank H. Sommer, John H. Wigmore, Burton A. Zorn.

Arbitration Journal, Joint Advisory Board, 1937

Charles L. Bernheimer, James S. Carson, Charles T. Gwynne, Frances Kellor, William H. Knox, Frank H. Sommer.

Arbitration Journal, Business Advisory Committee, 1937

Thomas H. McInnerney, Chairman; William H. Baldwin, Louis K. Comstock, Lawrence B. Elliman, Francis P. Garvan, Samuel McRoberts, Sidney J. Weinberg.

Arbitration Journal, Foreign Collaborators, 1938

René Arnaud, Paris; F. Arroyo Parejo, Caracas; Algot Bagge, Stockholm; Marco I. Barasch, Bucharest; H. M. Barbour, Salisbury, S. Rhodesia; Ruben Barrientos, Tegucigalpa; E. H. v. Baumhauer, Amsterdam; André Boissier, Paris; F. W. Bradshaw, St. John's, N. F.; Antonio S. de Bustamante, Habana; Manuel Castro Quesada, San José; H. Craandijk, Rotterdam; H. Dietler, Zurich; W. T. Creswell, London; Aquiles Elorduy, Mexico, D. F.; Herbert Ertl, Vienna; Ottakar Flanderka, Paris; Manuel Foster R., Santiago; R. S. Fraser, London; F. I. Goloschekin, Moscow; H. C. Gutteridge, Cambridge; J. H. Hamilton, Vancouver; Bernt Hjejle, Copenhagen; Emil v. Hofmannsthal, Vienna; Thomas C. Jackson, Hull; H. J. V. James, Wellington, N. Z.; J. E. James, London; Enrique A. Jaminez, Panama City; J. L. Johnston, Winnipeg; W. P. M. Kennedy, Toronto, Ont.; P. W. Kuo, Shanghai; Roman Kuratow-Kuratowski, Warsaw; Luis F. Latorre, Bogota; James D.

McKenna, St. John; Josef Machek, Prague; Mme. E. N. Makovetskaya, Moscow; Fernand Marquet, Antwerp; Robert Marx, Paris; T. S. Miao, Shanghai; K. W. Middleton, Edinburgh; H. E. Muncks, Berlin; J. Maitland Paxton, Sydney; Roberto Pozzi, Milan; R. Simpson, Capetown; Raymond Streat, Manchester; Seichi Takashima, Tokyo; A. C. Tannahill, Nairobi; Geza Ujlaki, Budapest.

Arbitration Journal, Editorial and Advisory Boards, 1947

Board of Editors: Martin Domke, Ferris Faulkner, Jr., Frances Kellor, Sir Lynden Macassey, Eugene F. Sitterley, Wesley A. Sturges.

Advisory Editorial Board: Thomas W. Ashwell, Algot S. Bagge, William H. Baldwin, Daniel Bloomfield, Edwin M. Borchard, John F. Budd, Leo M. Cherne, Hermann Cooper, Emma Doran, Carl W. Drepperd, Thomas I. Emerson, E. C. K. Finch, Benjamin Fine, Frederick C. Kendall, W. P. M. Kennedy, Leo Nejelski, Stanley T. Olafson, Dwayne Orton, Sylvia F. Porter, Joshua B. Powers, George E. Quisenberry, Morris S. Rosenthal, Frances L. Roth, Chet Shaw, George W. Taylor, Victor Weybright, Thomas F. Wiesen.

Arbitration Magazine, Advisory Editorial Board, 1943

William H. Baldwin, M. F. Bannell, Leo M. Cherne, Carl W. Drepperd, E. C. K. Finch, Frederick C. Kendall, Joshua B. Powers, Maxwell J. Rice, J. E. Sitterley, Gladys G. Straus, Ordway Tead.

American Arbitration Association War Service Committee

Thomas J. Watson, Honorary Chairman, William Fellowes Morgan, Jr., Chairman. Robert E. Allen, Robert W. Atkins, Jules S. Bache, Willis H. Booth, John S. Burke, W. Gibson Carey, Jr., James S. Carson, Ralph F. Colin, Morton R. Cross, Kenneth Dayton, Cleveland E. Dodge, H. Bartow Farr, David M. Goodrich, Sylvan Gotshal, William J. Graham, Charles T. Gwynne, Lewis A. Hird, Fred I. Kent, Mrs. Harry Orland King, S. Whitney Landon, Robert Lehman, John T. McGovern, James H. McGraw, Jr., John L. Merrill, Malcolm Muir, W. W. Nichols, Warren Oakes, Frank C. Page, Arthur M. Reis, Raymond Rubicam, Eugene F. Sitterley, Kenneth M. Spence, Mrs. Roger W. Straus, Eugene P. Thomas, Frank A. Tichenor, Evan E. Young.

National Labor Advisory Council, 1943

Honorary Chairmen: Emil Rieve, President, TWUA-CIO; Matthew Woll, Vice Pres., AFL.

Leo Abernathy, Pittsburgh Central Labor Union; Harry Acreman, Texas State Federation of Labor; Roy W. Atkinson, Washington State Industrial Council; Arnold Atwood, UAW-CIO; J. A. Bell, ACWA-CIO; Norbert Berger, Allied Printing Trades Council, AFL; William Berger, Beilenson & Berger; Carl Bersing, UERMWA-CIO; Charles Binna, Denver Industrial Council; Frank Bonacci, CIO; George W. Brayfield, Colorado State Federation of Labor; R. H. Brazzell, WPB; Roy Brewer, Nebraska Federation of Labor; J. W. Brown, Attorney; Ray F. Brown, Hotel Peabody Printing Department; Frank Bruno, National Maritime Union; H. J. Burbach, Upholsterers International Union, AFL; Frank Burke, USA-CIO; John P. Burke, International Brotherhood of Pulp, Sulphite & Paper Mill Workers, AFL; Hamilton Camos, New Orleans Metal Trades Council; Floyd Case, Meat Cutters L. U., AFL; Dale Cashdollar, Dist. Carpenters Council AFL; Gordon W. Chapman, American Fed. of State, County and Municipal Employees; John Chizzoni, United Mine Workers; Wade Church, Arizona State Fed. of Labor; Harry C. Clark, Attorney; James J. Clerkin, Connecticut State Fed. of Labor; Ralph Cline, TWUA-CIO; Sidney Cohen, OWIU-CIO; William L. Connolly, R. I. State Fed. of Labor; Rudolph Cook, IAM; W. H. Crawford, Steel Workers Organizing Committee, CIO; Robert J. Davidson, CIO; Robert Davis, CIO; James P. Dean, CIO.

John Despol, Steel Workers Org. Committee, CIO; F. M. Dickinson, URWA-CIO; Al Dietrick, Teamsters Joint Council #40, AFL; Joseph M. Dillon, ILWU-CIO; Benjamin J. Dorsky, Maine State Fed. of Labor; William Doyle, Mass. State Fed. of Labor; Stanley Earl, Oregon State Industrial Union Council; Dan Edwards, IUMMSWA-CIO; Paul Elzea, United Cannery, Agricultural Packing & Allied Workers, CIO; Irving Fagan, Philadelphia Industrial Union Council; P. T. Fagan, UMW-CIO; Anthony J. Federhoff, CIO; John A. Feigel, Typographical Union 7, AFL; Harold V. Feinmark, New Haven Central Labor Council; H. Y. Feldman, Int'l Printing Pressmen and Assistants' Union, AFL; James Geelan, U. S. Senator; Charles H. Gillman, CIO; Daniel J. Goggin, Central Labor Union of Boston; Joseph A. Goney, USA-CIO; C. Harry Goodell, Marine Engineers, CIO; George L. Googe, AFL; Hugh Gormley, AFL; Albert W. Gossett, Atlanta Fed. of Trades, AFL; Harry Grages, Boston Central Labor Union; John W. Grajciar, USA-CIO; Louis Guilmet, TWU-CIO, C. J. Haggerty, California State Fed. of Labor; Charles E. Handy, Meat Cutters & Butcher Workmen, AFL; James Hanley, USA-CIO; Powers Hapgood, CIO; Michael Harris, USA-CIO; W. J. Harris, Dallas Labor Temple, AFL; Marion Hedges, IEWO-AFL; Henry Herbolsheimer, Engineers LU #1, AFL; W. L. Hines, Miss. State Fed. of Labor; Sal B. Hoffman, Upholsterers Int'l Union, AFL; Julius Holzberg, Attorney; Bert Hough, USA-CIO; Arthur Huggins, Int'l Bro. of Paper Makers, AFL; Paul R. Hutchings, IAM.

Clyde Ingram, Texas State Industrial Union Council; Earl Ingram, Metal Trades Council, AFL; George Jaber, Maine Industrial Union Council; Joseph M. Jacobs, Attorney; Ernest A. Johnson, Bldg. & Const. Trades Council, Metropolitan Dist., AFL; A. E. Joiner, New Mexico State Fed. of Labor; Walter Kenefick, IBEW-AFL; O. A. Knight, OWIU-CIO; Joseph Kres, UERMW-CIO; Fred Kruse, Seattle Metal Trades Council, AFL; Leonard Lageman, Minn. State Industrial Union Council; J. H. Lake, Electric Workers #48, AFL; George Lambert, ACWA-CIO; Rubin Latz, Minneapolis Bd of Business Agents; George W. Lawson, Minn. Federation of Labor; Joseph Leeds, TWUA-CIO; John W. Livingston, UAW-CIO; Lev.

Loring, Memphis Trade and Labor Council; M. J. Lyden, Ohio State Fed. of Labor; Lloyd McBride, Missouri St. Industrial Union Council; Edward McCrone, CIO; James L. McDevitt, Pa. State Fed. of Labor; A. B. Martin, USA-CIO; Perrin D. McElroy, Kansas City Building Trades Council; Eugene Maurice, USA-CIO; H. E. Miller, IUOE-AFL; John J. Murphy, AFL; Agnes Nestor, Int'l Glove Workers Union, AFL; Joseph I. Nichols, Utah State Fed. of Labor; Emmett M. Norment, Tenn. Employment Service, AFL; John O'Neill, Iron Workers #41, AFL; Patrick J. O'Neil, CIO; Judge Joseph A. Padway, General Counsel, AFL; Herbert W. Payne, TWUA-CIO; I. A. Peck, Automotive Machinists Lodge, AFL; F. C. Pieper, CIO; Ted Rhodes, United Retail, Wholesale and Dept. Stores Employees, CIO; A. W. Richter, Attorney; Reid Robinson, IMMSWA-CIO; Charles Rosen, ACWA-CIO.

August Scholle, Michigan CIO Council; Paul Seeds, Wichita Falls Trades and Labor Council; William Sentner, UERMWA-CIO; William G. Serota, United Retail, Wholesale & Dept. Store Employees, CIO; E. Shay, Retail Clerks Union, AFL; C. C. Smith, CIO; William Smith, Am. Fed. of Hosiery Workers, CIO; W. O. Sonnemann, Attorney; John J. Stack, Albany Typographical Union #4; T. J. Starling, UAW-CIO; Jos. Stuhldreier, IAM; Ralph Sturdevant, Denver Trades & Labor Assembly; P. E. Terzick, Editor of Carpenter's Journal; Hugh Thompson, CIO; Florence Thorne, AFL; H. F. Tucker, Int'l Bridge Structural and Ornamental Iron Workers, AFL; William B. Van Houten, Georgia School of Technology; S. M. Vottis, Capital Dist. Industrial Union Council, CIO; Martin J. Walsh, USA-CIO; Alexander Watchman, San Francisco Bldg. Trades Council; Will Watts, USW-CIO; Roy W. Weir, Minneapolis Central Labor Union; Edward H. Weyler, Kentucky State Fed. of Labor; Hunter Wharton, Pittsburgh Building Trades Council; Al Whitehouse, USA-CIO; George Wilson, San Francisco CIO Industrial Council; George A. Wilson, Houston Trades and Labor Council; Herbert Woods, Operating Engineers, AFL; Peter Zanghi, UAW-CIO.

INTER-AMERICAN COMMERCIAL ARBITRATION COMMISSION MEMBERS, 1947

Tomas Amadeo, Luis Anderson, James R. Angell, J. Arturo Arguedas, Julian A. Arroyo, Jose Aviles, Erwin Balluder, Luis Beltranena, Francisco Caceres Bendana, Valentim F. Boucas, Spruille Braden, Jose Brunet, Kenneth H. Campbell, Adolfo Cardenas, Julio Caro, James S. Carson, Roberto Casas Alatriste, Jorge Chamot, T. Jefferson Coolidge, Edmundo da Luz Pinto, Renato de Azevedo, Jose I. de la Camara, Daniel A. del Rio, Francisco de Sola, Donato Diaz Medina, James H. Drumm, Phanor J. Eder, Edward F. Feely, J. M. Fernandes, Enrique Finot, Luis Fiore, Farris A. Flint, Carlos Garcia Gastaneta, Enrique Gil, John B. Glenn, Gaston Goyeneche, David E. Grant, Manuel Gual Vidal, Julio Guzman Tellez, Frederick E. Hasler, R. W. Hebard, W. R. Herod, Rafael A. Huezo, Adolfo Ibanez, Frances Kellor, James S. Kemper, Arthur S. Kleeman, W. E. Knox, Otto T. Kreuser, Vicente Lecuna, Fidel Lopez Arteta, Miguel Lopez Pumarejo, J. Kirby

McDonough, M. T. McGovern, Brasilio Machado Neto, Geo. W. Magalhaes, Percy C. Magnus, Joseph M. Marrone, Modesto Martinez, Arnaldo Massone, Rodolfo Mezzera, J. M. O. Monasterio, Juan Antonio Montoya, Jose Nabuco, Joseph Nadal, Louis Naetzker, F. W. Nichol, Rodolfo Ogarrio, J. Rafael Oreamuno, Ismael Ortega B., Leopoldo H. Palazuelos, Eurico Penteado, Warren Lee Pierson, Stanley Powell, Joshua B. Powers, Antonio Maria Pradilla, Alejandro Quijano, Manuel Resumil Aragunde, German Riesco, Edward S. Rogers, Joseph C. Rovensky, Juan Sabates, Orlando Sagrera, Eduardo Salazar, Francis Salgado, Juan Samper Sordo, Gilberto Sanchez Lustrino, E. Schaeffer, Santiago Schulze, Percy Seibert, Fermin Silveira Zorzi, Eugene F. Sitterley, Luis Soto, William R. Strelow, Eugene P. Thomas, W. V. B. Van Dyck, Charles H. Wanzer, Thomas J. Watson, George H. White, John W. White, Fernando Wiese, George W. Wolf, Jorge B. Zalles.

Inter-American Business Relations Committee, 1947

Rodolfo Ogarrio, Chairman; P. G. Agnew, Thomas W. Ashwell, Albert J. Barnaud, Edward Beattie, James L. Brown, John F. Budd, J. Francis Cross, E. H. Gaither, Christopher de Groot, H. F. Heron, Stanley E. Hollis, Jean U. Koree, William M. Le Brecht, Robert C. Lee, Fred Leighton, Henry C. Maher, Frank Mason, Robert D. Merrill, Paul E. Moss, John Quirk, George E. Quisenberry, Harry S. Radcliffe, Morris S. Rosenthal, Joseph A. Sinclair, J. M. Thompson, Ralph H. Thomson, Thomas J. Watson, Jr., Albert Welsh, Edwin Whitehouse.

Inter-American Law Committee, 1947

Phanor J. Eder, Chairman; Edwin M. Borchard, James L. Brown, William C. Cannon, L. A. Crosby, Allen Foster Dulles, Leslie Freeman, Gordon Ireland, Philip C. Jessup, E. G. Lorenzen, Dr. J. Rafael Oreamuno, Jackson H. Ralston, F. Bayard Rives, Dr. Eduardo Salazar, Otto Schoenrich.

Inter-American Banking Committee, 1947

J. A. Allis, H. F. Boettler, A. S. Brueggemann, O. L. Carlton, Horace M. Chadsey, R. R. Claghorn, Paul Dietrich, Mario Diez, James H. Drumm, A. W. Faragher, Roderick P. Fraser, J. G. Geddes, Carl K. Giesse, W. L. Gray, T. W. Gregory, Jr., Einar Hammer, W. J. Hartney, H. A. Hayward, Clinton C. Johnson, P. A. Kinnoch, Otto T. Kreuser, F. C. Lexa, Egil Mack, J. F. McRae, J. W. McHaffie, Elliott McAllister, W. Granville Meader, Harry O. Metzger, Jo Zach Miller, III, Louis Naetzker, Wilbur H. Roberts, Howard J. Rogers, J. A. Rouveyrol, Joseph W. Rowe, Stephen E. Ruth, Harry Salinger, William H. Schroeder, Russell G. Smith, Harry W. Sontag, A. M. Strong, Ralph Wahlborg, G. H. Zimmerman.

Inter-American Arbitration Committee, 1947

Phanor J. Eder, Leslie E. Freeman, David E. Grant, Frances Kellor, Edward S. Rogers.

United States Committee of the Inter-American Commercial Arbitration Commission, 1947

John Abbink, New York; Charles R. Allen, Charleston, S. C.; Charles W. Applegate, Camden, N. J.; Leo E. Archer, Los Angeles; Julian B. Baird, St. Paul, Minn.; Thomas C. Ballagh, Philadelphia; R. G. Barnett, Portland, Ore.; R. F. Bausman, New York; Faye G. Bennison, Los Angeles; B. B. Bowen, Memphis; F. E. Briber, Denver; Samuel Broers, Akron; F. E. Brookman, Los Angeles; Sherman T. Brown, New York; A. G. Cameron, Akron; Henry Munroe Campbell, Detroit; James S. Carson, New York; E. L. Caswell, Cleveland; Reginald F. Chutter, Philadelphia; N. E. Clark-Hunt, New York; C. W. Coker, Hartsville, S. C.; Harold Colee, Jacksonville, Fla.; John L. Connolly, St. Paul, Minn; L. G. Coveney, San Francisco; E. S. Crosby, New York; J. E. Crosby, Shamrock, Fla.; J. Anton De Haas, Boston; W. J. de Winter, Minneapolis; John W. Doty, New York; James H. Drumm, New York; E. A. Emerson, Middletown, Ohio; Felix Ferraris, Providence; Jerome A. Flexner, St. Louis, Mo.; Leslie E. Freeman, New York; Harold W. French, Bridgeport, Conn.; Alfred C. Fuller, Hartford, Conn.; John C. Gallagher, New York; W. R. Gammage, Cincinnati; W. G. Garlan, Philadelphia; John D. Garrett, Hartford, Conn.; John L. Gillis, St. Louis, Mo.; J. J. Halloran, Boston; Mark Harris, Philadelphia; Michael Harris, Los Angeles; Wm. J. Hartney, Boston; Douglas F. Heuer, Memphis; W. G. Hillen, Syracuse, N. Y.; Miss M. J. Hine, Cleveland, Ohio; Miss Lorena J. Hitch, West Norfolk, Va.; P. A. Hoyt, Oakland, Cal.; S. Foster Hunt, Providence; Frank M. Inman, Atlanta; C. Bissell Jenkins, Jr., Charleston, S. C.; Harry B. Jones, Seattle; John Kinsey, Detroit; Arthur S. Kleeman, New York; T. A. Lambert, San Antonio, Texas; H. J. Leisenheimer, New York; Dr. Ben F. Lemert, Durham, N. C.; Alfred A. Leon, Memphis; A. G. Lindsay, Hollywood, Cal.; Wm. Frank Lowell, Boston; W. H. Lukens, Camden, N. J.; W. C. MacFarlane, Minneapolis; Egil Mack, Seattle; L. F. Macklem, Seattle; Colin C. MacRae, Los Angeles; F. L. Marshall, Chicago; Greenhow Maury, Jr., Richmond, Va.; J. Kirby McDonough, Dallas; Paul B. McKee, Portland, Ore.; Earle G. Moore, Tampa, Fla.; A. D. Neal, Denver; John H. Neubert, Rochester, N. Y.; John D. Nichols, New York; N. P. Oliver, New Orleans; G. R. Olliphant, Jacksonville, Fla.; Ralph Plowman, Wilmington, Del.; Stanley Powell, San Francisco; A. E. Pradilla, New Orleans; C. A. Richards, New York; Gustav Riedlin, Los Angeles; Caffey Robertson, Memphis; David Robinson, Portland, Ore.; Frank J. Roderick, Philadelphia; Antonio M. Romero, New York; R. A. Romero, Huntington, W. Va.; M. R. Sacra, Towson, Md.; Eugene A. Schwarz, Buffalo, N. Y.; R. W. Showalter, Indianapolis; A. D. Simpson, Houston, Tex.; David A. Skinner, Columbia, S. C.; J. P. Spang, Jr., Boston; Emerson Spear, Los Angeles; W. H. Stanley, Chicago; Roland C. Stevens, Los Angeles; E. Taranger, Richmond, Va.; Charles Taussig, New York; Arthur R. Upgren, Minneapolis; Henry C. Von Elm, New York; J. C. Wickliffe, Augusta, Ga.; Col. J. E. Yonge, Miami, Fla.

Commercial Associations Committee of the Inter-American Commercial Arbitration Commission, 1947

United States:

Association of Commerce, South Bend, Indiana; Baltimore Chamber of Commerce, Baltimore, Maryland; Boston Chamber of Commerce, Boston, Mass.; Chamber of Commerce of Kansas City, Kansas City, Missouri; Buffalo World Trade Association, Buffalo, New York; Commerce and Industry Ass'n of N. Y., New York; El Paso Chamber of Commerce, El Paso, Texas; Hampton Roads Maritime Exchange, Inc., Norfolk, Virginia; Houston Chamber of Commerce, Houston, Texas; Jacksonville Chamber of Commerce, Jacksonville, Florida; Los Angeles Chamber of Commerce, Los Angeles; The Manufacturers Ass'n of Conn., Inc., Hartford, Conn.; Memphis Chamber of Commerce, Memphis, Tennessee; Miami Chamber of Commerce, Miami, Florida; Mishawaka Chamber of Commerce, Mishawaka, Indiana; Mobile Chamber of Commerce, Mobile, Alabama; Nat'l Council of American Importers, Inc., New York; National Foreign Trade Council, Inc., New York; New Haven Chamber of Commerce, New Haven, Conn.; New York Board of Trade, New York; Norfolk Association of Commerce, Norfolk, Virginia; Dept. of Conservation & Development, Raleigh, North Carolina; Pensacola Chamber of Commerce, Pensacola, Florida; Portland Chamber of Commerce, Portland, Oregon; Providence Chamber of Commerce, Providence, Rhode Island; Richmond Chamber of Commerce, Richmond, Virginia; Rochester Chamber of Commerce, Rochester, New York; San Francisco Chamber of Commerce, San Francisco; Seattle Chamber of Commerce, Seattle, Washington; Springfield Chamber of Commerce, Springfield, Mass.; St. Louis Chamber of Commerce, St. Louis, Missouri; Syracuse Chamber of Commerce, Syracuse, New York; Tulsa Chamber of Commerce, Tulsa, Oklahoma; Virginia State Chamber of Commerce, Richmond, Virginia; Yakima Chamber of Commerce, Yakima, Washington.

Latin America:

American Chamber of Commerce for Brazil, Rio de Janeiro; American Chamber of Commerce of Cuba, Havana; American Chamber of Commerce of Mexico, Mexico, D. F.; American Chamber of Commerce of Sao Paulo, Sao Paulo, Brazil; The Chamber of Commerce of the U. S. of America in Uruguay, Montevideo; American Chamber of Commerce of the Dominican Republic, Ciudad Trujillo; Camara de Comercio, Cartagena, Colombia; Camara de Comercio, Medellin, Colombia; Camara de Comercio e Industria de Guatemala, Guatemala City; Camara de Comercio de Barranquilla, Barranquilla, Colombia; Camara de Comercio de Lima, Lima, Peru; Camara de Comercio de Quito, Quito, Ecuador; Chamber of Commerce of the USA in the Argentine Republic, Buenos Aires; Chamber of Commerce of the U. S. of America in the Republic of Chile, Santiago; Chamber of Commerce of Costa Rica, San Jose; Chamber of Commerce of the Dominican

Republic, Ciudad Trujillo; Chamber of Commerce of El Salvador, San Salvador; Chamber of Commerce of Caracas, Caracas, Venezuela; Confederacion de Camaras de Nacionales de Commercio e Industria, Mexico, D. F.

CANADIAN-AMERICAN COMMERCIAL ARBITRATION COMMISSION MEMBERS, 1947:

Brooke Claxton, Chairman; William H. Coverdale, Vice Chairman; *Canadian Section:* G. W. Bellevue, L. F. Burrows, F. A. Gaby, Clinton Henderson, J. D. Johnson, Wesley McCurdy, W. D. McGregor, S. S. McKeen; *U. S. Section;* James R. Angell, James S. Carson, Paul Fitzpatrick, Frances Kellor, Donovan O. Peters, Wesley A. Sturges, Thomas J. Watson.

CHINESE-AMERICAN TRADE ARBITRATION CONFERENCE MEMBERS, 1947:

U. S. Delegation: H. R. Boswell, Walter J. Braunschweiger, James S. Carson, Austin Flegel, Jr., Austin T. Foster, Cornell S. Franklin, Henry F. Grady, G. C. Hoyt, William P. Hunt, J. A. Keane, H. O. King, James A. MacKay, Clark H. Minor, Philo W. Parker, Alfred E. Schumacher, Blackwell Smith, Eugene P. Thomas, Joseph T. Wilson. *Chinese Delegation:* Li Ming, H. L. Hsieh, K. C. Li, T. C. Liu, S. D. Ren, T. S. Shih.

PHILIPPINE-AMERICAN TRADE ARBITRATION COMMISSION MEMBERS, 1947:

Philippine Section: Ramon J. Araneta, Salvador Araneta, Manuel Barredo, Conrado Benitez, Vicente Carmona, Manuel Elizalde, Vicente Fabella, Jose P. Fernandez, Santiago Freixes, Francisco Genato, Lino Gutierrez, Simon Paterno, Aurelio Periquet, Gil J. Puyat, Jose V. Ramirez, Ramon Roces, Eulogio Rodriguez, Mariano Salazar, Toribio Teodoro. *American Section:* William B. Craig, Kenneth B. Day, A. F. Dollar, Arthur H. Evans, J. H. Foley, John W. Haussermann, Erwin F. Koch, Ralph McKibben, T. Kevin Mallen, William E. Murray, Louis H. Pink, A. E. Rebollo, C. A. Richards, F. M. Satterfield.

INTERNATIONAL BUSINESS RELATIONS COUNCIL, 1947:

Barclay Acheson, Sam G. Baggett, William L. Batt, D. C. Beaulieu, John C. Best, H. R. Boswell, Spruille Braden, Samuel Broers, Herbert Brunn, George N. Butler, George S. Butler, Charles Cain, Jr., Curtis E. Calder, Owen L. Carlton, James S. Carson, E. L. Caswell, Wayne Chatfield-Taylor, John C. Cooper, W. L. Cunliffe, H. L. Derby, Chairman; Martin Domke, Georges F. Doriot, James H. Drumm, Vice-Chairman; Lincoln Filene, Austin T. Foster, Amos B. Foy, Arthur B. Foye, Sylvan Gotshal, Merrill Griswold, W. C. Haddon, Basil Harris, Frederick E. Hasler, Eldridge Haynes, R. S. Hecht, Henry H. Heimann, G. C. Hoyt, Leslie A. Jacobson, Henry R. Jahn, Frances Kellor, James S. Kemper, Fred I. Kent, H. Donn Keresey, Meyer Kestnbaum, Arthur S. Kleeman, Robert C. Lee, Robert J. Lynch, Vice-Chairman; W. C. MacFarlane, George B. Markle, Jr., Rene May, Sidney A. Mitchell, Thomas A. Morgan, Marcus A. Nadler, Richard C. Patterson, Jr., C. M. Peter, Frank Phillips, J. G. Phillips, Warren Lee Pierson, Joshua B. Powers, George E. Quisenberry, Philip D. Reed, Morris S. Rosenthal, John F. Rudy, Raymond Rubicam, Clarence E. Searle, Frank Shepard, George H. Sibley, Eugene F. Sitterley, Blackwell Smith, J. P. Spang, Jr., W. H. Stanley, Henry E. Stehli, Eugene P. Thomas, Juan Trippe, A. Lightfoot Walker, Thomas J. Watson, Jr., Willard W. Wirtz.

Special Research Contributions from Foundations

Lucius and Eva Eastman Fund, Inc.; Economic and General Foundation; Lincoln and Therese Filene Foundation; Michael Friedsam Fund; Daniel and Florence Guggenheim Foundation; Home Ship Corporation; New York Foundation; William S. Paley Foundation; Rosenwald Family Association; Felix and Frieda Schiff Warburg Foundation.

Recipients of Distinguished Service Awards

American Arbitration Association—Gold Medal for Distinguished Service in Arbitration (Commercial): 1928, Charles M. Schwab; 1929, Harry F. Guggenheim; 1930, Frederick Brown; 1930, Richard Evelyn Byrd; 1931, Frank Gillmore; 1936, Thomas J. Watson; 1938, Juan T. Trippe; 1939, Frank H. Sommer; 1942, Charles T. Gwynne; 1944, Charles E. Wilson; 1945, Lincoln Filene; 1946, R. S. Hecht.

American Arbitration Association—Gold Medal for Distinguished Service in Industrial Arbitration: 1938, Edward F. McGrady; 1942, William H. Davis.

Western Hemisphere Award: 1943, Thomas J. Watson; 1944, Eugene P. Thomas (for the National Foreign Trade Council); 1946, Spruille Braden.

Inter-American Commercial Arbitration Commission—Gold Medal for Distinguished Service in Inter-American Arbitration Peace and Friendship: 1937, Spruille Braden; 1939, Cordell Hull; 1940, L. S. Rowe; 1940, Senator Juan Samper Sordo; 1943, Eric A. Johnston; 1945, James S. Carson.

Inter-American Commercial Arbitration Commission—Commercial Associations Award, 1944: Albany Chamber of Commerce; Boston Chamber of Commerce; Buffalo Foreign Trade Association; Chicago Association of Commerce; Dallas Junior Chamber of Commerce; Denver Exporters Club; Foreign Trade Association of Southern California; Indianapolis Chamber of Commerce; Foreign Traders Association of Philadelphia, Inc.; Portland Chamber of Commerce; Foreign Trade Bureau, St. Louis Chamber of Commerce; Foreign Commerce Association of San Francisco, Chamber of Commerce; Santa Fe Chamber of Commerce; Seattle Chamber of Commerce.

Importer's Guide Award—Presented under the Auspices of the American Arbitration Association, and Guia Award—Presented under the Auspices of the Inter-American Commercial Arbitration Commission: 1941, Foreign Commerce Association of San Francisco Chamber of Commerce; 1942, Chamber of Commerce of the State of New York; 1943, New Orleans Association of Commerce; 1943, Mexican Confederation of National Chamber of Commerce; 1944, Commercial Association of Rio de Janeiro; 1945, Los Angeles Chamber of Commerce; 1946, Chamber of Commerce of Bogota, 1947, Argentine Chamber of Commerce.

ANNEXES

ANNEX I

COMMERCIAL AND LABOR ARBITRATION RULES

The following text of the Commercial Arbitration Rules of the American Arbitration Association are sufficiently identical with the Commercial Rules of the Inter-American Commercial Arbitration Commission and Canadian-American Commercial Arbitration Commission to be generally applicable in principle, practice and arbitration administration. They may be accepted as expressing the Western Hemisphere commercial arbitration policy and practice.

These Commercial Rules have also served as a model for the Voluntary Labor Arbitration Rules. The important differences are indicated by the appropriate footnotes in the Rules.

Text of Commercial Arbitration Rules

I. RULES A PART OF THE ARBITRATION AGREEMENT

1. *Agreement of Parties* The parties shall be deemed to have made these Rules a part of their arbitration agreement whenever, in the Submission or other written agreement, they have provided for arbitration by the American Arbitration Association or under its Rules. These Rules and any amendment thereof shall apply in the form obtaining at the time the arbitration is initiated.

II. TRIBUNALS

2. *Name of Tribunal* Any Tribunal constituted by the parties for the settlement of their dispute under these Rules, shall be called the Commercial Arbitration Tribunal, hereinafter referred to as Tribunal.
3. *Administrator* When parties agree to arbitrate under these Rules or provide for arbitration by the American Arbitration Association and an arbitration is initiated thereunder, they thereby constitute the American Arbitration Association the Administrator of the arbitration. The authority and obligations of the Administrator are limited in the manner prescribed in the agreement of the parties and in these Rules.
4. *Director of Tribunals and Tribunal Clerks* The duties of the Administrator may be carried out through a Director of Tribunals or other officers

of the Administrator or such Tribunal Clerks, Committees or Agents as the Administrator may direct.

5. *Panels of Arbitrators* The Association shall establish and maintain Panels of Arbitrators and shall appoint Arbitrators therefrom in the manner prescribed in these Rules, and such Arbitrators shall hereinafter be referred to as "Panel Arbitrators".

6. *Office of Tribunal* The general office of a Tribunal is the headquarters of the Administrator. The Administrator, however, may assign the administration of any arbitration to any of its branch offices or to a designated Tribunal Clerk.

III. INITIATION OF THE ARBITRATION

7. *Initiation under an Arbitration Provision in a Contract* Any party to a contract containing a clause providing for arbitration by the American Arbitration Association or under its Rules, or any party to a contract containing a general arbitration clause, when the parties have agreed, by stipulation or otherwise, to arbitrate under the Rules of the American Arbitration Association, may commence an arbitration in the following manner:

(a) By such party giving written notice to the other party of intention to arbitrate (Demand), which notice shall contain a statement setting forth the nature of the dispute, the amount involved if any, the remedy sought;[1] and

(b) By filing with the Administrator at any of its offices two copies of said notice, together with two copies of the contract or such parts thereof as relate to the dispute, including the arbitration provisions.

The party upon whom the demand for arbitration is made may, if he so desires, file an answering statement with the Administrator within seven days after mailing of such Demand, in which event he shall also send a copy of his answer to the other party. If no answer is filed within the stated time, it will be assumed that the claim made is denied. Failure to file an answer shall not operate to delay the arbitration.

After the filing of the claim, and answer if any, if either party desires to make any new or different claim such claim shall be made in writing and filed with the Tribunal Clerk and a copy thereof mailed to the other party who shall have a period of seven days from the date of such mailing within which to file an answer with the Tribunal Clerk.[2]

However, after the Arbitrator is appointed no new or different claim may be submitted to him except with the consent of the Arbitrator and all other parties.

8. *Initiation under a Submission* Parties to any existing dispute may commence an arbitration under these Rules by filing at any office of the Administrator two copies of a written agreement to arbitrate under these Rules (Submission), signed by the parties, and containing a statement of the matter

[1] Under the Labor Rules, it is not required to specify any amount.

[2] This paragraph does not appear in the Labor Rules.

in dispute, the amount of money involved if any, and the remedy sought.[3]

9. *Administrative Fee* The Initial Fee in the amount prescribed in the Schedule in Rule IX shall be paid to the Administrator by each of the parties at the time of initiating the arbitration.[4]

10. *Fixing of Locality* The parties may mutually agree on the locality where the arbitration is to be held. If the locality is not designated in the contract or Submission, or if within seven days from the date of filing the Demand or Submission, the parties do not notify the Administrator of such designation, it shall have power to determine the locality and its decision shall be final.

IV. APPOINTMENT OF ARBITRATOR

11. *Qualifications* No person shall serve[5] as an Arbitrator in any arbitration if he has any financial or personal interest in the result of the arbitration, unless the parties, in writing, waive such disqualification.

12. *Appointment from Panels* If the parties have not appointed an Arbitrator and have not provided any other method of appointment, the Arbitrator shall be appointed in the following manner: Immediately after the filing of the Submission or copy of a Demand, as required under Rule III, the Tribunal Clerk shall submit simultaneously to each party to the dispute, an identical list of names of persons chosen from the Panels. Each party to the dispute shall have seven days from the date of the mailing of such lists in which to examine said list, cross off any names to which he objects and number the remaining names indicating the order of his preference, and return the list to the Tribunal Clerk. When any party or both parties fail to return the list within the time specified all persons named therein shall be deemed acceptable. From among the persons who have been approved on both lists, and in accordance with the designated order of mutual preference if any, the Tribunal Clerk shall invite the acceptance of an Arbitrator to serve. If the parties fail to agree upon any of the persons named or if those named decline or are unable to act, or if for any other reason the appointment cannot be made from the submitted lists, the Administrator shall have power to make the appointment from other members of the Panels without the submission of any additional lists.

13. *Direct Appointment by Parties* If the Submission or other agreement of the parties names an Arbitrator or specifics any direct method by which an Arbitrator is to be appointed, that designation or method shall be followed. The notice of appointment, with name and address of such Arbitrator, shall be filed with the Tribunal Clerk by the appointing party. Upon the request of any such appointing party the Tribunal Clerk shall submit a

[3] See footnote (1) on p. 220.

[4] Under the Labor Rules, the amount is specified as $25.00 for each party for the first hearing and $15.00 for each party for subsequent hearings.

[5] The Labor Rules read: "A member of the Panel shall not serve. . . ."

list of members of the Panels from which the party may, if he so desires, make the appointment.[6]

If the Submission or other agreement specifies a period of time within which an Arbitrator shall be appointed, and any party fails to make such appointment within that period, the Administrator shall have power to make the appointment.

If no period of time is specified in the Submission or other agreement, the Tribunal Clerk shall notify the parties to make the appointment and if within seven days thereafter such Arbitrator has not been so appointed, the Administrator shall then have power to make the appointment.

14. *Appointment of Additional Arbitrator by Named Arbitrators* If the parties have named their Arbitrators or either or both of them have been named as provided in Section 13, and have authorized such Arbitrators to appoint an additional Arbitrator within a specified time and no appointment is made within such time or any agreed extension thereof, the parties, under these Rules, authorize the Administrator to appoint such additional Arbitrator who shall act as Chairman.

If no period of time is specified by the parties within which such Arbitrators are to appoint an additional Arbitrator, a period of seven days from the date of the appointment of the named Arbitrator last appointed, shall be allowed for their appointment of the additional Arbitrator. In the event of their failure to make the appointment within such seven days, the parties, under these Rules, authorize the Administrator to appoint such additional Arbitrator who shall act under the agreement with the same force and effect as if he had been appointed by the named Arbitrators and he shall act as Chairman.

If the parties have agreed that their named Arbitrators shall appoint the additional Arbitrator from the Panels, the Tribunal Clerk shall furnish to the named Arbitrators, in the manner prescribed in Section 12, a list selected from the Panels and the appointment of the additional Arbitrator shall be made as prescribed in such Section.

15. *Appointment of Arbitrator in an International Commercial Arbitration*[7] If one of the parties is a national or resident of a country other than the United States, the sole Arbitrator or the third Arbitrator shall, upon the request of either party, be chosen or appointed from among the nationals of a country other than that of any one of the parties.

16. *Designation of Number of Arbitrators* If the arbitration agreement does not specify the number of Arbitrators, the dispute shall be heard and determined by one Arbitrator, unless the Administrator in its discretion specifically directs that a greater number of Arbitrators be appointed.

17. *Notice of Appointment to Arbitrator and Parties* Notice of the appointment of the Arbitrator, whether appointed by the parties or by the Administrator, shall be mailed to the Arbitrator by the Tribunal Clerk and the

[6] The last sentence does not appear in the Labor Rules.

[7] This section does not appear in the Labor Rules.

signed acceptance of the Arbitrator shall be filed with the Tribunal Clerk prior to the opening of the first hearing. Together with such notice to the Arbitrator, the Tribunal Clerk shall enclose a copy of the Rules and call attention to the requirements of Section 11 and 18 of these Rules.[8]

18. *Disclosures by Panel Arbitrator of Disqualification* At the time of receiving his notice of appointment, the prospective Panel Arbitrator is requested to disclose any circumstances likely to create a presumption of bias or which he believes might disqualify him as an impartial Arbitrator. Upon receipt of such information, the Tribunal Clerk shall immediately disclose it to the parties who, if willing to proceed under the circumstances disclosed, shall, in writing, so advise the Tribunal Clerk. If either party declines to waive the presumptive disqualification, the vacancy thus created shall be filled in the same manner as the original appointment was made.

19. *Vacancies* If any Arbitrator should resign, die, withdraw, refuse or be unable or disqualified to perform the duties of his office, the Administrator shall, on proof satisfactory to it, declare the office vacant. Vacancies shall be filled in the same manner as the original appointment was made and the matter shall be reheard by the new Arbitrator.

V. PROCEDURE FOR ORAL HEARING

20. *Time and Place* The Arbitrator shall fix the time and place for each hearing. The Tribunal Clerk shall mail at least five days prior thereto notice thereof to each party, unless the parties by mutual agreement waive such notice or modify the terms thereof.

21. *Representation by Counsel* Any party may be represented by counsel. A party intending to be so represented shall notify the other party and file a copy of such notice with the Tribunal Clerk at least three days prior to the date set for the hearing at which counsel is first to appear. When the initiation of an arbitration is made by counsel, or the reply of the other party is by counsel, such notice is deemed to have been given.

22. *Taking of a Stenographic Record* The Tribunal Clerk shall make the necessary arrangements for the taking of a stenographic record of the testimony whenever such record is requested by one or more parties. The requesting party or parties shall deposit the estimated cost of such record with the Tribunal Clerk.

23. *Interpreters*[9] The Tribunal Clerk shall make the necessary arrangements for the services of an interpreter upon the request of one or more of the parties who shall deposit the cost of such service with the Tribunal Clerk.

24. *Attendance at Hearings* Persons having a direct interest in the arbitration are entitled to attend hearings. It shall be discretionary with the Arbitrator to determine the propriety of the attendance of any other persons. The Arbitrator shall have the power to require the retirement of any witness or witnesses during the testimony of other witnesses.

[8] The last sentence does not appear in the Labor Rules.

[9] This provision does not appear in the Labor Rules.

25. *Adjournments* The Arbitrator for good cause shown may take adjournments upon the request of a party or upon his own initiative and shall take such adjournment when all of the parties agree thereto.

26. *Oaths* Before proceeding with the first hearing, or with the examination of the file as provided under Rule VI, each Arbitrator may take an oath of office, and if required by law, shall do so. The Arbitrator may, in his discretion, require witnesses to testify under oath administered by any duly qualified person, or, if required by law or demanded by either party, shall do so.

27. *Majority Decision* Whenever there is more than one Arbitrator, all decisions of the Arbitrators may be by majority vote. The award may also be made by majority vote unless the concurrence of all is expressly required by the arbitration agreement or by law.

28. *Order of Proceeding* A hearing shall be opened by the filing of the oath of the Arbitrator, where required, and by the recording of a Minute by the Tribunal Clerk. The Minute shall set forth the place, time and date of the hearing, the presence of the Arbitrator and parties, and counsel if any, and the receipt by the Arbitrator of the Submission or of the statement of the claim, and answer if any. The Tribunal Clerk shall keep as part of the record a list of the names and addresses of all witnesses.

Exhibits, when offered by either party, may be received in evidence by the Arbitrator, and when so received shall be numbered by the Tribunal Clerk and made part of the record.

The Arbitrator may, at the beginning of the hearing, ask for statements clarifying the issues involved.

The complaining party or his counsel shall then present his claim and proofs and his witnesses who shall submit to questions or other examination. The defending party or his counsel shall then present his defense and proofs, and his witnesses who shall submit to questions or other examination. The Arbitrator may in his discretion vary this procedure but shall afford full and equal opportunity to all parties for the presentation of any material or relevant proofs.

29. *Arbitration in the Absence of a Party* Unless the law provides to the contrary, the arbitration may proceed in the absence of any party, who, after due notice, fails to be present or fails to obtain an adjournment. An award shall not be made solely on the default of a party. The Arbitrator shall require the other party to submit such evidence as he may require for the making of an award.

30. *Evidence* The parties may offer such evidence as they desire and shall produce such additional evidence as the Arbitrator may deem necessary to an understanding and determination of the dispute. When the Arbitrator is authorized by law to subpoena witnesses or documents, he may do so upon his own initiative or upon the request of any party. The Arbitrator shall be the judge of the relevancy and materiality of the evidence offered and conformity to legal rules of evidence shall not be necessary. All evidence shall be taken in the presence of all of the Arbitrators and of all the parties

except where any of the parties is absent in default or has waived his right to be present.

31. *Evidence by Affidavit and Filing of Documents* The Arbitrator may receive and consider the evidence of witnesses by affidavit, but may give it only such weight as he deems it entitled to after consideration of any objections made to its admission.

All documents not filed with the Arbitrator at the hearing but which are arranged at the hearing or subsequently by agreement of the parties to be submitted, shall be filed with the Tribunal Clerk for transmission to the Arbitrator. All parties shall be afforded opportunity to examine such documents.

32. *Inspection or Investigation*[10] Whenever the Arbitrator deems it necessary to make an inspection or investigation in connection with the arbitration, he shall direct the Tribunal Clerk to advise the parties and obtain their consent in writing before such inspection or investigation may be made. The Arbitrator shall set the time and the Tribunal Clerk shall notify the parties thereof. Any party who so desires may be present at such inspection or investigation.

33. *Conservation of Property*[11] The Arbitrator, with the consent of the parties, may issue such orders as may be deemed necessary to safeguard the subject matter of the arbitration, without prejudice to the rights of the parties or to the final determination of the dispute.

34. *Closing of Hearings* The Arbitrator shall specifically inquire of all parties whether they have any further proofs to offer or witnesses to be heard. Upon receiving negative replies, the Arbitrator shall declare the hearings closed and a Minute thereof shall be recorded. If briefs are to be filed, the hearings shall be declared closed as of the final date set by the Arbitrator for the receipt of the briefs. If documents are to be filed as provided in Section 31 and the date set for their receipt is later than that set for the receipt of briefs, then such later date shall be the date of closing the hearing. The time limit within which the Arbitrator is required to make his award shall commence to run, in the absence of other agreement by the parties, upon the closing of the hearings.

35. *Reopening of Hearings* The hearings may be reopened by the Arbitrator on his own motion, or upon application of a party for good cause shown, at any time before the award is made. If the reopening of the hearings would prevent the making of the award within the time agreed upon by the parties, hearings shall not be reopened unless the parties agree upon the extension of such time limit. When hearings are reopened the effective date of closing the hearings shall be the date of the closing of the reopened hearings.

[10] This provision is abbreviated in the Labor Rules to read as follows: "*Inspection*—Whenever the Arbitrator deems it necessary, he may make an inspection in connection with the subject matter of the dispute after written notice to the parties, who may if they so desire be present at such inspection."

[11] Omitted from Labor Rules.

VI. PROCEDURE FOR OTHER THAN ORAL HEARINGS[12]

36. *Waiver of Oral Hearing* The parties by written agreement may submit their dispute to arbitration by other than oral hearing. The arbitration shall be conducted under these Rules except such provisions thereof as are inconsistent with this Rule.

If no method is specified by the parties, the Tribunal Clerk shall notify the parties to present their proofs in the following manner: the parties shall submit to the Tribunal Clerk their respective contentions in writing, including a statement of facts duly sworn to, together with such other proofs as they may wish to submit. These statements and proofs may be accompanied by written arguments or briefs. All documents shall be submitted within seven days from the date of the notice to file such statement and proofs in such number of copies as the Tribunal Clerk may request. The Tribunal Clerk shall forthwith transmit to each party a copy of the statement and proofs submitted by the other party. Each party may reply to the other's statement and proofs, but upon the failure of any party to make such a reply within a period of seven days after the mailing of such documents to him, he shall be deemed to have waived the right to reply.

The Tribunal Clerk shall then transmit all proofs and documents to the Arbitrator, who shall have been appointed in any manner provided for in Rule IV. The Arbitrator shall have ten days from the date of their mailing or delivery to him within which to request a party or parties to produce additional proof. The Tribunal Clerk shall notify the parties of such request and the party or parties shall submit such additional proof within seven days from the date of the mailing of such notice. The Tribunal Clerk upon receipt thereof shall forthwith transmit to each party a copy of the additional statement and proofs submitted by the other party. Each party may make reply to such statement and proofs, but upon the failure of any party to make such a reply within a period of seven days after the mailing to him of such documents, he shall be deemed to have waived the right to reply.

Upon mailing or delivery to the Arbitrator of all documents submitted as provided above, the arbitration shall be deemed closed and the time limit within which the Arbitrator shall make his award shall begin to run.

VII. SPECIAL PROVISIONS

37. *Waiver of Rules* Any party who proceeds with the arbitration after knowledge that any provision or requirement of these Rules has not been complied with and who fails to state his objection thereto in writing, shall be deemed to have waived his right to object.

[12] This Rule does not appear in the Labor Rules. However, Rule VI, Section 34, makes a similar provision, as follows: "The parties may provide, by written agreement, for the waiver of oral hearings; in such event the hearings shall be conducted in the manner specified by the parties and the Tribunal Clerk shall put into effect ths special procedure agreed upon."

38. *Extensions of Time* The parties may modify any period of time by mutual agreement. The Administrator for good cause may extend any period of time established by these Rules, except the time for making the award. The Administrator shall notify the parties of any such extension of time and its reasons therefor.

39. *Serving of Notices* Each party to a Submission or other agreement which provides for arbitration under these Rules shall be deemed to have consented and shall consent that any papers, notices or process necessary or proper for the initiation or continuation of an arbitration under these Rules and for the entry of judgment on an award made thereunder may be served upon such party (a) by mail addressed to such party or his attorney at his last known address or (b) by personal service, within or without the state wherein the arbitration is to be held (whether such party be within or without the United States of America);[13] provided that reasonable opportunity to be heard with regard thereto has been granted such party.

VIII. THE AWARD

40. *Time* The award shall be rendered promptly and, unless otherwise agreed by the parties, or specified by law, not later than thirty days from the date of closing the hearings, or if oral hearings have been waived, then from the date of transmitting the final statements and proofs to the Arbitrator.

41. *Form* The award shall be in writing and shall be signed either by the sole Arbitrator or by a majority if there be more than one. It shall be executed in the manner required by law.[14]

42. *Scope*[15] The Arbitrator in his award may grant any remedy or relief which he deems just and equitable and within the scope of the agreement of the parties, including, but not limited to, specific performance of a contract. The Arbitrator, in his award, may assess the arbitration fees and expenses in favor of any party or of the Administrator.

43. *Award upon Settlement* If the parties settle their dispute during the course of the arbitration, the Arbitrator, upon their request, may set forth the terms of the agreed settlement in an award.

44. *Delivery of Award to Parties* Parties shall accept as legal delivery of the award (a) the placing of the award or a true copy thereof in the mail by the Tribunal Clerk, addressed to such party at his last known address or to his attorney, or (b) personal service of the award, or (c) the filing of the award in any manner which may be prescribed by law.

45. *Release of Documents for Judicial Proceedings* The Tribunal Clerk shall, upon the written request of a party, furnish to such party at his

[13] Words in parenthesis do not appear in Labor Rules.

[14] Second sentence of this section does not appear in Labor Rules; but the Labor Rules provide as follows: "The Arbitrator may file an opinion, copy of which shall be mailed to each party by the Tribunal Clerk, at the time the award is delivered."

[15] Omitted from Labor Rules.

expense, certified facsimiles of any papers in the Tribunal's possession that may be required in judicial proceedings relating to the arbitration.

46. *Notice of Compliance* The Tribunal Clerk, for the purpose of closing the record, may request either party to notify the Administrator of compliance with the award.

IX. FEES AND EXPENSES[16]

(Amended and clarified March 1, 1945)

47. *Schedule of Administrative Fees* An administrative fee in the amount prescribed in the following schedule shall be paid to the Tribunal Clerk by each of the parties at the time of initiating the arbitration:

Where Amount involved is disclosed:—

Initial Fee:

$10.00 plus 1% of the amount involved up to $25,000;

plus ½% of the amount involved in excess of $25,000, to $100,000;

[16] Rule IX of Commercial Rules does not apply to labor arbitrations. Fees and expenses in labor arbitrations are regulated by Rule VIII of Labor Rules, reading as follows:

43. *Administrative Fee* Each party shall pay to the Administrator in advance of each hearing the sum of $25.00 for the first hearing and $15.00 for each subsequent hearing for its administrative service and facilities. For any adjournment after due notice of hearing, the party causing it shall pay an additional fee of $5.00. For hearings or parts thereof, held after 6 P.M. week days or after 12 noon Saturdays, there will be a charge to each party of $2.00 per hour.

44. *Expenses* The expenses of witnesses for either side shall be paid by the party producing such witnesses.

The total cost of the stenographic record, if any is made, and all transcripts thereof, shall be prorated equally among all parties ordering copies, unless they shall otherwise agree among themselves.

All other expenses of the arbitration, including required traveling and other expenses of the Arbitrator and Tribunal Clerk, and the expenses of any witness or the cost of any proofs produced at the direct request of the Arbitrator, shall be borne equally by the parties unless they agree otherwise, or unless the Arbitrator in his Award assesses such expenses or any part thereof against any specified party or parties.

The Arbitrator may award to the Administrator any expenses advanced or incurred by it and any fees due and remaining unpaid by any party responsible therefor.

45. *Arbitrator's Fee* If the parties desire to compensate the Arbitrator but do not agree upon the rate or amount of the compensation it shall be fixed by the Administrator on a *per diem* basis of $25 for each hearing, such fee to cover the making of the award and the preparation of the accompanying opinion.

Any arrangements for the compensation of a Panel Arbitrator shall be made through the Administrator and not directly by him with the parties.

46. *Deposits* The Tribunal Clerk may require the parties to deposit in advance with the Administrator such sums of money as he deems necessary to defray the expenses of the arbitration, including the Arbitrator's fee, if any, and shall render an accounting to the parties and return any unexpended balance.

plus ¼% of the amount involved in excess of $100,000, up to $200,000;
plus 1/10% of the amount involved in excess of $200,000.

The fee is based upon the amount of the claim as disclosed when the arbitration is initiated, and such fee is payable by each party. If, however, a claim in a larger amount is disclosed in the answer or in any amendment of the claim or answer filed later, an additional fee in accord with the above schedule shall be paid by the claimant for such larger amount.

Where Amount involved is not disclosed:—

Initial Fee:

$50.00 Subject (a) to adjustment with the Administrator.
or (b) subject to adjustment in accordance with preceding schedule if an amount is subsequently disclosed.

For Second and subsequent Hearings:—

(Payable before each hearing)

$30.00 or 50% of Initial Fee—whichever is lower amount.

Adjournment Fee:—

$5.00 (Payable only by party causing adjournment of hearing duly called by notice.)

Overtime Fee:—

$2.00 per hour payable by each party (Chargeable after 6:00 P.M. weekdays or 12 noon Saturdays.)

Apportionment of Fees:—

The Arbitrator may award to either party and against the other, an amount equal to the fee, or any part thereof, which was paid by such party to the Association.

Fee When Arbitration is Withdrawn:—

The minimum initial fee of $10.00 will not be returned or waived, but one half of any fee paid in excess thereof may be returned or cancelled if the arbitration is withdrawn before the date set for the first hearing.

48. *Fee When Oral Hearings are Waived* Fee when all Oral Hearings are waived under Section 36 shall be the Initial Fee as determined under Section 47 hereof.

49. *Expenses* The expenses of witnesses for either side shall be paid by the party producing such witnesses.

The total cost of the stenographic record, if any is made, and all transcript thereof, shall be prorated equally among all parties ordering copies, unless they shall otherwise agree among themselves.

All other expenses of the arbitration including required traveling and other expenses of the Arbitrator and Tribunal Clerk, and the expenses of any witness or the cost of any proofs produced at the direct request of the

Arbitrator, shall be borne equally by the parties unless they agree otherwise, or unless the Arbitrator in his Award assesses such expenses or any part thereof against any specified party or parties.

The Arbitrator may award to the Administrator any expenses advanced or incurred by it and any fees due and remaining unpaid by any party responsible therefor.

50. *Arbitrator's Fee* If the parties desire to compensate the Arbitrator but do not agree upon the rate or amount of the compensation, it shall be fixed by the Administrator.

Any arrangements for the compensation of a panel arbitrator shall be made through the Administrator and not directly by him with the parties.

51. *Deposits* The Tribunal Clerk may require the parties to deposit in advance with the Administrator such sums of money as he deems necessary to defray the expense of the arbitration, including the Arbitrator's fee if any, and shall render an accounting to the parties and return any unexpended balance.

X. INTERPRETATION AND APPLICATION OF RULES

52. *Interpretations and Application of Rules* The Arbitrator shall interpret and apply these Rules insofar as they relate to his powers and duties. When there is more than one Arbitrator and a difference arises among them concerning the meaning or application of any such Rules it shall be decided by majority vote. If that is unobtainable either an arbitrator or a party may refer the question to the Administrator for final decision. All other Rules shall be interpreted and applied by the Administrator.

ANNEX II

ARBITRATION CLAUSES

The American Arbitration Association and its co-operating organizations have from time to time recommended commercial arbitration clauses that are adapted to American and also to international trade. As these are referred to in the text, it seemed advisable to include the texts.

As labor arbitration clauses are recommended by the Association and are referred to in the text, these texts are also included. The Association recommends other labor clauses which appear in its publication —*A Guide to Labor Arbitration Clauses.*

AMERICAN GENERAL COMMERCIAL CLAUSE

Any controversy or claim arising out of or relating to this contract, or the breach thereof, shall be settled by arbitration, in accordance with the Rules, then obtaining, of the American Arbitration Association, and judgment upon the award rendered may be entered in any Court having jurisdiction thereof.

INTER-AMERICAN COMMERCIAL ARBITRATION COMMISSION CLAUSE

Any controversy or claim arising out of or relating to this contract, or the breach thereof, shall be settled by arbitration, in accordance with the Rules, then obtaining, of the Inter-American Commercial Arbitration Commission. This agreement shall be enforceable and judgment upon any award rendered by all or a majority of the arbitrators may be entered in any court having jurisdiction. The arbitration shall be held in   or wherever jurisdiction may be obtained over the parties.

WESTERN HEMISPHERE COMMERCIAL ARBITRATION CLAUSE

Any controversy or claim arising out of or relating to this contract or the breach thereof shall be settled by arbitration in accordance with the Rules then obtaining of the American Arbitration Association. If, however, one or more of the parties to this agreement is domiciled in one of the Republics of Latin America, the Rules of the Inter-American Commercial Arbitration Commission shall apply. If one or more of the parties to this agreement is domiciled in Canada the Rules of the Canadian American Commercial Arbitration Commission shall apply except where the other party is domiciled in a Latin American Republic in which case the parties may agree to arbitrate under the Rules of the Inter-American Commercial Arbitration Commission or of the Canadian American Commercial Arbitration Commission. Should any question arise as to which Rules are applicable under this provision, the Joint Arbitration Committee established by these organizations shall have power to determine which Rules shall be applicable. Judgment upon the award rendered may be entered in any court of any country having jurisdiction.

CANADIAN-AMERICAN COMMERCIAL ARBITRATION COMMISSION CLAUSE

Any controversy or claim arising out of or relating to this contract, or the breach thereof, shall be settled by arbitration, in accordance with the Rules of Procedure, then obtaining, of the Canadian-American Commercial Arbitration Commission, established by the American Arbitration Association and the Canadian Chamber of Commerce, and judgment upon the award rendered may be entered in any court having jurisdiction thereof.

GENERAL INTERNATIONAL COMMERCIAL CLAUSE

Any controversy or claim arising out of or relating to this contract, or the breach thereof, shall be settled by arbitration in accordance with the Rules, then obtaining, of the American Arbitration Association or such other Rules as it may designate. The Association is authorized to make arrangements for this arbitration to be held under such Rules in any locality or territory agreed upon by the parties or, failing such agreement, as designated by the Association. This agreement shall be enforceable and judgment upon any award rendered by all or a majority of the arbitrators may be entered in any court of any country having jurisdiction.

INTERNATIONAL CHAMBER OF COMMERCE—AMERICAN ALTERNATE CLAUSES

All disputes arising in connection with the present contract shall be finally settled by arbitration. Arbitration to be held outside the United States shall be conducted in accordance with the Rules of Arbitration of the International Chamber of Commerce unless by written agreement of the parties they adopt the Rules of the American Arbitration Association. Arbitration to be held in the United States shall be conducted in accordance with the Rules of the American Arbitration Association unless by written agreement of the parties they adopt the Rules of Arbitration of the International Chamber of Commerce.

Judgment upon the award rendered may be entered in any court having jurisdiction or application may be made to such court for a judicial acceptance of the award and an order of enforcement, as the case may be.

When the parties have stipulated in advance where the arbitration is to be held, the following clause is recommended:

All disputes arising in connection with the present contract shall be finally settled by arbitration.

The arbitration shall be held at .... and conducted in accordance with the Rules of the American Arbitration Association(*).
International Chamber of Commerce(*).
Judgment upon the award rendered may be entered in any court having jurisdiction or application may be made to such court for a judicial acceptance of the award and an order of enforcement, as the case may be.
(*) Delete the name of the Institution the Rules of which do not apply.

BRITISH-AMERICAN COMMERCIAL ARBITRATION CLAUSE

Any controversy or claim arising out of or relating to this contract or breach thereof shall be settled by arbitration. If the arbitration is held in England it shall be conducted under the Rules of the London Court of Arbitration and the construction, validity and performance of the contract shall be governed by the law of England. If the arbitration is held in the United States, it shall be conducted under the Rules of the American Arbitration Association. Judgment upon the award rendered may be entered in any court having jurisdiction thereof. In the event that the parties have not designated the locale of the arbitration and are unable to agree thereon, either party may apply to the International Law Association in London to decide the locale and its decision shall be accepted by the parties thereto.

MANCHESTER (ENG.)-AMERICAN COMMERCIAL ARBITRATION CLAUSE

This contract incorporates the 1946 America/Manchester (England) Arbitration Agreement by which each party hereto is bound.

PHILIPPINE-AMERICAN COMMERCIAL ARBITRATION TEMPORARY CLAUSE

Any controversy or claim arising out of or relating to this contract, or the breach thereof, shall be settled by arbitration in accordance with the Rules, then obtaining, of the Philippine-American Trade Arbitration Commission. If for any reason the arbitration cannot be conducted under the Rules of said Commission, then the arbitration shall be held under the Rules of the American Arbitration Association, which shall apply them in whatever locality the parties have designated for their arbitration.

CHINESE-AMERICAN COMMERCIAL ARBITRATION TEMPORARY CLAUSE

Any controversy or claim arising out of or relating to this contract, or the breach thereof, shall be settled by arbitration in accordance with the Rules, then obtaining, of the Chinese-American Trade Arbitration Commission. If for any reason the arbitration cannot be conducted under the Rules of said Commission, then the arbitration shall be held under the Rules of the American Arbitration Association, which shall apply them in whatever locality the parties have designated for their arbitration.

GENERAL LABOR CLAUSE

Any dispute, claim or grievance arising out of or relating to this agreement shall be submitted to arbitration under the Voluntary Labor Arbitration Rules, then obtaining, of the American Arbitration Association. The parties agree to abide by the award, subject to such regulations as any Federal agency having jurisdiction may impose. The parties further agree that there shall be no suspension of work when such dispute arises and while it is in process of adjustment or arbitration.

RESTRICTED LABOR CLAUSE

Except for disputes, claims or grievances concerning (here state matters which are excluded from arbitration) any dispute, claim or grievance arising out of or relating to this agreement shall be submitted to arbitration under the Voluntary Labor Arbitration Rules, then obtaining, of the American Arbitration Association. The parties agree to abide by the award, subject to such regulation as any Federal agency having jurisdiction may impose. The parties further agree that there shall be no suspension of work when any such arbitrable dispute arises and while it is in process of adjustment or arbitration.

LIMITED LABOR CLAUSE

Only disputes, claims or grievances arising out of this agreement and relating to (here specify the matters that may be determined by arbitration) shall be submitted to arbitration. Such arbitration shall be conducted under the Voluntary Labor Arbitration Rules, then obtaining, of the American Arbitration Association. The parties agree to abide by the award made in connection with any such arbitrable dispute, subject to such regulations as any Federal agency having jurisdiction may impose. The parties further agree that there shall be no suspension of work when any such arbitrable dispute arises and while it is in process of adjustment or arbitration.

ANNEX III

CODE OF ETHICS FOR ARBITRATORS

SOME BASIC PRINCIPLES OF RIGHT CONDUCT

Deliberation, fairness, conscientious appraisal of evidence, determination according to the facts, and the impartial application of the law, whether the controversies are decided in the courts or in administrative tribunals—these are the safeguards of society. For the law is naught but words, save as the law is administered.

IN THESE words, former Chief Justice Charles Evans Hughes, in an address before the American Law Institute, set forth fundamental principles for the administration of justice.[1] In his own particular field the Arbitrator undertakes, to the best of his ability, to apply these principles; for although he need only follow procedural arbitration law, he is none the less bound to be deliberate, fair and impartial and must conscientiously appraise the facts and decide accordingly.

The following description of the powers, duties and responsibilities of the Arbitrator and the standards pertaining to his office are observed in all Tribunals organized, maintained and administered by the American Arbitration Association; and in all of the instances where the Association acts in an advisory or consulting capacity; and in the Inter-American, Canadian-American and International Tribunals in which the Association participates; and in the manner specified in the Rules of these respective organizations.[2]

JUDICIAL CHARACTER OF THE OFFICE

The office of Arbitrator is not established by law or by official order. It is created by the private agreement of the parties. The office is of a judicial nature, for the Arbitrator is chosen to determine the respective claims of the parties by making a just and final award. In the performance of his duties, the Arbitrator remains independent and impartial,

[1] Delivered at the Sixteenth Annual Meeting of the *American Law Institute,* Washington, D. C., in May, 1938.

[2] This Code was issued in 1946 as a guide for members of the Panel of the American Arbitration Association. It is now being reviewed by a Special Committee of which Lloyd K. Garrison is Chairman.

acts within the powers bestowed upon him, is responsible for the conduct of the proceeding, offers a fair hearing and receives evidence—all acts of high judicial importance.

The Arbitrator need not consider it any reflection upon his office, if, during the proceeding, the parties mutually arrive at a settlement of their differences. If the Arbitrator creates, by his fairness, impartiality, integrity and courtesy, an atmosphere that leads to a settlement, the function of arbitration is fully met. His only responsibility is to avoid having any personal part in arranging a settlement, for he is a judge and not a compromiser.

Requirement of Impartiality

The office of Arbitrator is judicial in that a dispute is to be decided, not only deliberately and conscientiously, but with a fair appraisal of the evidence and according to facts. The element of honesty is satisfied when the Arbitrator fully believes that he is doing what is right. The element of independence is satisfied when he arrives at his decision by his own free will.

But more than this is required to satisfy the element of impartiality, for this includes not only an honest purpose and independent judgment, but the ability to maintain an even-handed attitude toward both parties alike. The Arbitrator must stand between the parties with an absolutely open mind. The amount of interest which will create a disqualification does not admit of any precise definition; but any circumstances indicating an evident bias in favor of either party will be open to suspicion. It is for the parties to decide whether the circumstance, thus disclosed, is such as to invite withdrawal by the Arbitrator.

Arbitration laws consider impartiality so important that they quite universally provide that, upon proof of bias, the award shall be set aside. Rules attach so much importance to it that they establish qualifications and contain provisions for vacating the office when bias is proved. But, finally, and ultimately, the responsibility rests squarely upon the parties: if they wish to appoint impartial Arbitrators they may do so, for the parties make their own choice.

When each party appoints a partisan or an advocate, the judicial character of the office is violated and it is the parties who pull down its high character. In interpreting the New York State Arbitration Law, the Court of Appeals has explicitly stated its opinion of this practice.[3]

> But first, the practice of arbitrators of conducting themselves as champions of their nominators is to be condemned as contrary to the purpose of

[3] See *In the Matter of American Eagle Fire Ins. Co. v. New Jersey Insurance Co.*, (1925) 240 N. Y. 398, 148 N. E. 562.

arbitration and as calculated to bring the system of enforced arbitrations into disrepute. An arbitrator acts in a quasijudicial capacity and should possess the judicial qualifications of fairness to both parties so that he may render a faithful, honest and disinterested opinion. He is not an advocate whose function is to convince the umpire or third arbitrator. He should keep his own counsel and not run to his nominator for advice when he sees that he may be in the minority. When once he enters into an arbitration he ceases to act as the agent of the party who appoints him. He must lay aside all bias and approach the case with a mind open to conviction and without regard to his previously formed opinions as to the merits of the party or the cause. He should sedulously refrain from any conduct which might justify even the inference that either party is the special recipient of his solicitude or favor. The oath of the arbitrators is the rule and guide of their conduct.

The court, however, is not in a position to maintain this principle unless a party challenges the award on this ground and thereby incurs the risk of its invalidation. Unless the Rules governing the proceeding provide for an earlier correction, arbitrations will continue with biased arbitrators and annulled awards.

The Rules provide a correction at the time the Arbitrator is appointed and during the proceeding. Qualifications as to impartiality are established, and the Arbitrator is invited to examine his own qualifications by these standards and to report any circumstances he thinks will create an assumption of bias. When the circumstance is reported to the parties, it is for them to waive it or request that the Arbitrator decline the appointment. If, in spite of these precautions, it appears, during a proceeding that a bias exists, a party may challenge the Arbitrator and an Arbitration Committee will hear the evidence and has power to declare the office vacant. When a partisan has been appointed by a party and it is pointed out to him that the appointment creates an inequality, the other party having appointed a neutral person, the tendency is for the party to withdraw his advocate-arbitrator.

Honorary Position of the Arbitrator

Carrying on an ancient tradition, the office of the Arbitrator is honorary.[4] Men have not hitherto been attracted to it either as a profession or as a source of regular income. The office as a rule seeks the man. Inherent in this concept is the belief that the Arbitrator not only

[4] This practice generally prevails under the Rules of the American Arbitration Association and under those of many trade associations. Where compensation is arranged for, it is an honorarium rather than payment for services and is so regarded by the men who receive it. Under the System established by the Motion Picture Consent Decree, compensation is authorized and has been fixed upon the basis of an honorarium. Under labor arbitration Rules, compensation may be arranged by agreement between the parties and the Arbitrator.

acts as a private judge for the parties but he renders a public service in ridding society of a dispute that threatens its tranquillity.

When the office is honorary, the Arbitrator is freed from all financial interest in the matter before him. He has none of the obligations or handicaps that attach to an advocate or employee paid by a party naming him; he is free to proceed expeditiously, for he is not interested in prolonging hearings; and he is wholly independent, being beholden to no man for an office that he did not seek.

Personal Responsibility

Arbitration is, in itself, nothing but a word, save as the Arbitrator clothes it with dignity, integrity, and authority. The office is precisely what the Arbitrator makes it. If he is conscientious, deliberate, fair, painstaking in arriving at the truth, and bases his decision upon the facts, arbitration becomes an instrument for advancing justice. If he follows the principles laid down in the Rules and those indispensable attributes of the law of evidence which makes the parties feel that they have had a fair trial, arbitration becomes a safeguard of society, for it eliminates disputes and promotes amity and contributes to the well-being of those it serves and those it influences. The responsibility of the Arbitrator is, therefore, to act to the best of his ability and with a conscientious regard for his office.

Public Responsibility

Such are the social implications of modern business society and so integrated are modern human relations that the old concept that a dispute is a personal matter between the parties and of no public concern no longer holds. A labor dispute is of public concern. When a trade association sets up an arbitration system for its members, it admits that disputes are the concern of the whole industrial group. When a chamber of commerce establishes facilities, it is with a view to serving not only the members but the community. When national and international organizations set up systems they have in mind something more than settling a dispute between individuals, namely, contributing to international peace and security. Private though the proceeding may be, friends, relatives, associates, organizations and communities may come to know of it. The office is, therefore, not only one of personal responsibility but of public importance.

Independence

Not only is the office of an Arbitrator honorary and judicial; it is independent. Once the Arbitrator is appointed he is free to arrive at his own decision. He need not frame his decision with the idea in mind that some other tribunal will upset it, for he is not bound by what someone has previously decided. The public, being unaware of the proceeding, does not bring public opinion to influence his judgment and he is not worried about what the press will say concerning his conduct and how it will affect his future. Threats of removal or reprisal do not influence him, for he resumes his regular occupation when that particular arbitration is closed and he may or may not be called upon again in his lifetime to act as an Arbitrator.

Oath of Office

The dignity of the office of Arbitrator is greatly enhanced by the solemnity of his taking an oath of office. When the arbitration law requires that it be taken, it must be in the prescribed form; when the Rules require it, a form is usually provided. When both are silent, it is still a sound rule of practice for an Arbitrator to take an oath of office, for it impresses upon him more deeply his responsibility and creates confidence in his office.

Source of Authority

The Arbitrator derives his express authority: (1) from the submission or clause executed by the parties, the terms of which he is strictly bound to obey; (2) from the prevailing arbitration law whose regulations, insofar as they relate to him, should be explicitly followed; (3) from the rules of procedure drawn up by the parties or adopted by them which, having been made expressly a part of the arbitration agreement, the Arbitrator is bound to respect and follow.

Panels of Arbitrators

For the convenience of parties, and in order to expedite the selection of the Arbitrator, Panels of Arbitrators are maintained by the administrative organization. Appointment as a member of a Panel may or may not mean a call to active service. Insofar as possible, appointments are made from these Panels for their members are committed in advance to serve wherever their personal circumstances permit, and to meet that obligation. A member cannot be chosen from a Panel until there is a case in which he qualifies as a competent expert, but the fact that he is a member of a Panel and possesses a certificate of appointment, in itself influences the making and keeping of peace and cooperation. For it is his *availability* that frequently persuades the parties in conflict to compose their difference without resort to an arbitration proceeding.

Method of Selection

The Arbitrator is selected for his office by the parties according to the method provided in their arbitration agreement or, if the agreement contains no specific provision under the Rules, in the manner specified. The number of Arbitrators chosen is also fixed in the agreement or if not so fixed, then by the Rules. An outstanding principle is the reservation to the parties of their mutual right to select their own Arbitrator. For this purpose lists of names are sent out to be approved or checked by the parties before an appointment is made. Only when they fail to agree upon names from such lists, or to make the appointment in the manner authorized under the prevailing Rules, is the appointment madc by an administrator.

Tenure of Office

Under the Rules, the Arbitrator is chosen by the parties and serves in that one case only. His office begins with his appointment and closes when he makes his award. The Arbitrator serves in as many or as few cases as he is chosen for by the parties, subject to his own inclination or time. He is under no obligation to accept the appointment, but once he does so, there is a moral obligation to see the matter through. This is implied when he accepts the appointment. Under collective bargaining agreements parties sometimes agree to have the Arbitrator continue for a definite period of time, or to act in several disputes arising out of that agreement. It is for the parties to determine what the tenure of office shall be under the terms of their arbitration agreement.

Effect of Taking Office

Upon accepting the office, the Arbitrator is immediately in a new position with respect to the parties, the subject matter and the public. As to the parties, he can no longer see them separately and privately at his convenience or enjoy their society until after the award is made. As to the subject matter, he cannot make private investigations, but must wait for the proofs to be presented to him at a hearing. As to the public, he has assumed the responsibility of ridding the community of a troublesome dispute. If there are other Arbitrators, each enters into a new relationship of judicial responsibility with the other. His relation in a trade may also be changed; for he is to decide a matter of importance to the entire group. His personal conduct during a proceeding is, therefore, directed to the maintenance of the confidence that was shown at the time of his appointment.

Powers of the Arbitrator

The powers of the Arbitrator are both judicial and administrative. His judicial powers are fixed by the agreement of the parties. He may decide no more and no less than the matter referred to him.

The administrative powers of the Arbitrator are fixed by the prevailing arbitration law and by the Rules. As arbitration laws provide for very little administrative detail, the Arbitrator is very largely guided by the Rules. They provide for the conduct of the proceeding from the time the dispute is submitted until it is disposed of in an award.

Requirements for Making an Award

The award is a properly executed decision of the Arbitrator, or where the law permits or where the Rules or the parties so provide, of a majority of the Arbitrators. There can be but a single award in any one arbitration for, with its making, the Arbitrator terminates his authority under the arbitration agreement, unless the parties have agreed to submit other matters to him.

The Arbitrator should draw up his award with the following requirements in mind, in order fully to comply with the intention of the parties in making his appointment:

(1) It should not go beyond the terms of the arbitration agreement.

(2) It should be a complete adjudication of every matter submitted by the parties.

(3) It should observe each and every condition set forth in the arbitration agreement.

(4) It should be rendered within the time limit, if any, specified in the arbitration agreement.

(5) It should be certain and definite and final in its terms.

(6) It should reserve to the arbitrators no duties to be performed after the award is made.

(7) The award should be made in clear and simple language, technical expressions of law being avoided. The award should be so phrased that its terms are possible of performance.

(8) The Arbitrator, unless the submission provides otherwise, is not required to state the reasons for the conclusions reached but may do so if he sees fit. In labor arbitrations, it has become a general practice to write an opinion to accompany the award, so as to promote a better understanding of the collective bargaining agreement and of the human relations involved.

(9) It is clearly the duty of the Arbitrator not to give any inkling of what his decision is to be before the hearing is closed and the award is made;

nor to indicate the nature of his thinking. This rule of conduct is most important, for nothing so discourages the presentation of full and conclusive evidence as for a party to get the idea that the Arbitrator's mind is made up or that he is no longer interested in taking evidence. It is also embarrassing to hear from outsiders what the decision is to be. These disclosures may lead a party to endeavor to upset the award in the belief that he has not had a fair hearing or that someone else enjoys the confidence of the Arbitrator more than he does.

Privacy of Proceeding and Award

The parties appoint the Arbitrator to decide an issue for them and to deliver the award to them. It is, therefore, their joint property and the Arbitrator is not in a position to release the award to anyone else or to give it publicity without the approval in writing of all the parties.

An arbitration proceeding is private and no information or publicity should be given by the Arbitrator concerning any matter that transpired during the proceedings, unless both parties have indicated their willingness to have the matter made public.

The Arbitrator should not betray any confidence or make use of any information which later would tend to bring disrepute upon his award.

Precedents

The Arbitrator is not bound to follow precedents in determining the merits of the matter submitted to him, but follows his own judgment. He is required, however, to observe certain principles established by arbitration law, violation of which may constitute grounds for nullification of the award by the court, upon the application of a party. These concern such matters as:

(1) An award procured by corruption, fraud or undue means.
(2) An Arbitrator who has exceeded his powers and decided matters not submitted to him or failed to exercise his powers.
(3) An Arbitrator found guilty of misconduct in refusing to postpone or adjourn a hearing for good cause shown.
(4) An Arbitrator who has refused to hear pertinent and material evidence.
(5) An Arbitrator found guilty of any misbehavior which has prejudiced the rights of any party.
(6) An Arbitrator who has so imperfectly executed his powers that a mutual, final and definite award was not made.

Precepts

Standards of practice which may be said to contain ethical principles or viewpoints appear in the following precepts:

The Arbitrator should decline an appointment when he has:

(1) Any personal, financial, or close family relation, or close business relation, such as partner or agent, to any of the parties.
(2) Any probable pecuniary interest in the outcome of the controversy.
(3) Any private understanding with, or obligation to, any party respecting the subject matter in controversy or making of an award.
(4) Any personal bias or prejudice in favor of, or against, any of the parties.

The Arbitrator should avoid:

(1) Acting as a conciliator. The duty of an Arbitrator is not to facilitate a compromise but to reach a fair decision and to make a just award.
(2) Acting as an advocate or agent for either party. His duty is not to argue or defend the case but to hear and decide it according to his best understanding.
(3) Delegating his duties or authority. Each Arbitrator is personally responsible and is obligated to perform the full duties of his office.
(4) Appearing to have a bias. The Arbitrator should not express opinions or views concerning the parties or the controversy before or after the award is made.

The Arbitrator should remember:

(1) That time is money and he should use his best efforts to expedite the proceeding by being on time, by taking few adjournments and by observing all time limitations imposed by the Rules or otherwise.
(2) That arbitration is a low-cost proceeding and he should keep down the costs by not incurring any unusual or unnecessary expense and by expediting hearings.
(3) That an arbitration is not a litigation and he should keep it free from technicalities or legal formalities and the spirit of litigation. Upon him devolves the responsibility for keeping the arbitration free from animosity, recriminations and conduct tending to impair the goodwill of the proceeding.
(4) That he is chosen to decide the issue impartially and fairly and not to act as counsel for either party, or to give legal advice or to aid one party more than another in their presentation of their case.

Upholding the Honor of the Panel

Members of Panels are the judicial branch of the organization that appoints them. Their appointment implies recognition of their high degree of qualification, by non-partisan, non-profit-making, wholly non-partisan, scientific and educational organizations that are devoted to the maintenance and advancement of high standards of arbitration.

The behavior of a Panel member when he acts as an Arbitrator either adds prestige or dignity to, and confidence in, the Panel as a whole, or reflects adversely upon it. Therefore, in justice to the parties who choose him by preference from the Panel and to his colleagues on the Panel and to the organization that appointed him to the Panel, his faithful observance of this Code is of high importance.

This concern for the integrity of the Panel should extend to the making of statements that would seem to identify them with the Panel as a whole, but which do not necessarily reflect its views. It is, therefore, advisable in making public statements for the Arbitrator to avoid implying that such statements are associated with his Panel membership.

INDEX

KEY

AAA=American Arbitration Association
CACAC=Canadian-American Commercial Arbitration Commission
IACAC=Inter-American Commercial Arbitration Commission
ICC=International Chamber of Commerce
ICAC=International Commercial Arbitration Committee

NAME INDEX*

* Partial list; see also Ch. XXV, *Builders of American Arbitration*, p. 181.